The New
Faculty Member

Robert Boice

The New Faculty Member

*Supporting
and Fostering
Professional Development*

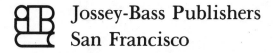 Jossey-Bass Publishers
San Francisco

For sales outside the United States contact Maxwell Macmillan
International Publishing Group, 866 Third Avenue, New York,
New York 10022

Printed on acid-free paper and manufactured in the
United States of America

The paper used in this book meets the State of California
requirements for recycled paper (50 percent recycled waste,
including 10 percent post-consumer waste), which are the
strictest guidelines for recycled paper currently in use in
the United States.

Library of Congress Cataloging-in-Publication Data

Boice, Robert.
   The new faculty member : supporting and fostering professional
development / Robert Boice.
      p.   cm — (The Jossey-Bass higher and adult education series)
   Includes bibliographical references and index.
   ISBN 1-55542-423-6
   1. College teachers—United States. 2. College personnel
management—United States. 3. Professional socialization—United
States.   I. Title   II. Series.
LB1778.2.B65 1992
378.1′2′0973—dc20   91-37579
                                                  CIP

FIRST EDITION
HB Printing   10 9 8 7 6 5 4 3 2 1   *Code 9219*

The Jossey-Bass
Higher and Adult Education Series

Contents

**Part Three:
Building an Institutional Support System**

Preface

As a rule, new faculty on our campuses are neglected resources whose development proceeds haphazardly. We know
too little about them, and we do too little for them. *The New
Faculty Member* shows why we must do better in a seller's
market and demonstrates proven support strategies.

The book's argument proceeds from five premises. First,
the best hope for improving professorial practices—including
teaching—lies with the cohorts of new faculty who come to
campus in increasing numbers each year. Second, because
new faculty are becoming harder to find and retain, campuses
must do a better job of making academic careers more enticing. Third, there is a dearth of research on what helps and
what hinders new faculty; effective support programs must
have a stronger basis in empirical study. Fourth, the best prospects for effective support programs await the involvement of
campus leaders (including higher administrators) with faculty
development practitioners. And fifth, support programs for
new faculty make sense as institutional investments; the costs,
both economic and human, of losing new hires to com-
petitors or to unproductive and unhappy beginnings are
clearly greater than those of setting up effective support
programs.

In this book, I advocate a holistic, data-driven approach

to nurturing new faculty. I argue for beginning with investigations, even of a casual sort, to determine what new faculty members need. I show how the enhancement of new hires' performance and satisfaction in any one area, such as teaching, depends on progress in related domains, such as collegiality and scholarship. And I propose a notion founded on the basic skills of academic success, IRSS theory, that helps clarify the kinds of simple interventions and plans that will be most effective for programs. Overall, *The New Faculty Member* is a blend of information, analysis, and action that has promise for application on all types of campuses.

Audience

The audience I envision for this book consists first and foremost of the academicians who most obviously figure in the socialization of new faculty—the chairpeople and colleagues who assess their progress and make decisions about their retention, tenure, and promotion. Then, of course, I hope to reach the practitioners, faculty developers and others, whose efforts could or already do encompass support programs for newcomers to campus. But I also want *The New Faculty Member* to reach the campus leaders and higher administrators whose involvement as advocates and participants is essential to successful programs. Thus, I have written this book for a broad audience—for everyone with a stake in hiring and nurturing gifted and diverse groups of new employees: campus presidents, deans, committees concerned with hiring and evaluation, individuals who orient new faculty members to campus, chairpeople and colleagues in daily contact with new faculty, and those who conduct instructional development and other support programs.

Overview of the Contents

I begin the book with an introductory chapter (Chapter One) that makes a case for campuses' spending increasingly restricted resources on support for new faculty, especially at this point in our history. The remainder of the book is organized into three main parts. Part One deals with the three obstacles facing most new faculty: collegiality, teaching, and writing. Chapter Two begins an exploration of the experiences of new faculty members as they adjust to new campuses; it identifies the obstacles to establishing collegial support and presents strategies for providing needed support in establishing social networks. As I present the methodology and results of interviewing new faculty semester after semester, I hope to reveal the fascination of observing new faculty coping with a difficult situation where complaints of loneliness accompany demands for autonomy.

Chapters Three and Four extend the study of new faculty experience to teaching and scholarly productivity. While in both areas the initial experiences of new faculty members are usually disappointing, the chapters do make two encouraging observations. First, we do see some "quick starters" who exemplify what contributes to success for teachers and writers. Second, by their third or fourth year on campus, most new faculty members have at last made progress toward managing the demands that often seemed overwhelming during the first two years. In the main, though, the qualitative and quantitative results from long-term studies reveal distressingly poor starts as teachers and published authors, which may make future progress difficult.

Part Two moves from observation to intervention. The chapters in this part portray new faculty overcoming obstacles, as colleagues, teachers, and scholarly writers in structured programs. Chapter Five, for instance, discusses building programs for social support around a traditional method: mentoring by more experienced colleagues. Chapter Six explores ways of helping new faculty members to develop their skills as teachers, both by improving already established interventions (such as early informal evaluations from students) and by enhancing skills usually overlooked (for instance, finding classroom comfort). And Chapter Seven shows how the most effective solutions to the usual procrastination and distress of scholarly writing rely on making it a more relaxed, less exclusionary activity. Throughout, I show the interdependence of these three kinds of support programs; the lesson of balance and moderation comes as a relief for new faculty members experiencing the busiest and most stressful years of their lives.

The conceptual device for making sense of the enormous task of promoting colleagues' success at teaching, social relations, and writing is IRSS theory. I use the ideas of student developers and composition teachers to argue that support efforts in every domain where new faculty can founder or find success must take into account the same four factors of usually untaught knowledge: involvement, regimen, self-control, and social skills (IRSS). Chapter Eight, the last chapter in Part Two, shows how a similar four-stage approach can be extended to self-help programs for new faculty who will work at development on their own. A central assumption is that even self-help needs help.

The chapters in Part Three discuss ways of building an institutional support system. Chapters Nine and Ten address the needs of new faculty and their supporters at special times: Chapter Nine deals with recruitment and orientation and Chapter Ten with retention and tenure. Chapter Eleven explores ways of meeting the special needs of nontraditional faculty, including women and members of minority groups. Through these three chapters, we find that the most important judgments may be about whom to hire, how to acquaint newcomers to campus with one another, and who gets to stay; without improving policies and practices in these areas, our other efforts at giving the best start to new faculty may be doomed to mediocrity. In Chapter Twelve, I show ways of enlisting the support and involvement of chairpeople and other administrators in such efforts. Finally, in Chapter Thirteen, I link the lessons learned from the discussions of minority faculty and other special challenges to an overview of essential points presented throughout the book and a review of better-established programs in fields such as organizational development. Most critically, Chapter Thirteen confronts the usual sticking points, funding among them, that arise in building campus programs for our new hires. The Resource at the end of the book presents the questionnaire used for the interviews of new faculty discussed throughout.

Acknowledgments

In presenting my first major book on faculty development after some twenty-five years of practice, I am especially thankful to the people who encouraged this unplanned diversion in my career. Among them were the usually grateful colleagues who came to me for informal help, even as I made my own beginnings as a new faculty member, and the deans and chairpeople who arranged increasingly greater support for what became faculty development programs. In the past decade, as I decided to make faculty development my full-time endeavor, a number of practitioners were memorably supportive and helpful. The late Joseph Katz, in particular, played a timely role in encouraging me to, as he put it, come out of the closet and do what I really enjoyed doing, no matter what my colleagues would think of my abandoning an already successful career in ethology.

From my first systematic contacts with new faculty, communicating what hinders and helps them has been a paramount goal. Now, years later, I have received generous help from my editor at Jossey-Bass, Gale Erlandson, whose keen insights and sense of what would work have helped shape this book starting with its initial proposal; and from my reviewers, Joanne Gainen, Robert J. Menges, and Jack H. Schuster, whose expertise and collegiality as scholars, practitioners, and writers have helped redirect and improve this manuscript.

Stony Brook, New York   Robert Boice
January 1992

Dedicated to Jimmie L. Turner:
Once a student but more typically a teacher,
many times a collaborator
on projects including some of the interviews portrayed in this book,
and always a cherished friend

The Author

ROBERT BOICE is professor of psychology at the State University of New York, Stony Brook, where he also directs the Faculty Instructional Support Office. He received his B.A. (1962), M.A. (1964), and Ph.D. (1966) degrees from Michigan State University, all in psychology, at first with joint training in organizational development and later in biology (ethology). He has published more than 150 articles and books, many on faculty development, including the self-help manual *Professors as Writers* (1990). He has also directed faculty development programs at the University of Missouri, Columbia; the State University of New York, Albany; and California State University, Long Beach. His proudest accomplishments over those years include the restoration of several antique cars and the acquisition of a few teaching awards.

The New
Faculty Member

 ONE

Introduction:
New Faculty—
A Neglected Resource

Many of us reading this book have something in common with new faculty: we were once new faculty ourselves. While this shared experience may make us more sympathetic to new hires, it can create a problem of overconfidence; we may think that we already know what new colleagues experience and need. This assumption helps explain why support programs for new faculty are often conducted without consultation with new faculty themselves. I shared many of these beliefs, at least implicitly, until a decade ago, when I looked back on an intensive study of faculty who were clearly unsuccessful at midcareer (see Boice, 1986b). Almost without exception, these individuals traced their failures back to critical incidents in their first few years on campus. This comment is typical:

> Once I discovered that I was getting hopelessly behind in all the things I had to do, especially in getting published, I began to give up. I never really did feel that I fit in or that I got the resources that I needed. I sometimes tried to tell myself that I got my satisfaction from teaching, but that was never really true. Somehow, I think that if I had gotten off to a better start, I could have had a much better career. What probably

1

was missing here was a caring attitude that translated into showing me how to manage the way
the people who did make it do.

This appreciation of what can undermine professorial careers
inspired me to concentrate my efforts on new hires. As I conducted repeated interviews and observations with hundreds of
new faculty members, I came to a pair of related insights: Somehow, I had forgotten or perhaps bypassed much of what my
new colleagues were experiencing. And things had changed
since my days as a new hire.

The aggregate of these inquiries, alas, does not reflect
the optimism that marks the arrival on campus for most new
faculty members. Nor does it signal the relief of having secured
a desirable job. Instead, what overshadows the experience of
many newcomers is the despair of isolation, insecurity, and
busyness. I remember one new hire who likened his first year
on campus to Admiral Byrd's account of a long antarctic winter in the book *Alone*. Another, returned from a successful
career in industry, marveled at the wasteful neglect of new
faculty members, including herself. Academe seemed a cost-
ineffective and inhumane place to her. And a third newcomer
mused over the distance that her colleagues showed once she
arrived on campus; just months before, she had been recruited
(*seduced* was her word for it) in the midst of enthusiastic plans
to build the cohort of minority faculty on campus. How, she
wondered, would she make it as a successful academic?

My experiences with new faculty prompted me to conduct yet another study of entry points in professorial careers.
In an ongoing survey of recent doctorate recipients who considered and then rejected academic careers, I am acquiring a
perspective on what campuses could do better. Promising prospects who avoid professorial lives most often do so because
they see us as running our new hires through gauntlets of
demands for mastering teaching and scholarship. Moreover,
these avoiders suspect that we offer little help to new faculty
with problems. They assume that professorial lives carry strong

likelihoods of failure or, at the least, of mediocre and unhappy careers (Boice, 1991e). Recruits who leave tenure-track positions after a year or two, with or without signs of failing at academic careers, cite the same reasons for fleeing academe.

Taken together, reports of avoidance, distress, and unproductive beginnings suggest that we fail our campuses and our new hires when we allow the processes of socialization and support to be inefficient and unpleasant. Still, given that many of us survived similarly trying circumstances, we might wonder how serious the problem is. Haven't we gotten along nicely by perpetuating the autonomy and organized anarchy that we cherish so much about academe (Weick, 1976)?

Why Attend to New Faculty Now?

The problems faced by new faculty are not new. Reports by new faculty of feeling overloaded, unsupported, and uninformed may be as old as academe itself (Fink, 1991). Yet observers of higher education, including Seldin (1987), conclude that the demands and stresses of professorial life are increasing. Added to these growing pressures for new hires are three more recent problems in recruiting and retaining new professors: First, some experts on higher education predict shortages of applicants, especially of the most qualified people (Schuster, 1990a). Second, pundits expect growing public clamor for more accountability in professorial activities, including teaching (Blum, 1990; Mayhew, Ford, & Hubbard, 1990). This, too, could mean that professorial careers will become even more demanding. Third, we may be a bit out of practice at nurturing new hires. Recall the lost generation of would-be professors who, in the face of shortages of positions and funds in the 1970s and 1980s, abandoned their dreams for other careers. During that lapse, departments have suspended customs associated with recruiting, socializing, and evaluating new hires. In fact, the reasons for paying more attention to new faculty have expanded to the point where they merit a pause for extended listing and reflection.

An Opportunity for Major Changes in Higher Education

Because they have not established firm habits as professors, new faculty are attractive prospects for changing campus cultures. Indeed, many universities and even colleges have used new hires to heighten emphases on research (Smith, 1990). That is, while senior faculty may remain committed to the expectations under which they were hired, new faculty can be hired and rewarded according to new expectations.

There is, moreover, a compelling reason for counting on changes by way of new faculty now. Campuses face growing demands for improved teaching as a means of both attracting and retaining students and meeting demands for accountability in expenditures of public funds (Mayhew, Ford, & Hubbard, 1990). Like it or not, the teaching reform movement is here to stay (Watkins, 1990a). Prospects for change lie, again, most explicitly with new faculty; the first few years for new faculty are formative and lasting (Jarvis, 1988). Early experiences in the classroom (McKeachie, 1987) and in other academic activities, such as publishing (Creswell, 1985), predict more about career habits than any other formative period, including graduate school. Once under way, career paths may be hard to change.

The Need for More Research on New Faculty

While this reason for paying more attention to new faculty is less obvious than some others, it is, in fact, based on a sound argument: a good justification for collecting data about support programs is that doing so will provide the information base we need to make better-informed decisions about designing them. Thus far, all but a few of the limited studies of new faculty have been descriptive or speculative (see Fink, 1991). We have had to proceed as much by guess as by certainty.

Why are we sometimes remiss in finding out which supports new faculty need most? One reason is that much critical information about professorial success is tacit knowledge, information usually untaught but critical to thriving (see Sternberg, Okagaki, & Jackson, 1990). We are apparently unaccustomed to studying or teaching the practical intelligence that contributes to success and happiness in academic careers.

The Need to Reinvolve Administrators in the Faculty

Even casual observers of academe see the rift that has grown between faculty and administrators, especially in the past decade or two. As administrations have enlarged, often at rates disproportionate to those of faculty (Mayhew, Ford, & Hubbard, 1990), faculty feel more and more remote from administrators. Articles in the *Chronicle of Higher Education* increasingly report faculty demands for downsizing of administrations. One correction for this division between "faculty" and "former faculty" is a more direct involvement of administrators in faculty well-being. Consider that in one of the best studies of faculty development programs yet reported, explicit backing from the higher administrators was among the most powerful predictors of program success (Eble & McKeachie, 1985). In the perspective taken here, the sensible place for administrators to reinvolve themselves in the faculty is with new hires.

Support Programs as Institutional Investments

Some of us may be eager to support new faculty for no more reason than making their beginnings more humane. History shows, however, the limited promise of this logic operating in widespread fashion. A more promising argument is economic (Exum, 1983). The dollar costs of recruiting and retaining new faculty who fare unhappily or unproductively may be too great to tolerate.

We are already in the midst of replacing a huge contingent of retiring professors (Bowen & Schuster, 1986). Schuster (1990a) estimates that 180,000 new faculty will be hired in the 1990s, 340,000 by the year 2005 on American campuses alone. One result of this demand for new hires will be intense competition between campuses and between academic and non-academic employers. Careers outside academe are becoming increasingly attractive to graduate students. Another outcome will be a bimodal faculty, with an older group that may be unlikely to nurture their junior colleagues as readily as they would a group less dissimilar to themselves (Boice & Thomas, 1989; Mooney, 1990). And, according to Schuster (1990a), the rush of hiring should bring an increase of faculty power for newcomers; as campuses compete for faculty, administrators will inevitably offer concessions, including reduced teaching loads. Moreover, increased power may have effects beyond initial concessions. New faculty members who suppose that they will be better supported and appreciated at another campus will have unprecedented opportunities to move. Thus, effective recruitment and retention of our faculties will mean making academic careers more nurturing and attractive. So far, as noted earlier, we have the reputation of exposing our new hires, especially those with nontraditional backgrounds, to harsh and capricious treatment. A related rationale for directing more attention to new faculty is related to pressures for recruiting women and minorities as professors (Epps, 1989). The coming shift in the demographics of academe, one that demands a more diverse faculty, necessitates even less reliance on trial-and-error learning of the skills essential to thriving as a professor.

Weigh, in addition, the three typical outcomes of new faculty who make poor beginnings. First, those who fare in mediocre or unhappy fashion often leave for other positions, in or out of academe (Boice, 1991e). Second, those who fare even less well often end up being rejected in the retention and tenure process, usually after sharing an uncomfortable experience with their colleagues. Third, marginally successful newcomers may remain in the department for unhappy and unproductive careers (Boice, 1986b). Any of these outcomes is cost-ineffective. The newcomers who leave or who are rejected must be replaced with new hires, requiring renewed recruiting and training. The new faculty who stay on despite ambivalence about their suitability often prove to be bitter and counterproductive campus citizens. And, to return to an earlier dilemma, the potential new faculty who reject us first are likely to come from underrepresented and badly needed kinds of professors—the very individuals we can least afford to lose.

In a recent informal survey of three campuses of differing sizes and missions, I asked higher administrators and chairpeople to estimate the costs of replacing new faculty who end up being unsatisfactory. The most surprising outcome of my inquiries was that while none of these administrators had ever made such calculations in a deliberate way, all of them found the exercise interesting and important. Overall, their estimates of typical costs for recruiting replacements ran to the following figures:

- About $500 to $6,000 in travel monies
- Perhaps $200 to $800 in wages for hourly employees
- In some cases, $2,000 to $40,000 (depending on the research mission of the campus) for laboratory setups
- $3,000 to $10,000 in faculty and administrator's time if charged against their salaries

Another surprising outcome in this inquiry was that these few moments of reflection usually caused administrators to comment about how little effort, given the costs that they had just listed, had gone into making sure that the best prospects were hired and then supported. As a rule, these same administrators volunteered the opinion that the greatest costs accrued were for new faculty who were retained after ambiguous and unhappy beginnings. A plenitude of anecdotes followed, most commonly about colleagues doomed to careers as permanent associate professors who reliably elicited complaints about their teaching.

Precedents for Support Programs

If we agree, at least tentatively, about the need for support programs, where do we begin? We owe it to ourselves to check on precedent. The outcome is mixed but promising. Tradition quietly favors social Darwinism as the mechanism for dealing with new faculty. Professors with the right stuff (and the right connections) survive; those without it are presumably better off elsewhere. The autonomous life of professors, we are often reminded, selects for individuals who can establish their own motivation and direction.

Faculty Development

Challenged by new demographics, tradition may be changing; no longer do we necessarily approve of "natural selection" as the best design. The first real step toward helping faculty develop their potential as professionals came, not surprisingly, during the cultural revolution of the 1960s. Faculty development began with a wealth of enthusiasm and plans (see, for instance, Gaff, 1975). From the outset, though, faculty development programs have disappointed close observers. Kunz (1977) struck a cynical note, one that still rings true, when he described faculty development as "an academic Catch-22 where those who seek help don't need it, those who do need it don't seek it, there are no incentives for improving, and everything is voluntary" (p. 329).

One the whole, faculty development has not produced compelling evidence of lasting changes in its clients; most campuses seem to remain unconvinced of the need to sustain major programs (Schuster, 1989). And to complete a discouraging picture, most faculty development programs have been narrowly conceived, usually to help faculty with nothing but teaching, and usually in brief, episodic fashion (Katz & Henry, 1988; Menges & Mathis, 1988; Schuster, Wheeler, & Associates, 1990; Young, 1987).

Still, the promise of useful precedents among faculty development programs is real. At least one major program for enhancing teaching has been carried out and evaluated with impressive results (Eble & McKeachie, 1985). And Menges and Mathis's (1988) Herculean review of the literature on faculty development and cognate areas offers new potential for making sense of what we know about helping our colleagues develop. We now have excellent directives for improving teaching (Weimer, 1990) and for improving the practice of faculty development (Lewis & Povlacs, 1988), but we are only beginning to help particular groups of faculty, such as new hires. Heretofore, Jarvis's (1991) guide for new faculty has been the only attempt to present a systematic program of support for new hires.

Written Advice

Another, more common precedent for helping new faculty, and one that is older than faculty development programs, is the custom of supplying new faculty with written advice and rules. Most such orienting documents outline faculty obligations (such as deadlines for turning in grades) and list campus resources (such as the location and hours of the faculty computer laboratory); some even discuss legalities of retention and tenure (Bledsoe, 1988). These pamphlets and handouts are undoubtedly useful, but they can be criticized on at least two counts: For one thing, they usually remain unread. For another, they do little to help new faculty with their most difficult problems—adjusting to conditions of isolation, insecurity, and busyness (Boice, 1991a).

Even handbooks that do give advice about making it in academe are often little more helpful than the casual lore already floating around. The best of such guidebooks, Zanna and Darley's (1987) *The Compleat Academic,* suffers the usual limitations. Its advice comes almost exclusively from the experience of a few already successful professors who pay little attention to what caused their less successful counterparts to fail. Moreover, the authors of *The Compleat Academic* and of kindred guidebooks are content to draw speculative conclusions that cannot be found in the more scholarly and research-based articles that helped ensure their credibility as advice-givers. Consider this example of advice that is both incorrect and potentially undermining: "Do not panic about the amount of time you are spending on coursework. You may not get anything else done while you are planning and delivering your first courses. Typically, no one does" (Taylor & Martin, 1987, p. 25). As we will see in Chapters Two through Seven, new faculty who fare best in finding comfort, success at teaching, and tenure *do* find time to manage more than preparing lectures. Conversely, new faculty who fail to find this kind of balance tend to prepare too much lecture material for reasonably paced delivery (or for active student involvement).

A Basic Plan for Nurturing New Faculty

If the usual anecdotes and opinions about what supports new faculty needs fall short of helpfulness, what might work better? This book is an attempt to offer alternatives, principally by way of a data-based and balanced approach. The view here is that making sense of the new experience and of what most effectively augments it is a matter of making patient observations and of juggling combinations of strategies on the basis of those observations. A brief note shows how such background information can aid in the planning of support programs. The passivity of new faculty as agents of change in their own teaching is well documented (Fink, 1984), but its source has not been readily apparent. The studies of new faculty as teachers reported in Chapters Three and Six suggest one reason. New faculty and their more senior colleagues commonly suppose that the nearly exclusive priority of new teachers is to lower the difficulty level of their lectures to suit the sophistication and motivation of undergraduate students. They assume, as we will see, that this adjustment can be learned only via direct experience. So it is that advice about teaching can seem superfluous. We will also see other reasons why new faculty often resist advice about improving their teaching. One of these again involves balance: many new hires suppose that until they master the problem of finding enough time to write and rewrite error-free lectures, they cannot address other issues about teaching.

While the approaches advocated in this book begin with patient observation, their key elements are structural;

successful programs at both complex and simple levels have been shown to depend on careful planning (for example, selecting optimal pairings for mentor-protégé duos), on tested formats for carrying out projects (for example, following up on pairings with biweekly calls to ensure that pairs meet regularly and form bonds), and on evaluations (to see which program components work and which need modification). Demanding as this sounds, these steps have already been put into practice at a variety of campuses and by a diversity of practitioners. Perhaps the single most important aid in managing so complicated a challenge has been the development of a simple and useful theory to explain what hinders and what helps new faculty.

A Theoretical Approach

A few words about my background and philosophical stance may help ease the journey of readers through this book. My own gestalt in setting up support programs comes from my training, recently as a clinical psychologist, originally as an ethologist (a field biologist who uses descriptive, mostly qualitative accounts of behavior to generate and test hypotheses). Whatever the label, my orientation has most closely resembled what William James (1899), John Dewey (1916), and Herbert Simon (writing as recently as 1991) might have called rationalism or pragmatism; my real models, such as Royce (1898) and Ribot (1906), simply called themselves practicalists. Whatever else, these pioneers strived to demonstrate alternatives to romanticism in accounting for ways to succeed at creative and intellectual endeavors.

Once I had formally committed myself to a career of faculty development, I was trained as a clinical psychologist. My "retreading" shows itself, I suppose, in my eagerness to intervene in problems beyond teaching skills, including the social components of professorial success. All of us who nurture fellow faculty, I suspect, spend some of our time as therapists. Despite that new layer of training, the old one remains intact; ethology more closely represents my personal style. It has the virtue of requiring little funding and of encouraging close acquaintance, even compatibility, with the individuals and cultures under study. Its heroes include nonromantics such as Jane Goodall, who characteristically took the time to understand her chimpanzee neighbors before prescribing help for them.

All in all, then, I approach new faculty with a duality of intentions, of getting to both know and help my colleagues, usually in purely inductive fashion. During the writing of this book, however, I discovered that I needed more. In assembling information about new faculty, I constructed a simple theory to help provide a sense of cohesion and direction for the wealth of material at hand. While the theory is by no means crucial to using the information and ideas presented in the following chapters, it can help stimulate and organize thinking about support programs. Here I present the theory briefly; in the chapters that follow, I expand on its details and implications.

This four-part theory (involvement, regimen, self-management, and social networks, or IRSS) deals with the most fundamental skills and attitudes that we can impart to our new hires, skills and attitudes so elementary that we may take them for granted. My notions of the roots of professorial success and satisfaction are based in part on observations of what exemplary new faculty do that helps them short-cut the socialization and mastery processes and in part on what components appear to be most helpful to other new faculty in achieving the same goals. We will examine these observations in chapters to come. IRSS theory also has origins in the ideas of other people, all of them from outside traditional faculty development. The discussion that follows outlines the four interactive components of IRSS theory and their kinship with better-known theories.

Involvement. My own notion that new faculty must first immerse themselves in activities that will teach and support them draws on Astin's (1985) theory of involvement. His view of the pivotal nature of involvement is based largely on student development, but it seems to apply equally well to faculty development: briefly, the first step in success and retention is immersion in campus life—in its social networks, in activities that provide supports such as getting to know professors and students, and in an optimistic sense of membership in one's campus.

Regimen. Sternberg's (1988) notion that the most vital skills and attitudes usually remain untaught but are critical to thriving in school also applies to what he calls task management. Sternberg finds that one of the most pivotal tacit skills is knowing how to apportion one's study time. For new faculty, as we will see, critical but usually untaught knowledge includes the skill of establishing balance between time expenditures for teaching (usually excessive) versus scholarly writing (typically nonexistent). What this skill comes down to is learning a regimen of moderation and efficiency.

Self-Management. Flower (1990) popularized the idea of self-management, at least among composition teachers, as a matter of learning to solve the right problem. She finds that effective learners start by attending to whether they are on task. Her strategies for finding the right problems to solve derive from her research on finding better ways of teaching the difficult task of mastering writing. Before many students can progress as writers, they must avoid the pitfall of misrepresenting writing tasks; without a clear sense of the assignment and the intended audience, writing efforts tend to be ineffective and unrewarding. In chapters to come, we will see numerous examples of how new faculty commonly try to solve the wrong problems. One of the most customary of misstarts occurs when struggling writers try to interpret their experience of feeling overwhelmed and unprepared. In the case of neglected writing, newcomers assume that the solution lies in finding more time, preferably in big, undisrupted blocks during weekends and vacations. In regard to mastering teaching, they commonly focus on writing errorless and well-organized lectures as the solution to dissatisfied students. One result of this misdirected effort is a disproportionate amount of time spent on teaching preparation.

Another aspect of the emerging notion of self-management comes from the research of Sternberg and his colleagues (for example, Sternberg et al., 1990) showing that the lack of usually untaught skills of emotional expression and learning from one's context is what keeps many poor students from thriving in school. An example of a related problem that we will encounter with new faculty is their tendency, when faced with tough problems such as writing for publication, to engage in negative self-talk that can undermine confidence and momentum.

Social Networks. Here again, the idea has origins outside the usual channels of faculty development. We have, as a rule, neglected the power of social networking in faculty development. Consider a single example of how new faculty can benefit from sociality: spending as much time at collegial socializing on and off campus as at other professorial activities, such as writing and teaching, is a key to success in areas such as scholarly productivity (Creswell, 1985). In the chapters ahead, we will see evidence that both productivity in scholarship and excellence in teaching profit from the building of social networks.

What IRSS Theory Promises

The four components of IRSS theory (involvement, regimen, self-control, and social networking) can do more than help focus the facts and ideas about how best to support the development of new faculty. Because it concerns the most fundamental components of what new faculty need to master, IRSS theory also promises generality. While much of what new faculty eventually learn in adjusting to their specialties and campuses may be situation-specific, basic components such as involvement and regimen should be essential to thriving at almost any campus.

The main findings to be reported here come largely from three study campuses; so far, the results have been replicated in their essentials at a variety of campuses. But even preliminary checks for generality have confirmed the expected: different campuses provide somewhat different experiences. For example, one small Catholic liberal arts university evidences more collegiality than the large study campuses; even so, its cohorts of faculty new to such a campus still experience the same sorts of imbalance and distress in trying to manage teaching, collegiality, and writing. A primary goal of this book is to stimulate kindred inquiries on campuses setting up or expanding programs for new faculty.

Given your involvement as a reader (an IRSS factor?), the rest is up to me. I have, at the least, tried to convey the enthusiasm and enjoyment of my decade of involvement with new faculty. In my experience, there are no more talented, more fascinating, more challenging, more deserving, or more appreciative people to whom we can offer help.

 *Part 1*

Obstacles Confronting New Faculty Members

The chapters in this part deal with three obstacles facing most new faculty: teaching, writing, and collegiality. No doubt, the categories of obstacles facing newcomers to campus could be increased beyond three; new faculty lead complex lives. In the main, though, they worry about and work hardest at teaching, scholarship, and collegiality. New faculty themselves often suppose that mastery of any one of the three is difficult and that mastery of all of them is miraculous. My own observations of new faculty suggest that success at any of the three activities rarely comes in isolation from success in the other two.

TWO

Gaining the Acceptance of Colleagues

To what should we first attend in getting to know new faculty? My own temptation was to begin my accounts with teaching (after all, what is more important to the academic enterprise?) or perhaps with scholarly productivity (what counts more toward academic rewards?). But I came to realize that success or failure in professorial careers begins with social supports. As new faculty reflect on their experience, they agree on one thing: no matter how much they value their autonomy as professors, they still rely most on colleagues for success as teachers, as productive researchers, and as contented professionals.

They also agree on something else. The most salient experiences of new faculty during their first few years on campus, the ones they most want corrected, are loneliness and understimulation. So we begin our examination with collegiality, a usually neglected area of adjustment by new faculty. While we may readily agree that newcomers depend on their colleagues for modeling and nurturance (Creswell, 1985), we have not matched that supposition with facts from the experiences of new faculty. We still have a lot to learn about new faculty as colleagues.

Nonetheless, there is a literature on new faculty experience that alludes to collegiality. Three of the best studies in this area illustrate the promises and limitations of existing studies of new faculty. One, by Braskamp, Fowler, and Ory (1984), reminds us that assistant professors are often narrowly oriented to scholarly productivity. The second study, by Fink (1984), confirms the impression that new faculty experience heavy work loads and want more support and feedback. The third study, by Sorcinelli and Near (1989), documents the peril of negative spillover, where new faculty's work affects their home lives. So while these studies speak to the need for social supports and to the problems that professorial work can pose for personal lives, they say little about how new faculty actually cope with problems of establishing collegiality.

This chapter, then, details the usual problems of establishing collegiality, including social and intellectual isolation, cultural conflicts with senior faculty, and passivity in accepting social support. It follows the tradition of researchers who have studied the careers of academics via life history accounts (for example, Evetts, 1989). And it attempts, in the style of other qualitative studies (for example, Beynon, 1985), to use descriptive data as a basis for understanding the new faculty experience.

A Study of New Faculty

In the core study of collegiality described here, all the new faculty came from one campus, a large regional university. Participation was voluntary and nearly unanimous. All but a few of the new tenure-track faculty in each of the four successive cohorts agreed to my program of repeated interviews and visits to their offices, classrooms, and laboratories. Even so, many newcomers had to be coaxed into agreement; initial contacts were marred by new faculty who missed appointments, carried out other business during interviews, and questioned my credentials. Eventually, however, all the participants came to welcome these visits, often commenting that my visits were the only occasions when anyone on campus took much interest in them. (Technical details of this study appear in Boice, 1991a.)

Cohorts

The four successively hired cohorts of new faculty began with twenty-nine, forty, forty-eight, and sixty-eight participants, respectively. Although no participants dropped out of the study as long as they remained on campus, numbers dropped to twenty, twenty-four, forty, and sixty-two, respectively, by the last set of interviews. Some new faculty in each cohort left campus for a variety of reasons that usually amounted to fleeing what was seen as an unrewarding, pressure-filled situation.

A key fact about the study campus is that these cohorts represented the first major hiring in fifteen years for most academic departments. Their sudden appearance caused initial tension among the entrenched faculty (Boice & Thomas, 1989). This influx of new hires also signaled another important change: new faculty were hired with a clear expectation that they would do research and publish. Faculty who had started a decade or more earlier had been hired to "concentrate on teaching."

As interviews progressed over the years, I noticed a critical distinction among new hires: new faculty obviously differed as a function of whether they came to campus as inexperienced (with less than three years beyond the terminal degree—the Ph.D. degree except for a few faculty in the fine arts), as returning (from careers outside academe), or as experienced (at full-time teaching on another campus).

Interviews and Other Visits

The interview questionnaire is presented in the Resource at the end of this book. Briefly, I used it to ask new faculty to describe and rate their recent experiences, including collegial interactions, academic philosophies, and career plans. I repeated the interviews for each successive semester that indi-

viduals were on campus, for periods as long as four years. My
visits, consisted of much more than structured interviewing.
Interactions lasted at least an hour, and all but a few new
faculty members added open-ended responses to their structured answers. Beyond my set questions, new faculty chose
what to emphasize and develop in our discussions. As a way
of organizing a lot of data, I present the experience of all new
faculty chronologically, regardless of when they began during
the four years.

First Semester: Awkward Beginnings

Almost immediately, as soon as the glow of welcoming cere-
monies was replaced with the day-to-day toil of managing
classes and laboratories, complaints began.

Loneliness

The primary complaint in these interviews surprised me. Given
the enthusiasm that I had seen when new faculty first came to
campus, I initially expected to hear continued accounts of
people enjoying new opportunities during interviews at mid-
semester. I soon discovered that what I had observed at the presemester orientation was misleading. Except for two or three
individuals per cohort, new faculty interviewed at the midpoints
of their first semesters accentuated feelings of loneliness and of
intellectual understimulation.

   Loneliness was new faculty's most salient complaint,
one with clear precedence over the next most common types
of concerns—of work loads and busyness. One assistant professor from the first of four cohorts typified her colleagues'
comments with this remark:

> In graduate school, I always had people around
> me to talk with, people who were doing similar
> things, people who worried about me and I about
> them. What worries me most about being here is
> not so much the lack of social contacts—I can

understand, I suppose, why most of my colleagues are rarely here on campus—as it is the
lack of ideas and of caring about my teaching
and research. I worry that I may never have ideas
of my own for research. I guess that I'm a lot
more dependent on the people around me for
ideas and motivation than I realized.

But feelings of isolation and understimulation were not exclusive to inexperienced new faculty. A returning faculty member
made this remark in a quiet, bemused fashion:

Now that I'm here, I realize that they hired me
only because they couldn't find anyone else qualified in my specialty area and with a Ph.D. Now
that I'm here, no one pays much attention to me.
That's disappointing, I suppose, but I should
have known that this would happen. The other
people in the department have their own business
to take care of. I wish this were a happier place,
one where we took more interest in what each
other teaches.

Experienced faculty were the most surprised about their
isolation, even more than their colleagues who came to campus with little professorial experience. Almost without exception, these faculty had been hired because they had already
been productive as researchers on other campuses. The recruitment process often set up the false expectations expressed by
this associate professor:

When they recruited me, they couldn't be com-
plimentary enough. They courted me. Now that
I'm on campus, I feel ignored. They not only
don't care about my lab and my research, they've
actually undermined my efforts to set it up. If I
had known what things would be like here, I

would never have come. It puzzles me. Does this
sort of thing happen to other new faculty?

Changes in Collegiality over Time

Not surprisingly, both the experience of isolation and that of
understimulation affected new faculty's perceptions of collegiality. When I asked them to rate their departmental colleagues in terms of collegiality, new faculty produced the data
shown in Table 2.1. The arresting result revealed in the table
is one repeated throughout this study: within and across
cohorts, the collegial climate seems to have improved over
time. Whereas newcomers of 1985 and 1986 routinely reported
hostile comments from colleagues with more seniority on campus, new faculty who began in 1987 and 1988 rarely noted
collegial animosity.

Although cultural conflicts decreased over the years, they
remained noteworthy. The most common reports of cultural
conflict that I recorded were (1) that senior faculty routinely
excluded new faculty from departmental decisions, (2) that
seniors openly grumbled about new faculty's interests in gaining
more national visibility than local visibility as professionals, (3)
that seniors showed undisguised disdain for new faculty's talk
about research projects, (4) that seniors complained of new faculty's narrow preferences for teaching specialty courses, and (5)
that senior faculty aggressively distinguished teaching and
research as mutually interfering activities.

Table 2.1. Reported Levels of Collegial Support or Help
During First Semester (in Percentages).

Level of Support or Help	Year Cohort Began			
	1985	1986	1987	1988
High	28	38	46	49
Medium	31	35	46	41
Low	41	27	8	10

Note: Percentages represent the numbers of interviewees reported
receiving collegial support.

Perhaps because these indices of cultural conflict declined over the four cohorts, the ratings of collegial support shown in Table 2.1 improved. A comment from an assistant professor in cohort 3 illustrates the point just made:

> I gather that things have gotten better for new people here. [A colleague] who started here two years ago told me some horror stories about how the old-timers treated him. They seemed threatened by the presence of someone new, someone who is doing research, someone whom the students seemed to like a lot. But, according to him, that tension or resentment seems to have lessened. As far as I can tell, the same people who had trouble adjusting to newcomers have quieted down. They generally leave me alone; they're friendly in a superficial way—when I see them. Sometimes I wish they would show more interest, but then I'm not sure they would understand what I'm doing.

The Substance of Collegial Help

One change may have led to another. As new faculty's colleagues came to seem friendlier, or at least more tolerant, the substance of reported help improved slightly. The number of new faculty citing useful advice about professional activities went up from 17 percent to 30 percent over successive first semesters for each cohort. Still, two other aspects of advice from senior colleagues disappointed new faculty across all cohorts. First, senior faculty gossiped more than new faculty would have preferred (gossip, defined as rumors and idle talk about the personal and private affairs of colleagues, constituted 50 percent of all advice given over first semesters). Second, of all work-related advice communicated by faculty with more seniority on campus, useful hints about teaching were the rarest (never exceeding 3 percent of the total content). These excerpts from my notes on two inexperienced assistant professors illustrate the point:

Most of my colleagues like to complain about each other. They warn me about the people to avoid because they are deadwood or because they are explosive. They tell me stories about assistant professors who have failed—I could do without that, especially considering that these stories don't really tell me much about how I can survive. [In response to my question about whether colleagues give much advice about teaching] No, almost none, except to complain about the poor quality of students here. As a matter of fact, when I've mentioned teaching in terms of wanting to do well, I've been looked at askance. Some of my colleagues seem to be more comfortable talking about almost anything else [cohort 1].

There are a few people, like [one colleague] and [another colleague], who talk to me, but I wish I could tell you that the conversations were worthwhile. It is mostly gossip, so much so that I wonder what they will say about me. Some of it is goodnatured, though. The problem is that very little of it is about what must be done to get tenure—except for some vague comments like "you'll have to publish" [cohort 2].

Another surprising outcome of these interview questions was that the three categories of new faculty (inexperienced, experienced, and returning) showed no initial differences in terms of help and support received. (In later years on campus, though, inexperienced faculty indicated greater levels of help.) There was a paradox here: while senior faculty often reported (in a more informal series of interviews) feeling that they should leave new faculty alone until they seemed settled, new faculty, as we have seen, felt very differently. Nonetheless, new faculty were remarkably passive about seeking collegial support; they generally expected others to come to them, much as had happened during the recruitment process.

In a separate question, I asked new faculty for specific plans about collaborating as researchers or teachers with colleagues on campus. The percentages went up over cohorts (from around 20 percent to nearly 40 percent for research, and from 7 percent to 21 percent for coteaching), but not as much as I had anticipated. As a rule, new faculty were not feeling very optimistic about being able to carry out hoped-for collaborations at this point.

Data from other campuses may help put these results into perspective. Sorcinelli (1985), for instance, found that faculty at a campus with a strong research tradition cherished the supports and the milieu that greeted them. At that research campus, new faculty may find collegial networking easier. At my own present campus, a research university with demographics similar to those of the campus studied by Sorcinelli and Near, I am finding a result far less positive than that found at theirs. It may be that campuses differ in spontaneous collegial supports for new faculty. And it may be that my own direct interviews with almost all new faculty, contrasted to the surveys used in their study, account for some of the difference. New faculty, in my experience, tend to become more self-disclosing once interviews are under way, especially (by their own admissions) once they develop trust in me.

New faculty were, for example, initially reluctant to criticize their colleagues. I helped ease their discomfort in part by reminding them of the confidentiality of the interviews. And then I did something else designed to encourage disclosure. I asked them to begin by describing their departmental colleagues in terms of positive qualities. In descending order, senior faculty were seen as *positive* with regard to their

1.   Liking both undergraduate teaching and their students
2.   Appreciating their job security
3.   Appreciating their geographical location
4.   Envisioning a brighter future for their campus

I then asked them to rank the same colleagues in terms of
their negative qualities. Senior faculty were seen as *negative*
with regard to their

1. Burnout as professionals
2. Overconcern with campus politics
3. Paranoia about campus administrators
4. Complaints about campus resources
5. Complaints about poor-quality students

The curiosity in these listings, one often pointed out by new
faculty, is that senior colleagues were rated as good and bad
on similar dimensions (for example, the same individual who
complimented life in southern California might add a lament
about having stagnated and burned out in his or her career).
The reason for this overlap in perceptions seems to be that
their senior colleagues were demonstrating ambivalence about
their campuses and jobs. For example, they might exhibit
suspiciousness about their department at one time and optimism about it at another.

  Another seeming oddity was the persistence of many
negative feelings toward senior colleagues. New faculty's perceptions of senior faculty as generally tired, unproductive,
inconsistent, cynical, and even embarrassing remained intact
during the four years of this study. Indeed, the senior faculty
presented a problem that is usually absent in the literature
about new faculty (for an exception, see Seldin, 1987); that is,
new faculty saw seniors as often unable or unwilling to provide the kinds of effective support and models that newcomers
said they wanted in the midst of making stressful transitions
and establishing lasting habits as professors. A sampling of
representative comments of new faculty in their first year on
campus helps substantiate this point:

> The older people here amaze me. They don't even
> look or act like professors. I don't think they're
> too comfortable having someone like me here.
> For sure, they haven't made me feel welcome. Let

me tell you about what one guy said to me. He said, "Listen, what you want to do is get settled in your courses and then enjoy life. You'll see me out sailing when I can. You think you want to do research, but you'll learn. I did" [assistant professor, inexperienced, cohort 1].

The old-timers in my department do things that interfere, including saying negative things to students. Students come to me and actually tell me that [one of the old-timers] told them not to work with me. Fortunately, the students think it's a joke. I don't [associate professor, experienced, cohort 3].

My problem here is the chairman and his friends. They have their own clique, and they're not interested in helping me. They stick me with courses that they don't want to teach. They act like they don't have information on how to teach my courses [associate professor, returning, cohort 2].

A final trend in semester 1 proved to be of particular interest. Over cohorts, the campus seemed to hire new faculty with decreasing needs for collegiality. The percentage of interviewees who rated collegial support as important for job satisfaction and professional success generally diminished over cohorts (72 percent, 82 percent, 58 percent, and 34 percent). Another explanation may account for the same data. Perhaps because they came to a campus growing more congenial to newcomers, succeeding cohorts felt less concerned about collegiality and thus rated their need for it lower.

Still, despite the mounting acceptance of new faculty on the study campus, some things about new faculty continued to rankle the people who had hired them. At a campuswide meeting for recruitment committees in 1987, for example, senior faculty talked repeatedly about inexperienced new faculty who already seemed eager to leave the campus for better jobs. The consensus in the meeting was that the campus would fare better by hiring faculty who would show more "loyalty."

Second Semester: Disappointed Expectations

Without exception, new faculty ending their first semesters supposed that things would soon get better. At last, they assumed, they neared semester breaks during which they would rest and catch up on writing. In fact, though, a month of vacation failed to meet expectations for getting caught up. Even successes in getting rested were unclear. Worse yet, the second semesters that followed were little better than the first semesters. Among other things, ratings of collegiality went down—across all cohorts.

Collegial Support

Spontaneous comments provided an idea of what had caused the drop in morale among new faculty during the second semester. By the time they had been on campus for a few months, realities had set in. In particular, new faculty reported feeling depressed about their own productivity and about the competence of faculty who had been on campus for a while; familiarity and inefficiency were breeding contempt. This meant that plans for collaboration, especially where new faculty had no junior colleagues with similar interests, were being abandoned.

Not all judgments of more senior faculty were negative. Of newcomers from the three kinds of backgrounds, inexperienced faculty were most generous in rating their seniors as being competent on the average (13 percent, 17 percent, 28 percent, and 20 percent of inexperienced new faculty gave such ratings for senior colleagues). Experienced and returning new faculty's ratings of colleagues' competence ranged from 0 percent to 15 percent over the four cohorts.

Intellectual Stimulation

As in semester 1, intellectual stimulation proved to be an important part of collegiality. Not only did satisfaction with collegiality reach a nadir in semester 2, but complaints of intellectual understimulation peaked. Table 2.2 shows the result in terms of descriptive data; the great majority of inexperienced new faculty rated intellectual stimulation as poor across all four cohorts.

Inexperienced new faculty expressed the most concerns about this deficit; they typically worried about how productive they could be as researchers if they weren't intellectually stimulated. They wondered how motivated they could remain if almost no one else around them seemed to care about teaching. Experienced and returning new faculty, on the other hand, hoped to be able to accept the situation as it was. Ideas could, after all, be garnered from reading journals and attending conferences. But even as they said these things, new faculty discounted their chances of finding success on their adopted campuses. They knew, at least at some level, that without social supports, their careers and happiness were handicapped.

Third Semester: Still Newcomers?

The second year brought some relief. By the midpoint of their third semester on campus, new faculty reported a rebound from the low point of the second semester. The result of that

Table 2.2. Percentage of New Faculty Rating Intellectual Stimulation as Poor During Semester 2 (by Background and Cohort).

	Background of New Faculty		
Year Cohort Began	Inexperienced	Returning	Experienced
1985	87	50	33
1986	88	50	42
1987	61	60	19
1988	70	60	28

rebound in terms of ratings of collegiality brought ratings back to and slightly past where they had been in semester 1. That is, each successive cohort continued to rate collegiality somewhat more highly, especially among inexperienced new faculty. New faculty's comments suggested reasons for continuing to give collegiality mediocre ratings: First, new faculty in their second years reported surprise at continuing to feel like newcomers. In the best scenarios, they had found a mentor and a friend or two, but they rarely knew most of their colleagues (who continued to seem invisible and frugal with help). Second, new faculty felt even more pressure than in semester 1 to get on with research and publishing; during the summer between years 1 and 2, they had not, as a rule, fulfilled their plans of doing much research and writing.

New faculty in year 2 now openly concluded that one reason for their lack of scholarly productivity was a dearth of supports, including collegial encouragements, physical facilities (such as equipped laboratories), and personnel (such as secretaries and assistants) seemingly essential to research and writing. For the first time, new faculty consciously held their veteran colleagues responsible not only for the lack of a friendly environment but also for the absence of either a research or a teaching culture:

> No, I don't feel that things are any more conducive to feeling good about the campus than last year. People seem no more interested than they were before; that's how things will probably stay. What I should be doing, what I planned to be doing, is to get some collaborations set up here. That's a big disappointment, not having anyone to share things with. And I can't see it changing soon; nobody else around here seems to be doing much. I didn't know how reliant I could be on other people to help get things done [assistant professor, inexperienced, cohort 3].

> What's wrong is that nobody seems to care what I do. No one cares about teaching. No one talks

about it except to complain. I haven't got any useful help. So what hope is there for me to become a better teacher when no one cares or helps? It makes me angry [assistant professor, inexperienced, cohort 4].

Experienced and returning faculty made few spontaneous comments about collegiality by semester 3. When asked, they typically responded with a sigh of resignation; they had come to see the campus as a commuter culture where senior faculty spent little time.

Fourth Semester: A New Low

New faculty continued to anticipate each coming vacation and semester with expectations of at last getting rested and caught up. Sadly, the holiday break and second semester of the second year on campus provided little escape from disappointing patterns. With the exception of some atypical newcomers, most of them inexperienced, new faculty persisted in reports of social isolation and intellectual understimulation. Some subgroups reported more isolation and understimulation than did others. The most distressed new faculty, it was now apparent, were women and members of minority groups. The comments from minority new faculty were the most discouraging:

When will it end? Or maybe I should say when will I end? I just don't see how I am going to make it here. . . . What's going to happen, if I don't go crazy first, is that I'll get to be just like my colleagues who spend very little time on campus. Some of them have businesses elsewhere, you know. But I don't want to be like that. I still like students and teaching. And I still want to do research, something worthwhile. I don't like what this place is doing to me [assistant professor, inexperienced, cohort 3].

What are we in, my fourth semester on campus, right? I'll have to admit that I'm surprised how hard it is to get to know people here. I end up spending all my time preparing for classes and, more than that, spending lots of time with students in my office. They're not hard to get to know. I fret over the things I'm missing in not having colleagues in the department to interact with, especially on my research. I notice that I'm not getting much done of what I told you I had planned to do [associate professor, experienced, cohort 4].

By the end of their second year on campus, new faculty could be dichotomized according to whether or not they had found substantial social support. In the fourteen cases where new faculty had found systematic mentoring, they reported a nearly unique feeling of acceptance on campus. Minority faculty were the least likely to find substantial mentoring.

Fifth Semester: Finally!

At last, by year 3, things began to change for the better. For most new faculty, the third year on campus brought the first substantial changes in coping with their jobs and campus. Regardless of how collegially assimilated they felt, newcomers returned to campus with a certainty that things were going to be easier. To some extent, they were right. The small number of new faculty members who already felt a part of campus attributed this feeling to finding social support, most commonly from other new faculty. New faculty members who still felt estranged, on the other hand, explained their new-found comfort in terms of having mastered the time-consuming jobs, especially for course preparations.

In either case, some new faculty members seemed to have completed the stage that developmental theorists call the entry period (Braskamp et al., 1984), but not until well after the predicted "compressed" period of one or perhaps two years. Two seemingly obvious reasons for the lengthy entry period are the social upheaval of bringing new faculty to a campus that had done little hiring for more than a decade and a new set of professional values for incoming cohorts. Still, it may be that entry periods are generally longer than had been supposed; new faculty face complex challenges that may require several years of adjustments. At my present campus, a research campus where hiring has been stable for years, the normative entry period for more than a hundred new faculty members appears to be two and a half to three years.

Socialization Rates

Even when new faculty had abandoned hope of collaborations with more senior colleagues, they persisted in looking for friends and collaborators among other new faculty. Inexperienced new faculty delighted in having at least one friend (defined as someone with whom they socialized off campus) and one potential collaborator (defined as someone with whom they discussed academic matters at least weekly and in ways that might lead to coauthored projects) by their third year on campus. By year 3, though, a near majority were still looking. Experienced and returning new faculty again reported less success in establishing these kinds of social networks (Table 2.3).

By their own admission, experienced and returning new faculty were not adjusting happily to campus life by their third year. The exceptions to this rule were the few experienced faculty members who themselves became mentors for new faculty or whose departments had agreed to hire their friends from other campuses as even newer faculty.

Table 2.3 shows another result worth mentioning. Rates of substantial social interactions (that is, more than small talk) with colleagues continued to be low. When I asked them why this happened, new faculty offered remarkably uniform answers:

> The answer couldn't be more obvious. I have been too busy to try to do much socializing. I

Table 2.3. New Faculty Reporting Various Social Contacts in Year 3.

Year Cohort Began and Type	Type of Regular Weekly Contact			
	Visits to Colleagues	Visits from Colleagues	Visits with Chairs	Discussion of Plans
1985				
Inexperienced	75	50	42	58
Returning	0	25	0	0
Experienced	40	30	20	30
1986				
Inexperienced	86	71	36	71
Returning	20	20	10	10
Experienced	58	43	29	29

meant to. I wanted to (and I still want to). But I just haven't had the time [assistant professor, inexperienced, cohort 2].

I think I know why. I expected the people here, especially the chair, to come to me, to display more interest in me. It's part of the responsibility of the senior people to help make people like me feel at home [associate professor, experienced, cohort 1].

One good reason is that I haven't done as much as I could have. I really haven't made the effort to go around and talk to people. Part of it is due to shyness. Part of it is due to busyness; I've put other things first. Besides, I should have expected this. I sort of knew that a campus wasn't going to be like industry, where they pay so much attention to you when you first arrive. Part of what attracted me here was being left alone to operate autonomously. But now I'm not sure I relish the result [associate professor, returning, cohort 2].

Collegiality as Evaluation

Year 3 also marked the emergence of another dimension of collegiality: experiencing one's colleagues as evaluators. Some peer evaluations by more senior faculty had already occurred in earlier semesters, but the fifth semester was when preoccupation with colleagues in this role reached salience. New faculty's treatment in the retention, tenure, and promotion (R/T/P) process became a major source of complaints, many of them accompanied by tears during our private conversations.

In my observations, the evaluators operated much as they do at most campuses. R/T/P committees consisted almost entirely of senior faculty who evaluated new hires in written formats (typically with added evaluations from departmental chairpeople). On the campus I studied most intensively, R/T/P committees acted with a caution, one implanted by higher administrators, against communicating unrealistically positive evaluations that could be used by unsuccessful tenure seekers in litigation.

Fifty-eight percent of new faculty found these evaluations unfair and disheartening. Moreover, complaint levels were nearly equal across experience types; even faculty who were used to being evaluated chafed over their evaluations. It was all too easy to collect complaints about the campus evaluation process. Spontaneous comments about R/T/P procedures remained similar across successive cohorts and took on this rank order:

1. Feedback emphasized criticisms and rarely included praise.
2. Standards were enforced that most evaluators (faculty who had been on campus for a while) could not themselves meet.
3. Single failings of new faculty, especially relating to poor student evaluations of teaching, were overemphasized and then reemphasized in subsequent evaluations.

Even the minority of new faculty who had not complained about the fairness of evaluations joined their peers in objecting to the generally unspecified criteria:

> I can't find out how much is enough. And no
> one else seems to know, either. It would help to

know how many publications are enough and to know what level of student evaluations I should aim for. But I guess that all this gets decided on an individual basis; it makes the whole thing seem political, capricious [assistant professor, inexperienced, cohort 2].

Let me tell you what the effect of the R/T/P process is on me. Because I really don't know how the system works and because most of what I hear about is rumor (most of it horror stories), I end up feeling like avoiding the whole issue. I end up not working on the things I know I should because the system makes me feel helpless [assistant professor, inexperienced, cohort 4].

The common concerns about an ill-defined process of evaluation may be seen in this datum: of the fifty new faculty members participating in semester 2, only five reported receiving specific, sufficient information on how much quantity and quality they probably needed to achieve for approval in the R/T/P process. What new faculty apparently wanted most in this study was what their kin on other campuses reportedly wanted—more support and useful feedback (Fink, 1984).

Sixth Semester: A Brief Regression

Once again, this series of interviews at the midpoint of a spring semester brought many reports of dysphoria; new faculty often ruminated about the hopelessness of finding success on their adopted campus. But amidst all that, collegiality was a bright spot for slightly fewer than half of all new faculty members (most so, as usual, for inexperienced new faculty). While their opinions of their departments remained low, new faculty showed less emotionality in disparaging their home bases. They were, in effect, showing some "distancing," a presumably healthy adjustment to some aspects of a new job.
Distancing also took on a discriminatory aspect. New

faculty actively decided which colleagues to ignore and which to pursue as resources and friends. Overall, though, distancing was proceeding with remarkable slowness. Some two-thirds of new faculty reported that they still carried strong resentment about unpleasant experiences with campus administrators during semester 1. Invariably, these reports included descriptions of rude managers or bureaucrats who treated new faculty in patronizing fashion, usually in regard to obtaining resources that had been promised during the recruitment phase. New faculty reported that the memory of these events still motivated them to try to move to another campus. The durability of these critical incidents suggests that campuses should pay more attention to the delivery (and the manner of delivery) of promised resources.

Seventh Semester: Stability in the Fourth Year

How much had collegiality changed over the four years? In their first year on campus, cohort 1 reported a surprisingly low level of collegial support and help; only 28 percent of them rated it as high, while 41 percent rated it as low (Table 2.1). Each succeeding cohort, as we have seen, rated collegiality somewhat more highly, suggesting that the climate became more congenial to newcomers. Consistent with that trend, members of cohort 1 reported more help and support in each of their four years under study; by year 4, some 40 percent of them rated collegiality as highly positive (most so for inexperienced new faculty).

Intellectual Stimulation

Even the low estimates of intellectual stimulation from colleagues showed modest improvement over the years: 87 percent of new faculty rated it as poor in year 1, while just under 50 percent rated it poor in year 4. Here again, those who elicited this sort of social support reported a discriminatory stance in seeking collegiality; clearly, only a few colleagues could be counted on to provide intellectual stimulation. New faculty who did not find this stimulation generally reported finding (or maintaining) sources off campus. Nearly as often, experienced and returning new faculty reported that they were learning to cope without the ideas and prods that they had hoped for.

Usefulness of Collegial Advice

Not all available social support improved; the quality of collegial advice, for example, did not. By year 4, new faculty reported getting advice on academic survival from more senior colleagues that continued to be as gossip- and politics-laden as in year 1. Even after my probes to consider their own role in encouraging this sort of advice, only about one-third of new faculty admitted to such a possibility.

Mentors

New faculty in cohorts 1 and 2 found the fewest mentors over the study period, at rates below 15 percent and 34 percent, respectively. But despite their continuing failure to receive mentoring, twelve faculty members in these cohorts became mentors for more junior new hires. While tradition might have dictated an expectation that these mentors would come from the ranks of experienced new faculty, two-thirds of the new faculty who mentored came from the inexperienced ranks. New faculty who acted as mentors were, not surprisingly, unusually well connected to social networks and satisfied with their jobs. As in earlier semesters, minority new faculty were proportionately unlikely to find mentoring spontaneously. They were even less likely to act as mentors for other new faculty.

Eighth Semester: No Longer New

In general, few observable changes occurred between semesters 7 and 8; at last, new faculty were settled into seemingly stationary and somewhat useful social patterns or, lacking those, had become silent about collegiality. The most notable development during the fourth year involved an aspect of sociality not yet covered in this consideration: social supports off campus, including family life.

In their first interviews, most new faculty members listed a desire to balance their professional and personal lives. When I reminded them of this plan during subsequent semesters, responses took on a comical note. Balance, if it would ever come, was not an immediately foreseeable reality; new faculty felt too overscheduled, too far behind on writing projects, too insecure about teaching and gaining tenure to even try to give social life off campus as high a priority as academic activities.

What new faculty exhibited in this regard through their first three years on campus can be called negative spillover. Sorcinelli and Near (1989) found that new faculty were especially likely to allow their jobs to overwhelm (that is, negatively spill over into) their homes lives. In the present study, new faculty in years 1 and 2 had routinely admitted that they were neglecting their social life off campus:

> I really don't have any social life at all. I always have work that I take home in the evenings and weekends. If I'm not preparing lectures, I'm grading papers. I'm waiting for Christmas vacation to get at some writing. Plus, when I do get some free time, I'm tired [assistant professor, inexperienced, cohort 2].

> My family seems to understand, but it seems awful to spend so little time with them. Sometimes I don't even play with my son for a week at a time. That may be the hardest part of this job, having to devote almost all my time to it and almost none to the things that matter more [associate professor, experienced, cohort 2].

> You must be joking. I gave up that fantasy long ago. I hardly remember what my family looks

like. Let's talk about something else [assistant professor, inexperienced, cohort 4].

By year 3, though, a near majority of new faculty began mentioning attempts (often unsuccessful) to find balance. They
talked about plans to do more with their friends from campus,
to pursue more friendships on campus, to take more vacations
with their families, and to resume a more regular schedule of
physical exercise (usually in social fashion).

By year 4, most new faculty members had taken concrete steps to reduce negative spillover. Fourteen of the twenty
members of cohort 1 detailed specific plans for community or
family activities (membership in a choir, weekend camping
trips), compared to a previous high of four such reports. Curiously, this move generally came in conjunction with a decision that could have undermined it. During this year, nearly
a third of these new faculty members had found part-time
employment as consultants off campus.

In new faculty's view, consulting had two impacts
beyond financial considerations. First, consulting provided
them with reminders of their competence as professionals;
outside jobs were clearly more likely to produce compliments
than was the campus. Second, having to fit the part-time job
into an already crowded schedule helped teach new faculty
that they could manage more than the lecture-related activities that had dominated their lives. This step, one that usually
preceded the move to develop a more substantial social life
off campus, assumed the special appearance of a milestone
activity. It seemed to coincide with the realization that new
faculty could get on with their lives. In a way, this may have
been the most telling end point of the entry period.

Conclusions About Obstacles to Establishing Collegiality

What can we learn in a patient look at new faculty such as
this one? First, we are reminded that new hires cannot flourish in isolation. Before they will feel comfortable and efficient,
they must find social supports and intellectual stimulation.

We also saw another advantage of getting to know new faculty better: they may surprise us. Some findings in these interviews were anticipated. For example, I expected that new faculty would complain of busyness. But the extent of overall complaining proved surprising, especially in regard to the slow rate of change from the social isolation of the first semester. Even new faculty members' personal plans for corrections translated into action slowly. For example, ambitions for taking up exercise regimens were realized only incompletely, if at all, over the four years. When new hires did manage such practices, most changes occurred socially, with colleagues acting as partners or support groups.

A related surprise was the length of the entry period, the phase during which new faculty still felt alien to campus. Its persistence for three and sometimes four years may have been partly a result of the commuter culture of the study campus; presumably, when colleagues are more often on campus, socialization is accelerated.

Other surprises involved differentiating new faculty according to backgrounds; for example, faculty already on campus assumed that only the inexperienced new faculty needed significant help and support. Senior faculty often reacted defensively to the strong publication records of experienced and returning new faculty. Returning new faculty faced particularly strong obstacles, including culture shock: they had been away from academe for a long time (the modal duration was ten years), and they had trouble adjusting to what seemed a peculiarly political and competitive situation, one that included little respect for their years of accumulated knowledge in real-world contexts. Curiously, several returning newcomers cited Henry Kissinger as the supposed author of a comment about politics in academe being so petty because the stakes are so low.

Some returning new faculty members offered an intriguing insight about why they were not fitting in. They supposed that there must be a critical period for effective socialization to campuses and that those critical periods when adjustments would have been made most easily had already been spent in other settings, in other work cultures.

The biggest surprise was the seeming neglect and mistreatment of new faculty at the study campus. Was this campus especially calloused in its treatment of new hires? My own consulting at a variety of other campuses suggests that this reaction of new faculty is typical. As a rule, new faculty report feeling neglected, isolated, overworked, and deprived of vital support and feedback. The critical point in looking for the generality of these findings is this: much of the real distress and abandonment experienced by new faculty may remain unapparent until they are engaged in repeated and patient interviews.

Where campuses vary in terms of the kinds of problems expressed in this study, most differences probably occur in terms of duration. For example, because the study campus had not hired many new faculty in more than a decade, it may have been slower than the norm to adjust to them. And to cite an instance from my more recent observations of new faculty at a research university, experienced new faculty are welcomed somewhat more quickly by colleagues already committed to scholarly productivity. But even at campuses where socialization and support occur more rapidly, the process seems maddeningly inefficient and inhumane to new hires.

Given the apparent commonality of social isolation for new faculty, we might wonder whether this tradition has adaptive value. New faculty themselves conclude that academe still operates on social Darwinistic principles; as one inexperienced new assistant professor commented,

> Just as graduate schools let many students sink
> or swim in the dissertation stage, we also seem to
> willingly let people, even good people, fail here
> if they don't figure things out on their own.

No one among the new faculty I have gotten to know could imagine a useful purpose for the neglect and isolation that they experienced.

For all my disappointments in getting to know new faculty as colleagues on the study campus, though, I readily found a glimmer of hope. In the midst of new hires who managed collegiality with measured slowness, a small group of exemplary new faculty members demonstrated a more effective pattern. I end this chapter with the suggestion that we can employ these quick starters as a model for understanding what coping with obstacles to establishing collegiality is like at its best. Therein may lie clues about how to improve things for other new faculty.

Quick Starters

In each cohort, a few inexperienced and experienced new faculty members stood out as exemplary. These were individuals who socialized quickly, usually by their second and third semesters on campus. Curiously, quick starters were no more likely to emerge among experienced than among inexperienced new faculty. To make the case most clearly about what actions and mind-sets accompany the most efficient adjustments to campus, I have chosen to depict only the inexperienced quick starters in this book.

On the study campus, I identified eleven such quick starters. At my present campus, after two years of similar study of all new faculty, I have identified an additional twelve. To make initial identification of quick starters, I use measures of teaching success. Quick starters must, first of all, score in the top quartile of their cohorts as student-rated, self-rated, and expert-observer-rated excellence in teaching by their second or third semester on campus. This preliminary index of quick starting does not, as a rule, exclude new faculty members who make fast starts as scholarly writers or as collegial networkers. Success for new faculty members as teachers, publishers, and networkers is commonly general to all three activities.

Some of the distinguishing characteristics of these exemplary newcomers are predictable. They were generally more likely than others to rate collegial and intellectual support as moderate to good. They had established regular relationships with colleagues who shared their interests within the first year. By the second year on campus, they felt highly identified with their institutions. But none of these accomplishments was what quick starters judged as pivotal in their exemplary progress. They rated achieving balance, including social networking, as the single most critical thing that they had learned to do as new faculty.

For quick starters, balance meant three related things. First, it connoted setting limits on lecture preparation so that it no longer dominated workweeks. As a general rule, quick starters devoted no more than two hours of preparation per classroom hour (while also aiming to go to classes less overprepared and more inclined to encourage student participation than were other new faculty). Second, balance meant finding time during most workdays to do scholarly writing, typically about four to five hours per week. Third, and most surprising, quick starters generally spent as much time on social networking, on and off campus, as they did on scholarly writing. This finding of balance between time spent in productive writing and socializing, incidentally, resembles the well-established connection between research productivity and moderate but balanced investments in writing and networking (Creswell, 1985).

Lessons from Quick Starters

We will return to quick starters throughout this book, especially in Chapters Five through Eight, where we deal with intervention programs for new faculty. Here, though, we will take a look at the general principles that emerge from an examination of quick starters as colleagues. In each case, the characteristic habit or attitude is linked to the IRSS factors that we encountered in the introductory chapter. Each of the four attributes of quick starters is, as we will see, a matter of mastering elementary things.

Involvement. The first emergent characteristic of quick starters studied so far is their proactive immersion in the campus community. More than other new faculty, they are actively involved. They ask colleagues for help and advice far more commonly than do other new faculty members. They arrange collaborations for research projects, for writing grant proposals, and for coauthoring manuscripts for publication, activities almost nonexistent in counterpart new faculty members. And they socialize about teaching. They ask advice about teaching, sometimes by seeking out renowned teachers on campus with specific questions. They ask colleagues to guest lecture in their classes, and they reciprocate. They get to know students in and out of class, especially as laboratory assistants. Moreover, nearly half of them have taken or audited classes in areas where they wanted to experience new thinking or to brush up on old material.

Regimen. Quick starters also show relatively unique inclinations to manage their time to include writing and social networking. Their own consensus is that the real problem is not time management but task management. By limiting periods of involvement in activities such as class preparation and writing to brief, nonfatiguing sessions, they are able to "get more from less." Thus, finding time, usually about a total of an hour per weekday, for social networking (including visits, phone calls, and letters) is not difficult once they learn to put limits on the durations and fatigue of other activities.

One thing that happened in the wake of establishing this balance was especially interesting. As they practiced moderation in activities such as class preparation, new faculty noticed (as did I) a sharp drop in "busyness displays" (that is, complaining about feeling busy; feeling rushed). Soon after, they noticed an accompanying change in the readiness with which colleagues sought them out. One of the quick starters stated it this way:

> When I started feeling less rushed, less behind on everything, I began to do a better, more reflective job of things. Another thing: I notice that I haven't talked as much about how busy I am. And that, I'm sure, is a signal to my colleagues

and students that I can be approached. Busyness displays, as you call them, are really social signals that tell the people around us not to bother us. Some of the people who have known me for a while still preface their comments with a concern about how busy I am. Students will say, "You're probably too busy to talk to me now, right?" When I reassure them that I am no longer busy, they smile in relief [assistant professor, inexperienced, cohort 2, campus 2].

Self-Management. One reason why the successes of quick starters are so uncommon may be that they are typically based on tacit knowledge. We rarely impart these basics, for several reasons. One is that the skills and attitudes are so simple and basic that we may expect others to learn them on their own. A related reason why knowledge about things such as task management and social networking remains tacit for most new faculty is that we may not know exactly what it is that needs to be taught. So it is that we and they may spend a lot of time trying to solve the wrong problems.

In the case of quick starters, the types of usually tacit knowledge that they report valuing include balance, including social networking; proactiveness in establishing rapport and supportive interactions with colleagues and students; a spontaneous style of taking risks (for example, seeking communications with superstars in their disciplinary specialties and going to classes feeling less than perfectly prepared); and building self-esteem.

Social Networking. This fourth part of IRSS theory follows from what has just been listed. A key to the involvement, the task representation, and the learning of tacit skills is collegiality. That is, the kinds of wisdom and encouragement that colleagues can provide come only after involvement (for example, in a faculty fitness club), after solving the right problems (for example, in dropping busyness cues), and after learning what is essential to thriving but might otherwise remain unrecognized (for example, learning to talk with superstar colleagues without seeming ingratiating or demanding and yet appearing eager to learn). But this stage of mastering first-factor competencies includes something else. It relies, for its maximization, on letting others do some of the work. It means relaxing the usual proud autonomy so often character-istic of new faculty so that colleagues can assist as coteachers, as coauthors, and as mentors. It means, as the popular litera-ture on excellence puts it (Covey, 1989), moving past inde-pendence to interdependence.

Each of these four components of the success of quick starters will be developed in greater detail in our considera-tions of new faculty as teachers and writers. But for now, we can see what it is that other new faculty could be doing to help short-cut the usually slow and painful process of suc-ceeding in professorial careers. Clearly, collegial supports play an enormous role in augmenting or delaying that process.

Parallels to Quick Starters Outside Academe

While we are only beginning to learn about what distin-guishes new faculty who make quick starts, investigators out-side faculty development have been carrying out equivalent studies for decades. The corporate world provides some inter-esting comparisons in examinations of executives in fast-track career slots. The most thorough and famous of these, by How-ard and Bray (1988), suggests that employees become more autonomous and less affiliative with age. A similar process was evidenced among new faculty described here, most readily by non-quick-starters.

Colleagues of Howard and Bray (London & Stumpf, 1986) propose three critical predictors of how new employees will adjust and thrive: (1) resilience (how effectively they per-sist in the face of frustrations), (2) insight (how realistically they see their problems and potentials), and (3) identification (how much they felt a part of their organization). Each of these factors played a crucial role in the collegial adjustment of new faculty studied in this chapter. Resilience occurred here where new faculty persisted in seeking collegial support and identified the few senior faculty who could be helpful. Resilience also meant depersonalizing feelings of isolation and understimulation. On self-ratings and observer ratings of resilience, quick starters scored more highly than did other new faculty.

Insight, as the AT&T researchers studied it, was tantamount to what new faculty depicted here did while expressing realistic concerns about problems facing them (London & Stumpf, 1986). Insightful new faculty avoided the temptation to catastrophize and to value gossip. Identification, finally, was reflected in the readiness with which new faculty felt a part of campus. On both these measures, again, quick starters were clearly superior to their counterparts among new faculty.

The chapters that follow look to the four basic characteristics of IRSS theory and to their kin, such as resilience, as predictors of success in coping with obstacles. Among these portents of success for new faculty, we might suppose, will be balance of a sort that includes collegial networking. Taken together, the chapters to come show that the three domains of collegiality, teaching, and research work in concert.

THREE

Establishing Teaching Styles and Skills

My own efforts at supporting the teaching of new faculty began much as I imagine most other people's have: I looked to books of tips about teaching. When I shared copies of these books and articles with my new colleagues, often discussing the advice in small groups, the response was puzzling. New faculty agreed that these materials undoubtedly contained good ideas. We had a nice time discussing the collegially private activity of teaching. But they felt certain that the authors of these books had not understood the special problems faced by new hires. Almost without exception, new faculty talked about wanting to manage comfort in classrooms, to figure out unsophisticated students, and to find more time to do a proper job at lecture preparation. Later on, they added, they might worry about refinements.

As a result, I decided to learn more about the experience of new faculty as teachers before prescribing remedies. I began, more than a decade ago, by looking to the literature for hints about how other campuses had made similar inquiries. I found less help than I had hoped for. I eventually found an enormous literature about growing concerns for college teaching (for example, Association of American Colleges, 1985), and I was impressed to see that the field is producing more and more useful advice about ways to

improve instruction (for example, Katz, 1985). Yet few of
these books on instructional development told me much
about how (and how quickly) professors establish their
teaching styles. There is, in fact, a literature relevant to new
teachers (see Eble, 1972; Nyquist, Abbott, & Wulff, 1989;
and Reynolds, 1989), especially teaching assistants and newcomers teaching at K–12 levels. But none of it is based on
the widespread experiences of new faculty at colleges and
universities. An oddity is this: if campuses provide instructional development at all, it is usually for teaching assistants. The assumption seems to be that, once graduate
students (with or without experience as teaching assistants)
join a campus as faculty members, they already know how
to teach (or else can figure it out on their own).

Only a small fraction of the new faculty I have gotten
to know at large universities come to their adopted campuses with any substantial training and experience as
teachers. And even at campuses with stronger teaching missions, new faculty typically cannot specify what they have
learned in the sporadic bits of training that they received as
teaching assistants. Evidently, we need to preface our plans
for instructional development with studies of the backgrounds and earliest experiences of faculty as teachers. We
may err if we suppose that our new hires are well prepared
as teachers.

This chapter, like the ones before it, begins at the
beginning. It queries new faculty about their experiences
and plans as teachers from their arrival on campus. It examines their failings and successes, including some that are
not immediately apparent. And, somewhat sadly, it shows a
surprisingly slow pattern of establishing comfort and student approval; moving beyond defensive strategies, including overpreparation of lecture content; and looking for
supports in improving teaching. Overall, it depicts new faculty as colleagues badly in need of help, badly in peril of
establishing poor habits of teaching that will persist. If the
need for support programs was not apparent before, it
should, I believe, be now.

A Study of Two Campuses

This story of new faculty as teachers at two study campuses, one already replicated at other campuses, is largely one of initial failures. But given the complexity of teaching and the usual lack of training for classroom instruction, we may need to steel ourselves for an unpleasant picture. Only when we have analyzed what goes wrong will we be ready to determine what can accelerate the development of new teachers.

But that's not all. The task of examining the experience of new faculty as teachers is not always easy. As I describe their development, I depict diverse experiences and even hint at the outlines of an empirically derived "theory" of how teaching careers develop. And I complicate the picture by introducing three subgroups and reporting data from two campuses. The caution is this: shoals lie ahead, particularly for readers not comfortable with social science reports. I have a suggestion as to how those shoals might be negotiated—by skimming the text for the essentials and going back for any details that need sorting out. (After all, one of the consistent findings about students who are best in school is that they know when to skim and when to focus; it's all a matter of timing.)

In the end, much as in white-water canoeing, you may find the shoals worth navigating. There is, I think, an inherent fascination in learning more about ourselves, especially how we get to be the way we are. Most of the formation, evidently, lies in experiences as new faculty.

Cohorts

The four cohorts of new faculty depicted here came from two campuses where I worked as a faculty developer: a comprehensive university and a research campus. Both campuses hired similar numbers of new tenure-track faculty during the study years of 1985 to 1990, from forty to seventy per year. Details of the samples and of other procedural considerations can be found elsewhere (Boice, 1991c).

Again, new faculty were ready participants. At campus 2, all but twelve to fifteen new faculty members volunteered to participate in the same format of interviews. Campus 2, much less publicly committed to teaching than campus 1, also differed in the influence of department chairpeople; at campus 2 (but never at campus 1), several chairs advised their new faculty not to participate in a program that might interfere with research productivity. Many new hires rejected that prohibition by participating in low-profile fashion. All involvement was confidential.

In most other ways, the two groups of new faculty were alike. They came to campus with similar levels of scholarly productivity, teaching experience, and doctoral credentials from prestigious universities (although the new faculty at campus 2 were more often from elite private universities). While new faculty at both campuses declared an interest in teaching well and in establishing themselves as visible members of their disciplines, newcomers at campus 1 differed in one express way: they wanted to avoid the pressures for publication at research universities such as campus 2.

The most obvious difference between the two campuses in the view of new faculty themselves was teaching assignments. Campus 1 had an official load of twelve classroom hours a week (that is, four separate courses per semester). Most of its new hires received three hours of release time in year 1 on campus; thereafter, only a minority of successful applicants received reduced teaching loads. Campus 2 had a two-course (six hours a week) assignment except for some humanities faculty, who carried three courses.

The key faculty under study here are the inexperienced newcomers and returning newcomers; experienced new faculty serve as comparisons (see Chapter Two for definitions of these categories of new faculty). Most inexperienced and returning new faculty in this sample had minimal or no experience as classroom teachers during graduate school (fewer than 20 percent at campus 1 and 15 percent at campus 2 had taught their own classes or parts of classes as graduate students). Fewer still (eight at campus 1; three at campus 2) reported any systematic training, including teaching practicums. The interview format was the same as that described in Chapter Two; I visited each participant in his or her office during successive semesters. I asked new faculty about their experiences and plans as teachers, colleagues, and scholarly writers, and I made at least one brief visit to the classrooms of all the new faculty members except for a minority (fewer than 4 percent) who did not volunteer permission for my observations.

Results

My scheme for presenting this complex of information here is straightforward: for each semester on campus, data are presented as an aggregate of all four cohorts studied. Then, contrasts are drawn between backgrounds (as inexperienced, returning, and experienced) and between campuses. In places, I depict individuals' responses to give a sense of how new faculty experienced problems and supports.

First Semester: Overpreparation and Underappreciation

My first impressions about how new faculty would cope with teaching proved misleading. Initial contacts with new faculty at presemester orientations (at least a month before the onset of formal interviews) revealed common concerns that eventually changed. For example, because both campuses required publication for tenure, newcomers supposed that they would feel more pressure to write than to teach. Their concerns about teaching were limited to preparation of content; well-prepared lectures, they imagined, would result in well-taught classes. They expected to spend a minimum of time and energy at teaching while they got on with their careers.

Later, when first-semester interviews were well under way, two unforeseen realities had come to the fore. First, the lack of collegial support and of intellectual stimulation for teaching on campus dominated complaints at campus 2 as at campus 1 (Chapter Two). Second, time spent in lecture prep-

aration dominated workweeks to the near exclusion of socialization and scholarship. Perceived pressures were far greater
for teaching than for publishing; activities that could wait
were put aside until new faculty had time and energy left
over from teaching.

Collegiality and Teaching

The two campuses produced collegial experiences in regard
to teaching that were surprisingly alike. Campus 1, despite its
teaching mission, generally fared no better than did campus
2: First, helpful levels of collegial support for teaching were
anything but universal; senior faculty were unlikely to say
much beyond initial small talk. Second, most of what senior
faculty did say ran to rumors and grievances; again, of all the
kinds of counsel, advice directed at teaching was least common. This comment from an inexperienced newcomer at
campus 2 was normative:

> No, no one has said much about teaching.
> Mostly, I've been warned about colleagues to
> avoid. A lot of it is gossip and complaining. I
> can only think of two specific things that have
> been said about teaching here. One that I hear a
> lot is how bad the students are—about how
> unprepared and unmotivated they are. The other
> one, that maybe two people mentioned, was a
> warning about the need to set clear rules and pun-
> ishments on the first day of class. All in all, I'm
> pretty disappointed with the help I've gotten.

The nearly total public inattention to teaching by colleagues surprised new faculty at both campuses. Neither inexperienced nor returning faculty were confident that they knew
how to teach. Moreover, few new faculty got the help as
teachers that they expected. What was most expected but least
likely to materialize was concrete help such as syllabi from
previous courses. Another unmet need was for advice about

managing difficult students, especially those who might complain about new faculty members' teaching to department chairs. (At both campuses, rumors about new faculty members who suffered punishments as a result of such complaints spread quickly).

From a variety of measures of colleagues' inattention to teaching, one more merits mention: fewer than 5 percent of new faculty members in their first semesters at either campus could identify any sort of social network in their departments for discussing teaching (in ways akin to departmental discussions about, say, the scholarly literature—moderately common events).

My questions about social support for teaching produced another surprise. At both campuses, patronage was no greater for inexperienced or returning faculty than for experienced newcomers, despite the seemingly greater need for guidance by the former two groups. At campus 2, curiously, experienced new faculty received the most useful advice and encouragement about teaching; this was part of a general pattern where already accomplished professors were more likely to feel welcomed than at campus 1, where resident senior faculty, because of their own inactivity as scholars, were apparently alienated by the productivity levels of incoming colleagues.

When I asked inexperienced new faculty why they thought so little help was forthcoming, their answers were typically as terse as this one:

> It is because they only care if we teach adequately. So long as there are few complaints about my teaching, my teaching will remain a very private activity [assistant professor, inexperienced, cohort 2, campus 2].

When I asked new faculty about what kind of help they needed most as teachers, the answer was nearly universal: they envisioned the hardest tasks as learning what level of lecture difficulty was appropriate for students and managing reasonable preparation times for classes. Significantly, all but a few new faculty planned to manage this learning entirely on their own; no departmental colleagues had offered help in these regards, and new faculty showed little interest in soliciting it. They supposed, when they thought about it at all, that they would learn to teach by trial and error.

In another question, I asked for specific plans to coteach. Clearly, this potentially useful strategy for acculturating newcomers to teaching was not on their minds (or in the plans of their more senior colleagues). Few planned to coteach (12 and 20 percent for the two cohorts at campus 1, 8 and 4 percent for the two cohorts at campus 2). Fewer still were already doing it.

Finally, new faculty in the inexperienced and returning categories commonly reported some distress over their senior colleagues' attitudes about teaching. At campus 2, interviews with new faculty produced this rank-ordered list of what they disliked about their seniors: (1) overconcern with campus politics, (2) complaints about campus resources, and (3) negativism toward students. Except for the omission of burnout as one of the unlikable qualities of senior colleagues, this list matches the one for campus 1 that we saw in Chapter Two. Of all these complaints, the one about colleagues' negativity toward students caused the most confusion among new faculty. Newcomers routinely wondered whether, after some time on campus, they too would develop cynicism toward students.

By this point, a disappointment was taking form. At campus 1, only five new faculty members specified seniors who acted as positive models for teaching (three instances were department chairs); at campus 2, only six such specifications were made (three of them chairs). Teaching was proving to be, as one newcomer put it, "a surprisingly private experience—except for those transients known as students."

Work and Plans

Next in commonality after complaints about a lack of collegial supports came about work loads. New faculty's predic-

tions of typical workweeks during the rest of year 1 emphasized a hoped-for balance of time expenditures, usually seven
to thirteen hours per week each for both lecture preparation
and scholarly writing. But those estimates only remotely
reflected ongoing patterns at the midpoint of semester 1. New
faculty members, including the two experienced associate professors quoted here, invariably portrayed their patterns as temporary aberrations:

> As soon as I have my classes under control, I'm
> going to spend a lot more time on my writing. I
> need to get at least two papers finished (actually
> one just needs revision) this semester. [In response
> to my question about how ready he was to teach
> his classes] I have taught these courses before. And
> I spent some time this summer going over my
> notes. I thought that I would be spending very lit-
> tle time preparing for classes. But now I find that
> I'm doing a lot of modification. I'm trying to sim-
> plify some things. And much as I always have
> done—now that I think about it—I find myself
> always trying to improve the content of my notes.
> I want to be sure that I'm up to date [campus 1].

> I am not settled down yet. I'm still trying to fig-
> ure out what will work with students here. So
> my typical workweeks, as you call them, are not
> typical yet. I find myself spending much more
> time than I planned on my classes. I want to find
> a way to make the students a little less obviously
> bored and disinterested. Once I do that, I will get
> back to writing and the other things I have to do
> [campus 2].

Self-Descriptions as Teachers

When new faculty were asked to list their strengths as teachers, the result was remarkably uniform across groupings. My

rank orderings of the most common answers sorted themselves into the following categories:

Campus 1	*Campus 2*
1. I am well-prepared and knowledgeable.	1. I am well-prepared and knowledgeable.
2. I am interested in students.	2. I am good at explaining and conceptualizing.
3. I am good at explaining and conceptualizing.	3. I am a motivator.

In this context, new faculty implied what they considered the basis for good teaching in a uniform definition: clear, knowledgeable, and, possibly, inspiring lectures.

Self-generated lists of weaknesses as teachers produced this rank ordering:

Campus 1	*Campus 2*
1. I ask too much of students.	1. None.
2. None.	2. I ask too much of students.
3. I am too disorganized.	3. I am too disorganized.

My inquiries into faculty's limited concerns as teachers (note the commonality of new faculty who supposed that they had no weaknesses in the list above) produced some related outcomes. First, a near majority of new faculty members had no plans for improving their teaching (and all but a few who did specified improvements in content, organization, and motivation). Second, fewer than four faculty members per cohort described their classroom styles as anything more than what Fink (1984) and others have labeled "facts-and-principles lecturing." And, third, only two newcomers at each campus had firm plans to visit the classrooms of colleagues for models and insights in regard to teaching. When I asked new faculty to explain this disinclination, they answered much as these inexperienced new hires did:

No way. I wouldn't want anyone, any colleague, coming to my classes. Why would I expect someone else to tolerate it? [campus 1].

Frankly, I never thought of it. I'm not sure what I would learn. I really think it's a matter of simply learning what the students here can handle and of lowering my standards in general. Besides, I'm not sure I would be welcome in my colleagues' classes [campus 2].

Second Semester: Weathering the Storm

As did improvements in collegiality, other changes came slowly. By second semesters, new faculty felt no more settled in, successful at teaching, or productive at the things that teaching supplanted than they had in semester 1. When most of these new faculty members reflected on their experiences as teachers, they felt that semester 2 was the nadir.

Collegial Support for Teaching

Estimates of collegial support for teaching declined by about 10 percent in all four cohorts during semester 2. This drop in perceived collegiality by semester 2 had a reliable correlate. New faculty talked openly about a growing sense of disillusionment with their colleagues as teachers and as inspirations for teaching. More than before, new hires worried aloud about what the lack of collegiality would do to their teaching:

One thing I worried about in returning to a campus job was whether I could handle the teaching. I guess I didn't presuppose that I would get lots of help, but I certainly didn't expect to be surrounded by colleagues who don't seem to care about teaching. When I talk about it in the department, I feel like I am violating a rule of silence [campus 1, returning].

One big reason why I left my job at [my last cam-
pus] was because I thought I would enjoy teaching. Now I wonder how I can avoid becoming
just as negative about teaching as this campus is.
It isn't just that people don't care; teaching is
seen as a negative and as something that we
rarely discuss except to complain about [campus
2, returning].

Self-Descriptions as Teachers

There were almost no changes in self-descriptions from
semester 1 except from a few handfuls of new faculty members, many of whom had become participants in campus
faculty development programs. (As a rule, new faculty preferred to wait until years 4–6 to seek help with teaching,
usually after a warning by their retention and tenure committees.) While participants persisted as facts-and-principles
lecturers, they began to look forward to encouraging more
classroom discussions.

Work Patterns and Teaching

Although in semester 1, new faculty in all groupings predicted
changed work patterns that would allot equal time to teaching
and to scholarly writing by the next semester, once in semester
2, their habits had changed little since initial interviews (Table
3.1). Core workweeks (time spent per week on invariable, necessary activities), usually an estimated thirty-five to forty hours,
remained far shorter than predicted. By semester 2, average
investments in lecture preparation remained far higher than
deemed desirable by new faculty; campuses 1 and 2 evidenced
means exceeding twenty-one and sixteen hours, respectively,
across all experience types. Even the small subgroup of newcomers to science departments at campus 2 with teaching loads
of one course or less routinely expressed surprise that they had
spent three to four hours a week preparing for each hour of
classroom presentation.

Table 3.1. Mean Hours per Week Spent
in Core Academic Activities During Semester 2.

Academic Activity	Year Cohort Began			
	1987 (Campus 1)	1988 (Campus 1)	1988 (Campus 2)	1989 (Campus 2)
Teaching	8.5	8.2	4.0	4.1
Lecture preparation	23.7	21.0	17.2	16.1
Scholarly writing	0.8	0.6	1.1	0.3
Research	2.2	0.7	3.9	2.9
Committees	3.3	2.8	4.0	3.8

Accordingly, anticipations of spending far more time at writing by semester 2 went unfulfilled. Despite original estimates of workweeks with an equilibrium of hours per week spent on teaching and writing, the ratio of the two activities remained at more than 15:1. These imbalances were nearly as characteristic of experienced faculty as of other new hires. New faculty's immediate concern with this pattern was related to a virtual absence of scholarly and grant writing. The result was an increasing frustration with teaching as a task whose demands seemingly overshadowed its rewards. But with nudges to reflect about the reasons for spending so much time preparing lectures, new faculty realized their own contributions to the problem. The majority of them spontaneously admitted to overpreparing (having too much material to present without hurrying their lectures) and to perfectionism (going beyond the level of detail and correctness that could be rewarded in most classes). These insights did not, however, lead to immediate action.

A final, more optimistic pattern characterized new faculty. Despite having no immediate plans to effectively change their workweeks, new hires invariably predicted more productive and effective schedules in the near future; nearly all new faculty saw upcoming summers as times when they would at last catch up on writing.

Teaching Evaluations

During semester 1, all but a few new faculty members declined offers made during the first rounds of interviews to help them conduct early, informal student evaluations of their teaching. The stated reasons at both campuses are typified in these comments:

> No, no, not yet. I don't want you to see me yet. Maybe next semester would be better, once I'm doing a better job [campus 1, inexperienced].

> I already do that in my own way. I ask students to tell me how I am doing and if they have any questions. I think I'm doing fine in that regard— I don't really see the need to go through this [campus 2, inexperienced].

By semester 2, at both campuses and across all groupings, disappointing teaching ratings became a reality for the majority of new faculty. Table 3.2 shows that most new faculty were rated as mediocre according to campus-generated, compulsory teaching evaluations administered at the end of semester 1. In response to this measure, new faculty reported that they generally fared far worse in terms of teaching ratings than they had anticipated.

While this result held across campuses, two limitations

Table 3.2. Percentage of New Faculty Scoring Below the Mean
on Student Evaluation Scores (Semester 1).

Year Cohort Began	Background of New Faculty		
	Inexperienced	*Returning*	*Experienced*
1987 (Campus 1)	63	75	57
1988 (Campus 1)	55	50	44
1988 (Campus 2)	68	83	57
1989 (Campus 2)	69	67	64

merit mention. First, faculty at campus 2 were less surprised at their generally poor ratings; their undergraduate students were apparently more open in expressing their dissatisfaction during classes through bored expressions, audible conversations among themselves, and early exits from classes. In retrospect, new faculty at campus 2 realized that they should have paid more attention to obvious signs that students would rate them unfavorably. Second, nearly half of new faculty members at campus 2 failed to receive the printouts of the analyses of their student evaluations during semester 2. Even though this campus had made special efforts to devise and institutionalize a student evaluation instrument, no one had followed up to see that faculty were getting the results.

While campus 1, which prided itself on caring about teaching, did a far better job of getting feedback from its teaching evaluations to faculty, it did little better in terms of supplementing printouts with consultation from chairs or colleagues. Only a handful of new faculty members at either campus (five at campus 1 and four at campus 2) were counseled by anyone in their departments about what their numerical ratings meant or how they translated into alternative ways of teaching (see Menges and Mathis, 1988, p. 105, for information about the potential usefulness of such counseling).

Third Semester: More Disillusionment

What had the long-awaited summer vacation after the first year on campus brought? Before it began, new faculty hoped that their return to campus after their first lengthy respite from teaching would mark the end of a life-style of busily catching up. They expected to be rested, to have finished a manuscript or two, and to assume a less harried schedule. They were, once again, disappointed.

I began contacting new faculty as soon as they returned to campus for the fall semester of their second years on campus. Our informal meetings left the impression of disappointing progress during first summers since joining the campus. As a rule, new faculty had not settled down to productive writing as planned; instead, they had spent most of the summer recovering from what they described as the busiest, most stressful year of their lives. Then, when and if they felt compelled to work during the last parts of their first summers, they prepared and revised course plans and lectures:

> What I realized when I finally felt like getting back to work was that I needed to be better prepared for my classes than I was last year. I realize that as long as I'm struggling to have good enough notes and problems, I will never get around to writing [campus 1, inexperienced].

> All I did was rest. I needed it. I didn't do anything else, and I don't think I could have. When I finally started to think of coming back, I could only worry about getting ready to teach [campus 2, inexperienced].

Collegial Support for Teaching

During initial contacts and, later, during regular interviews, newcomers reported feeling another disillusionment upon returning for year 2: they still did not feel that they were a real part of the campus. Nonetheless, reports of collegial support had reached new (albeit still modest) heights. New faculty at both campuses continued to complain about loneliness and understimulation, but they were often better able to identify colleagues with whom they had regular and substantial interactions. Teaching continued to be the least discussed topic in such interactions. This improvement was not, however, universal. Two groups evidenced no gains in collegial support for activities such as teaching: returning faculty at both campuses and experienced faculty at campus 1. Their comments about this continuing predicament are echoed in this remark:

> No point kidding myself; I'm a bit hurt by it all. I thought that by now I would have some

friends—or at least some colleagues who feigned
an interest in what I'm doing. But evidently, this
is how things are going to be. I'm just going to
have to make the best of a bad situation. It's
hard to want to spend time at things like teaching when no one here seems to care [campus 1,
returning].

And for new faculty where collegiality had improved, changes
came from unexpected sources (not counting the senior faculty who invited some new hires for one-time welcoming
dinners in their homes). As a rule, inexperienced newcomers
who found collegial support for teaching got it from other
new faculty. An oft-heard comment in this part of interviews
was that "It's like the blind leading the blind."

Self-Descriptions as Teachers

In the main, new faculty's self-descriptions continued unchanged; improvements in teaching would come slowly, if at
all. The great majority of new faculty members in their second year on campus still saw good teaching in terms of little
more than content and, sometimes, enthusiasm. Few had
thought seriously about possibilities of someday winning a
teaching award on campus.

By semester 3, six more individuals identified themselves as having brought more enlightened concepts of teaching to classes than they had displayed or even discussed
during year 1. This enlightenment always included a plan to
have parts of classes devoted to student participation. The
single reason these new faculty stated for this delay was that
they had waited to feel settled as teachers before taking risks.

The great majority of new faculty members in year 2
persisted in describing their classroom styles as strict facts-
and-principles lecturing. My brief visits (with prior permission and with appearances at unpredictable times) to the classrooms of samples of ten of these faculty members at each
campus confirmed these self-descriptions. This comment from

an inexperienced assistant professor at campus 2 helps explain what I mean by a facts-and-principles style of teaching:

> You're right in calling it facts-and-principles. I organize my lecture notes so that most of what I have to say consists of lists (where I might say "the five kinds of phenomena are . . .") and of conceptual explanations (where I might give a definition and where I would want to give an illustrative example or so). I suppose, now that you mention it, that the limitation with my style is that I have everything worked out in advance. Students just sit and take notes. But I would argue that it offers the advantage of clear organization. Students know what to expect.

What I would add to that insightful description is that facts-and-principles styles are the epitome of lecturing, approaches that typically equate good content with good teaching. But what about the new faculty members who did not identify with facts-and-principles lecturing? In a similar sample of visits to the classrooms of new faculty members who claimed to be using student-oriented approaches (see Weimer, 1990, for a recent definition of this concept), more than half of them failed to confirm their self-descriptions. These self-described "innovators" were lecturing in "content-only" fashion during my visits, not in the student-oriented styles such as discussions and problem-solving groups that they had described to me earlier. They usually offered an explanation such as this:

> You have to realize that I don't always do this. When I have a better class, one that is better prepared and better prepared to participate, then I can focus around break-out groups and that sort of thing. Besides, to be honest with you, I don't feel all that confident here yet. These students are not shy about letting professors know when they don't like something [campus 2, experienced].

Student Evaluations

Given the formalized student rating systems for teaching employed at both campuses, new faculty had to wait for print-outs about semester 2 until semester 3. Two things stood out in my discussions of these ratings with new faculty: First, student ratings (except for some of the teachers with student-oriented styles mentioned earlier and for a near majority of experienced new faculty) had not improved. Second, new hires reported feeling ambivalent about attending to these generally discouraging results from the previous semester, now rather remote in time. Still, these ratings finally forced many new faculty members to admit to an unanticipated, unhappy outcome that had to be addressed. At last, some of them began thinking of ways of improving their teaching (or at least their ratings).

Work Patterns and Teaching

New faculty's disappointments about teaching were matched by frustrations with continuing imbalances. Semester 3 produced a result closely similar to that already seen for semester 2; teaching preparation continued to dominate other activities.

Plans

By the third semester, new faculty set more modest goals. More than ever, they looked forward to the time when they could temper the demands of teaching:

> I just need to get to the point where I feel that I am in control of my classes. I mean that my notes and overheads have to be better organized. I mean that the materials have to be at a level appropri-ate for students. [In response to my question about when he would know that his notes were well enough prepared] Good question. Maybe

never; I might always be repreparing my notes.
[In response to my question about when he
would feel comfortable about balancing teaching
preparation with other activities, such as social
life and writing] I think, really, that will come
when students seem to like what I'm doing—
and when I like what I'm doing [campus 1, in-
experienced].

Again, new faculty were asked to specify their plans for
improving their teaching. Rank orderings of their most common responses were nearly identical to the list for semester 1.
Overall, notions about the best ways of improving teaching,
classroom comfort, and student acceptance revolved around
better lecture preparation and lowered standards. In the face
of continuing frustration with teaching, though, one thing
had changed by the third semester. Suddenly, most new faculty attributed at least some of their pessimism about improving teaching to students, specifically to their lack of
preparation and motivation. "How," the question often went,
"can you expect me to do much with such poor students?"

Fourth Semester: A Critical Period?

While they persisted in hoping that each new semester would
bring feelings of acceptance by students, new faculty usually
found that semester 4 failed them in this regard. Instead, it
brought another self-rated low for new faculty. Exceptions to
this trend were inexperienced new faculty who found strong
bonds with other junior faculty in regard to scholarly productivity, inexperienced new faculty at campus 1 who participated in a campus faculty development program, and
experienced newcomers at campus 2 who had reestablished
some research productivity. In contrast, returning new faculty
showed the most obvious signs of maladjustment. By their
own admission, returners did not fit in. They had been treated
differently in their prior careers, usually with far more supports as new hires. The lack of sustenance for the things that

they valued most, especially teaching, simply made them retreat in disbelief.

Collegiality and Teaching

Overall, new faculty at both campuses, especially campus 2, rated collegial support for teaching as lowest in semester 4. Returning new faculty, as just mentioned, were most vocal in making this complaint. They had expected more friendly and appreciative colleagues:

> Sometimes I feel like a failure here. No one cares what I'm doing—except in the critical comments I got in my annual review. They make a big deal of my one poor teaching rating, but not one of them has offered to help. This system would be considered madness in industry. They wouldn't go to the trouble to recruit a doctoral-level specialist and then watch her fail [campus 1].

Semester 4 may have been a critical period of sorting out people who would establish commitments to teaching from those who would remain estranged. Overall, about half the new faculty members studied in semester 4 showed signs of establishing social networks and of finding increased comfort with teaching. While they had not yet, as a rule, found the kind of balance mentioned several times in this chapter, they were at least moving toward it. Their counterparts evidenced no real progress as teachers, during this or subsequent semesters. Apparently, new faculty who were going to improve as teachers made moves to do so by this critical juncture.

Student Ratings

Semester 4 brought feedback on student ratings of new faculty's teaching from semester 3, the point at which many new faculty members reported expecting a turnaround in student appreciation. As a rule, this did not happen; increases in rating levels over semesters 1 and 2 were slight except for participants in faculty development programs, a group of quick self-starters to be described later, and most of the group of experienced new faculty.

Three things about new faculty's reactions to these ratings stood out in interviews. First, new faculty tended to attribute disappointing ratings mostly to their students, especially to the inability of students to handle challenging material. Second, new faculty almost never (except for the minority of quick starters, many of whom participated in faculty development programs) sought out advice for ways of translating ratings into alternative styles of teaching. Third, even in the face of two disillusioning ratings, new faculty supposed that their usual plans for improvement (better organization, lowered standards) offered the best prospects for improved ratings.

Self-Descriptions as Teachers

Consistent with what we have just seen, new faculty showed few changes from earlier answers about their self-images. One slight change at both campuses was the valence associated with teaching; increasingly, teaching was depicted as even less fun than it had been during semester 1. A related change was that some interviewees, especially returning new faculty, grudgingly volunteered that they would never be considered good teachers.

Work Patterns and Teaching

By this fourth interview, new faculty expressed open dismay about how they were allotting their time. With the exception of small groups who were making regular time for scholarly productivity, new faculty showed workweeks similar to those seen earlier (Table 3.1). On the average, new faculty at both campuses were producing manuscripts at rates well below the mean of one and a fraction per year necessary to meet campus expectations for tenuring. For the first time, new faculty in this unbalanced pattern openly expressed resentment toward the demands of teaching as they saw them. That is, in addition to its signal lack of rewards, teaching seemed to demand preparation to the exclusion of other important things.

Plans

At the end of their second year on campus, new faculty placed heavy expectations on the coming summer session. Here again, they hoped to catch up on neglected activities, especially social life and writing. But this time, new elements crept into interview comments. New faculty no longer reported being as busy and stressed as they had been in semesters 1 through 3; they surmised that they would not have to spend the coming summer resting. Moreover, plans for writing seemed more realistic; suddenly, intentions were accompanied by realizations that, for most interviewees, *any* writing of substance would be progress. Thus, plans now specified, say, mornings at writing and afternoons at other things (and not the entire days and weeks of writing imagined in plans made a year earlier). This excerpt from my notes reflects the tone of a new faculty member, an unusually insightful one, trying to be realistic amid a disillusioning semester:

> Things are overdue, that's for sure. Maybe this summer will be the turning point. I have to make something work; I have to take better care of myself and of my career. Students may have to accept me for what I am—I am not perfect, but I try hard to bring good material to class. And, when I think of it, I may have to accept myself for what I am [campus 2, inexperienced].

Comparisons of Novice and Experienced Teachers

As I analyzed the results of these interviews over semesters, I integrated them with other observations, especially my direct

observations of teaching. My repeated samplings of the classroom performance of inexperienced new faculty, returning
new faculty, and experienced new faculty suggested surprisingly few differences in superficial teaching styles during
semesters 1 and 2. That is, most faculty members new to campus, regardless of prior experience as teachers, were lecturing
in facts-and-principles style: all but a few focused on presenting lots of content organized in terms of definitions, concepts,
and lists. All but a few lectured in rapid-fire fashion, with
limited opportunities for student involvement beyond occasional pauses for clarification.

The obvious difference between veteran and novice
teachers emerged in other dimensions, including classroom
comfort and confidence, often in covert fashion that became
apparent only as I walked to and from classes with veterans.

By semesters 3 and 4, nearly half of the experienced
new faculty had relaxed their styles from year 1 on campus to
encourage more student participation, not always with success in lower-division classes. During comments to me immediately after classes, they attributed this change to feeling
settled and comfortable with the students. Curiously, experienced new faculty who evidenced no apparent alterations in
classroom behaviors from year 1 reported having experienced
similar improvements in comfort. Changes for them came
primarily in the form of worrying less about preparing sufficient and error-free lecture material.

Inexperienced and returning new faculty generally
reported no such transitions in comfort or in time saved during years 1 and 2 at either campus. They were, according to
my observations and their own comments, still primarily concerned about avoiding punishment, especially the widely
feared complaints that students made to campus administrators. These new faculty were, in a few words, continuing to
teach defensively. And according to my notes made after I
walked to and from classes with them, they were experiencing
teaching as an anxiety-provoking and fatiguing task.

How persistent is this general pattern? In an extensive
pilot study with two cohorts at campus 1 that started before

the cohorts depicted here, I found that inexperienced ($n = 18$ and 13) and returning ($n = 3$ and 6) new faculty persisted in this same pattern during their first three and four years on campus. Where they had, on occasion, ceased overpreparing lectures (usually by semesters 5 or 6), they almost invariably stuck to the same "content-only" style that had characterized their performances in semester 1. Overall, only the high anxiety of going to classes had abated, but not for all inexperienced, returning, or even experienced new faculty.

A reminder about data presented earlier corroborates the notion that faculty tend to stick to initial styles: the majority of experienced new faculty sampled here were lecturing, by their own reckoning, in the same facts-and-principles manner that they had used as novices. Curiously, only a few of them were able to specify any significant changes over the years beyond increases in the comfort and confidence that come with experience and decreases in the demands that they made on students in terms of assignments and tests.

When I reflected on the persistence of teaching styles, I undertook two related inquiries: I asked what characterizes novice professors who seem to start as excellent teachers and what causes other colleagues to move in similar directions by their second year on campus.

Inexperienced Newcomers Who Made Quick Starts

I selected three inexperienced new faculty members in each cohort who began as exemplary teachers. Criteria for inclusion were (1) student ratings as teachers, (2) my own classroom ratings of comfort, enthusiasm, organization, student rapport and involvement, and clarity of presentation, and (3) new faculty members' own self-descriptions as comfortable, innovative, and interested in active student learning that were in the top quartile for all new faculty. These determinations were made during semesters 2 and 3 on campus.

Analysis of my notes about these twelve quick starters produced the following list of characteristics that, in combination, distinguished them from their peers: (1) positive attitudes about students at these state universities, (2) lectures paced in relaxed style so as to provide opportunities for student comprehension and involvement, (3) low levels of complaints about their campuses, including collegial support, (4) evidence of actively seeking advice about teaching (especially the mechanics of specific courses), often from a colleague in the role of a guide or mentor, (5) a ready transition to moderate levels of lecture preparation (less than 1.5 hours per classroom hour), usually by the third semester, (6) a generally moderate but meaningful investment in time spent on scholarly and grant writing (mean = 3.3 hours per workweek), and (7) a greater readiness to become involved in campus support programs.

Ten new faculty members who were not quick starters made transitions that brought them to obvious comfort and above-average student ratings during year 2. All but four of the individuals who met this description were experienced new faculty members. The four inexperienced newcomers in this category evidenced gradual movement toward items 1–3 of the list above; by semesters 3 and 4, for example, they were complaining less about colleagues and students. These new hires, however, did not seem to seek out the collegial support characteristic of the sample just described. Instead, they showed a determination to adjust on their own.

Reflections on How New Faculty Start as Teachers

This study at two large campuses suggests the following generalities about how new faculty begin as teachers (where my own observations confirm earlier, more impressionistic and theoretical accounts, I cite examples of relevant literature in parentheses):

1. They teach as they were taught, equating good teaching with good content (see Weimer, 1990). Thus, most faculty observed here stuck to what Axelrod (1973) called a facts-and-principles style of lecturing.

2. They teach defensively (see Eble, 1972). New faculty routinely worried aloud about public failures at teaching, especially the sort that would earn repeated listings in the reports of tenure committees. This meant that new faculty tried to get their facts straight; whatever else, they did not want to be accused of not knowing their material (see Feldman, 1988). Other factors, such as students who seemed to complain capriciously and maliciously, seemed beyond the control of new faculty.

3. They often blame external factors for teaching failures as indicated in student ratings. Three of the most common of these attributions were to poor students, heavy teaching loads, and invalid rating systems.

4. They are passive about change and improvement (see Fink, 1984), in part because of what Weimer (1990) calls a lack of teaching awareness. They assume that casual comments from vocal students (and perhaps from colleagues) are sufficient to gauge prowess at teaching. They reluctantly seek outside help from resources such as faculty development programs. And when asked to specify plans for improvement, even in the wake of poor ratings and admitted dissatisfaction, they are unable to specify alternatives beyond improving lecture content and making assignments and tests easier.

5. New faculty's primary goals as teachers revolve around time management and punishment; they do not expect to enjoy teaching until they no longer have to spend large amounts of time preparing for it and until it no longer offers prospects of public criticism. Only then, they suppose, can they get on with subtle aspects of teaching, such as moving beyond a content-only format (for example, to teaching critical thinking). These new faculty members, like those studied elsewhere, wanted a sense of control over their environment (see Cares & Blackburn, 1978); until they got it, their actions were dominated by narrow, short-term, self-directed goals (Braskamp et al., 1984).

6. Experienced new faculty claim that their defensive and factual styles of teaching are temporary regressions from

how they had taught most recently at other campuses. They, too, worried about public complaints and about heavy investments in new lecture notes.

7. Most new faculty members establish comfort, efficiency, and student acceptance only slowly, if at all. In preliminary studies at campus 1, large groups of new faculty were systematically interviewed and observed for periods as long as four years. Only a minority made verifiable progress in any of these areas except for decreased preparation time. Broader progress in the samples studied here was typical of the handfuls of new faculty members who persisted as participants in campus faculty development programs.

8. Some new faculty members were able to quickly establish comfort and acceptance in teaching. The same faculty members also showed a higher level of collegiality and scholarly productivity, which coincided with greater satisfaction and success in their careers.

Although this evidence about exemplary new faculty must be considered preliminary, the last generality offers bright promise in an otherwise dreary picture of how new faculty develop as teachers. It suggests, as we just saw, how new faculty can be aided in finding balance; quick starters displayed practices as teachers that offer no obvious difficulty for emulation.

Another conclusion concerns the generality of the findings just reviewed across two campuses with different priorities for teaching. That is, new faculty at the research campus showed the same practices and attitudes as their counterparts at the "teaching campus." In fact, the two groups were closely similar in terms of all the commonalities listed above; they resembled each other in regard to observable teaching performance, students' ratings (in approximately similar rating forms), in stated interests in teaching, in time spent with students outside class, and in attempts to seek help in improving teaching. This finding surprised faculty at the teaching campus, who commonly asserted the teaching superiority of their campus to research campuses.

Overall, what this direct and sustained examination of new faculty as teachers suggests is that professors often begin and persist in disappointingly narrow styles. One implication is that we might do better to initially safeguard new faculty from all but private and formative evaluations of their classroom performance. Such precautions might reduce the reliance of new faculty on facts-and-principles lecturing formats as ostensible defenses against possible criticisms. But the most tantalizing implication is that we can do more to support new faculty as teachers by showing them alternatives to how they already teach.

Development of these ideas for facilitating the teaching of new faculty is the subject of Chapter Six. Meanwhile, the subject of the next chapter, new faculty as scholars, is an indivisible part of new faculty experience. This chapter has shown that the newcomers who were most comfortable and successful as teachers had found balance as colleagues, as scholarly writers, and as lecture preparers and presenters. Similarly, I believe, the most effective programs for new faculty will show a parallel kind of balance. A brief return to the IRSS theory helps reinforce notions of balance—and of hope for remedying the usual poor starts of new faculty as teachers.

IRSS Theory and the Teaching Experience

The first component of the theory, involvement, was obviously critical to faring well at teaching. Quick starters stood out for their immersion in learning about teaching. They read about teaching. They observed colleagues as teachers. They asked colleagues for specific advice about teaching. They got to know students, and they paid attention to what about their teaching was most clearly connected to student learning. And they were willing to take risks with innovations in classes. Immersion meant a suspension of the defensiveness that characterized the teaching of most new faculty.

The second component of IRSS theory, regimen, also helps make sense of the teaching experience of new faculty.

Those who persisted in trying to come up with better and more error-free lectures made little progress in finding comfort, student acceptance, or time for other activities. Those who moderated and balanced time spent on teaching preparation fared far better as teachers.

The third component, self-management, was also critical to thriving at teaching. Those new faculty who mastered usually untaught skills (such as achieving classroom comfort first) and attitudes (such as deciding to see things from the perspective of students and to like students) were better rated and happier as teachers. They were, by their own recognition, working to solve the right problems, including ways of making teaching an efficient enterprise where students and others do some of the work.

Finally, in regard to the fourth component of IRSS theory, those new faculty who made teaching a collegial and sociable venture found the task of teaching easier and more rewarding. The stark absence of collegial support, such as coteaching and mentoring, that directly affect teaching reinforces the need for support programs. Clearly, we need to find ways to change the culture of teaching to one that makes teaching a more public and publicly supported activity.

 FOUR

Developing Habits of Writing Productivity

The facts about academicians as scholarly writers are well established but rarely discussed. Most of us write little if at all (Simonton, 1988). Fewer still seem to enjoy it (Boice & Jones, 1984). Yet we readily recognize its rewards (Hartley & Branthwaite, 1989), and, at the least, we expect our new faculty to evidence some proficiency at it (Zanna & Darley, 1987).

Paradoxically, the overscheduled conditions under which most new faculty try to master productivity seem to encourage procrastination and distress (Boice, 1989a). While those of us who write for publication are creative in conjuring up reasons why writing benefits our colleagues (Weaver, 1982), we do little to help make this difficult activity easier. Add to these facts another: prospects for writing in one's career and thus for successes such as promotion, salary, and portability (Boice & Jones, 1984) are established early. That is, patterns of productivity are solidified when one is a new faculty member—not when one is a graduate student and not later, after settling into a professional role (Creswell, 1985; Reskin, 1977).

Yet we know almost nothing about the experiences of new faculty in establishing productive habits. Given the increasing problems in recruiting and retaining the best and brightest people in professorial careers (Bowen & Schuster,

1986), we need more information about how new faculty fare as writers. This chapter examines new faculty coping with pressures to write; it explores what helps and what hinders their productivity, what distinguishes those who write fluently from those who block, and what imperils the success of women and members of minorities in meeting retention and tenure requirements as writers. It also completes the picture of what new faculty must do to prosper in their first few years; none of the three main activities studied here (collegiality, teaching, and writing) stands alone. Newcomers only rarely succeed in just one.

A Tale of Three Campuses

This last of three looks at the experience of new faculty is the broadest. By extending my sample to three campuses and nine years of study, I reflect the value that new faculty themselves placed on writing.

Cohorts

The nine cohorts of new faculty under study came from three campuses where I worked as a faculty developer: a doctoral university, a regional comprehensive university, and a research university. Details of the nine cohorts and of other methodological considerations appear elsewhere (Boice, 1991b). Additional information about the second and third cohorts may also be found in Chapters Two and Three.

In most ways, the three groups of new faculty were alike. They came to their campuses with similar levels of scholarly productivity and with credentials from prestigious universities. While newcomers to all three campuses expressed a strong interest in establishing themselves as visible, portable scholars and as adequate teachers, new faculty at campus 2 struck one distinctive note in this recital of aspirations. They talked vigorously about wanting to avoid the pressures for publication that exist at research universities. Another difference between campuses, one critical to this study of scholarly productivity, was teaching loads. At campuses 1 and 3, the usual assignment for newcomers was two courses per semester. At campus 2, the usual load was four courses.

The key faculty members under study here are the inexperienced and returning newcomers; their experienced counterparts serve as a comparison group. (See Chapter Two for definitions of these labels based on the backgrounds of new faculty.)

Interview

I used the same interview format as in Chapters Two and Three. Two cohorts, one at campus 1 and one at campus 2, were interviewed over four years (or eight sequential semesters). The other cohorts were interviewed for as long as I stayed on their campuses.

Again, interviews produced both qualitative and quantitative results. In regard to new faculty's estimates of their productivity, I asked for verifiable measures ("May I see the manuscript pages you produced in the last week?") and got careful specification of experiences ("With how many campus colleagues are you collaborating on manuscripts?"). The usual practice of relying solely on faculty self-estimates of productivity was deemed inadequate here (see Boice, 1987b, for an explanation of the shortcomings of usual estimates of faculty productivity, including unreliable memories and exaggerations). Briefly, I asked interviewees to recheck initial numbers of hours per week spent on various activities by reconstructing the events of the past few days. During this reevaluation, participants often revised estimates of workweeks, almost always in the direction of less generous totals.

Of all questions I asked new faculty, inquiries about scholarly productivity met with the most resistance. Respondents were reluctant to share something that they considered private. They sometimes felt that my questions implied incompetence on their part. And they especially resented reminders that they were getting less done as writers than they had expected. Nonverbal manifestations of this resistance during initial interviews occurred mostly during discussions about writing and most commonly took the form of disruptions (answering phone calls; letting students who had been waiting in the hall into the office for brief interactions). By the third interviews, however, such resistance had disappeared; faculty came to value these contacts as demonstrations that the campus cared about them and as opportunities to complain confidentially. They also had come to realize that they needed to get more writing done to survive the retention and tenure process.

As in Chapters Two and Three, I present the results of these interviews in terms of successive semesters on campus, of backgrounds (as inexperienced, returning, and experienced new faculty), and of campuses. I describe individual cases of new faculty to give a sense of how new faculty (1) weathered problems and successes as scholarly writers, (2) showed ready promise as producers, and (3) responded to opportunities as writers. Because this portrayal includes a campus not considered in the prior chapters, I make brief mention of their experiences as colleagues and as teachers.

First Semester

Again, initial impressions were misleading. At campuswide orientations, before the onset of my more formal interviews, new faculty at all three campuses worried most about getting enough writing done; they assumed that their teaching would suffer in the process of establishing productivity. One original impression proved to be durable, however. Almost no new faculty members had a clear sense of how much and what sort of writing would be satisfactory for tenure considerations. Moreover, no one had a clue about where to get such information beyond the grapevine; rumors about the capriciousness of tenure decisions were already circulating. As a rule, new faculty members simply concluded that they should do lots of writing:

> How much is enough? I imagine that you can
> never do enough. I plan to write like a madwo-
> man [campus 1, experienced].

Later, by the midpoint of the first semester, when interviews were well under way, new faculty's comments about
writing had changed in three ways. First, they said little about
writing compared to collegiality and teaching. Their concerns
were dominated by what they perceived as collegial isolation
and finding acceptance as teachers (Chapters Two and Three).
Their workweeks were dominated by lecture preparation, even
with light teaching loads.

Second, when new faculty were prodded to discuss their
achievements as writers, they acknowledged that they had
done little or no writing during semester 1. They also admitted that their plans had been very different, as in this typical
comment:

> I know what I should be doing. No doubt about
> it, all this time I'm spending on teaching isn't
> going to have much payoff. [In response to my
> question about how much time he had hoped to
> spend per week on writing during semester 1]
> Oh, at least 10 hours a week. Maybe more. I had
> no idea that teaching would take so much time
> [campus 2, inexperienced].

Accordingly, new faculty of all three experience types made
similar plans for balancing writing and lecture preparation
during semester 2.

Third, although new faculty expressed concern about
procrastinating about scholarship, they reported being much
more worried about avoiding the punishments that could
result from student complaints about their teaching. Single
visits by disgruntled students to chairs could result in widespread concern among colleagues. Single poor student evaluations of a class could find mention in repeated reports from
retention and tenure committees. Writing, in the view of

almost all new faculty, would have to wait until teaching was under control. Writing, it seemed, should be postponed until writers had large blocks of time for undisrupted, calm reflection. At best, it would have to be put off until the semester break and the next semester.

Second Semester

By the second semester, new faculty, except for experienced newcomers at campuses 1 and 3, reported anxieties about finding supports for writing manuscripts and grants:

> How am I going to get it done here? No one pays much attention to me. There aren't any opportunities for collaboration that I can see. I can work on my own, to an extent, but I need to work with other people. The other people just seem to go their own ways; they don't seem to care about anyone else [campus 3, experienced].

Workweeks

By the midpoint of semester 2, workweeks had changed little from semester 1; new faculty at all three campuses were still allotting time for teaching and writing at a ratio of about 15:1. Furthermore, very few new faculty had done any manuscript writing over the semester break; instead, they had rested after what they described as a harrowing first semester.

Productivity

By second interviews, new faculty members, including experienced newcomers, still had done little or no writing. Almost to a person, they hoped to find time for writing before the semester was over. Follow-up checks at the end of the semester showed virtually no changes in writing productivity; the periods between midterm exams and semester finals were the nadir of satisfaction with new jobs. Teaching continued to take the bulk of time. Plans for writing now became the focus of catching up during the coming summers. With teaching and fatigue prospectively under control, plans for semester 3 projected a reversal of imbalance in favor of writing. Presumably, the momentum of productivity established during the summer would continue into the fall.

Third Semester

As new faculty returned to their offices, it became apparent, except in the case of experienced new faculty at campuses 1 and 3, that class preparation and resting had been the focus of first summers. Hoped-for blocks of undisrupted time for writing that would appear after everything else had been taken care of rarely materialized.

Productivity

Table 4.1 shows the low levels of writing output, in terms of manuscript pages completed, during first summers across campuses for inexperienced new faculty. Outputs for returning new faculty were even lower; across all campuses and cohorts, they evidenced particular difficulty in terms of teaching, collegiality, and writing. Experienced new hires, by contrast, showed gains in writing outputs, especially at the two campuses (1 and 3) with the clearest research orientations.

Workweeks

At the midpoint of semester 3, workweeks remained unchanged from semesters 1 and 2. So, too, did productivity. By this juncture, new faculty began to express concerns about their visibility and portability as professionals. These comments from inexperienced new hires at each of the three campuses exemplify that growing uneasiness:

> Maybe I'm not going to be able to leave here. I'm not going to get many job offers at this rate.

Table 4.1. Mean Number of Verified Manuscript Pages Completed
During Summer Between Years 1 and 2 on Campus.

| | Background of New Faculty | | |
Cohort	Inexperienced	Returning	Experienced
1	4.3	0	6.8
2	6.3	0	10.0
3	6.3	3.3	12.5
4	8.0	4.0	9.0
5	2.1	0.2	1.0
6	3.4	0	4.2
7	1.9	3.5	8.3
8	3.0	0.7	5.5
9	3.6	6.6	25.7

Maybe I'm not even going to get tenure here. I'm
surprised that I have to spend so much time on
teaching [campus 1].

I guess it must be obvious to you that I'm no
great producer. I certainly have not spent my time
the way I had planned. I really don't understand
it. I certainly didn't expect to devote almost all
my time to teaching—I'm not even enjoying
teaching [campus 2].

What can I say? I feel embarrassed. I am at the
point where all I want is to feel that I have my
lectures well organized and my students reacting
with a little less boredom and rudeness. Until I
get to that point, I'm just not going to get much
of anything else done. I definitely don't like it
[campus 3].

By semester 3, another pattern had emerged. Untenured
new faculty began to show concern about campus norms for
the productivity expectations of retention and tenure com-

mittees. Much as when I first asked them (in semester 1) how well they understood campus expectations, they still had received no specific information. At all three campuses and across all cohorts, rumors were rife about new faculty who made tenure without publications or newcomers who published at strong rates but, nonetheless, were denied tenure. Indeed, the tendency of new faculty to procrastinate about writing was apparently exacerbated by anxieties about the seeming capriciousness of the retention and tenure systems. In the face of not knowing how much was enough, of not feeling secure about the fairness of campus evaluation processes, new faculty preferred to concentrate on immediate demands.

My own notes of oral and written feedback received by new faculty during semester 3 verify the sense that standards for productivity went unspecified. Some newcomers who were doing no writing got no warnings to do more. Most new faculty members who were admonished to be more productive were told so only in the most general terms ("We encourage you to devote more effort to writing"). The actual number of new faculty members in the nine cohorts who received specific suggestions from departmental committees or chairpeople about how much and what to write during the first three semesters was less than a handful.

Fourth Semester

The end of the second year brought another low point in morale, particularly in regard to scholarly productivity. As a rule, teaching was going little better in terms of student response or preparation time required, except among a near majority of experienced new faculty. Collegiality for inexperienced and returning new faculty had not yet improved. And at all three campuses, writing outputs languished. Increasingly, however, I found exceptions in this regard for inexperienced (but rarely for returning) new faculty. Although most new faculty still had not found collegial support, acceptance from students, moderation in preparing for teaching, and

hope for engaging in research and scholarship beyond dissertation issues, a growing minority did. These quick starters
are depicted toward the end of this chapter.

For the moment, though, two characteristics of exemplary newcomers deserve mention. First, they were atypical in
terms of their positive attitudes about campus and their willingness to seek out social support, including mentoring, starting by at least semester 3. Second, they were rarely women or
members of minorities.

Workweeks

On the whole, workweeks had still not changed sufficiently
to please new faculty. Although time spent on teaching preparation had dropped as much as one-third at campuses 1 and
3, it had been more than replaced by growing responsibilities
in other activities, such as committees. Time spent on writing
was still minimal, with a mean of less than one hour per
week across cohorts.

Productivity

Outputs mirrored work habits and produced commonly verbal-
ized distress about the slim likelihood of gaining reputations. By
semester 4, no cohort was producing more than a mean of 0.6
manuscripts per year submitted to refereed outlets. Table 4.2
depicts verified outputs in semesters 3 and 4 in terms of a more
generous measure of productivity, manuscript pages completed.
Overall, new faculty estimated that typical manuscripts com-
prised thirty pages. Given that all three campuses expected about
1.0–1.5 juried publications per year, productivity levels were inadequate. Predictably, though, the majority of inexperienced and
returning new faculty members who had not yet produced a manuscript on campus had ready rationalizations. Writing was, as they
often reminded me, something that should not be rushed:

> Yes, I know that you're worried about me. And I
> often worry too. But I'll get to writing later, when

conditions are right. I've been too busy to do a proper job of it so far. Once I settle down to writing, I'll be able to get a lot done in a hurry. So you don't need to worry [campus 1, inexperienced].

You just don't understand how mathemeticians write papers. You're a psychologist, and you have to work on papers gradually. We work differently. We think about things for a long while, we do a lot of reading, then we sit down when we have some time and we write it all at once. [In response to my question about what he thought of data that I had gathered in areas such as theoretical mathematics showing that his argument correlated negatively with productivity and peer-related success] I'm not sure I can believe it [campus 2, inexperienced].

The most common response to my queries about productivity referred to plans for the coming summer. Estimates remained at the level predicted for first summers, with a mean of about 1.5 manuscripts to be completed before the start of semester 5.

Table 4.2. **Mean Number of Verified Manuscript Pages Completed During Second Year on Campus.**

	Background of New Faculty		
Cohort	Inexperienced	Returning	Experienced
1	5.5	0	18.4
2	2.5	0	13.0
3	8.5	5.3	22.7
4	4.0	0	12.7
5	2.2	1.5	7.0
6	6.1	1.1	5.0
7	3.1	0.6	11.3
8	2.0	1.7	10.3
9	4.0	8.6	17.1

Fifth Semester: A False Sense of Relief?

Second summers, in retrospect, were unproductive in regard to manuscript pages. On average, new faculty in their second summers required less recuperation, but these respites were again the occasion, presumably the last of a major sort, for another round of generating and revising lecture notes. Still, all three types of new faculty returned to campus for the third year with a sense of relief. They felt certain that things were finally going to go more easily. At the least, they felt reasonably prepared for the kinds of state university students that they taught (although they generally felt no more positive about the sophistication and motivation of their pupils).

For the first time, the majority of inexperienced (but not returning) new faculty members were finding social supports. In the main, though, collegiality and collaboration came from other new faculty members.

Workweeks

As new faculty reported feeling more settled, they expressed more confidence about being able to manage writing. Nonetheless, as semester 5 proceeded, workweeks generally resembled those of recent semesters. The ratio of time spent on teaching versus research and writing, across cohorts of all background types, remained at more than 10:1. Unquestionably, writing had yet to assume equality, let alone dominance, among academic activities. My inquiries about how new faculty decided whether to write or do something else typically elicited this kind of response:

> In fact, the activities make the decision for me. Things like reorganizing my lectures or grading papers can't wait. Writing demands a whole morning or day where I can concentrate. Usually, I haven't had those openings [campus 3, inexperienced].

Productivity

Outputs remained unchanged except for two categories of new faculty: (1) a slight majority of experienced newcomers who were producing manuscripts at rates of about 0.8 per year across cohorts and (2) about 15 percent of inexperienced new faculty who were also finding success as colleagues and as teachers. When I asked new faculty to list their strengths as scholarly writers, all cohorts responded in similar rank-ordered fashion:

1. I am good at conceptualizing the field and what needs to be investigated.
2. I work on interesting problems.
3. I can't think of one.

Curiously, fewer than 4 percent of this sample, usually from humanities departments, rated themselves as skilled writers. The equivalent outcome occurred when I asked similar groups of new faculty to list their strengths as teachers (see Chapter Three); answers were generally limited to organizational skills in lecture preparation. Weimer (1990) ascribes this sort of answer to a lack of "teaching awareness" in faculty who simply are not used to thinking about what they do as teachers. New faculty here also showed a lack of writing awareness. As with teaching, they tended to equate prowess with nothing but knowledge and organization of the material. Some new faculty members seemed to lack what Creswell (1985) calls a template for writing a journal article; that is, they were uncertain about how to proceed and about what the finished manuscript should look like. When asked to list weaknesses as writers, however, new faculty were a little more specific than they were as teachers. Responses were equivalent across cohorts and can be represented by this rank ordering:

1. I am too perfectionistic.
2. I put it off.
3. I don't always finish what I start.
4. English is not my native language.

When I asked new faculty how they felt about the lists that they had generated, they almost invariably indicated an ironic acceptance of these flaws (except for number 4). As one interviewee put it, "that's the way writing is." As a rule, they externalized their perfectionism and procrastination to the difficult art of writing.

In semester 5, as before, evidence from the small groups who balanced activities and successes continued to make a point about the usual pattern of coping with writing. Not only did these exemplary new faculty refuse to accept writing as inevitably difficult and delayed, but they got far more of it done, and they rated it as more enjoyable.

Sixth Semester: Belated Pressures

The end of year 3 on campus reinforced whatever anxieties had been felt earlier about pressures to write. On all three study campuses, this was the time when collegial evaluation came to the fore; here, far more than before, emphasis was on feedback in the retention and tenure process. Most new faculty members talked at length about the unfair and demoralizing aspects of this departmental evaluation. Nonetheless, once complaints had been vented, the reality remained. Feedback to them from senior colleagues had made the point, however obliquely, that many new faculty members might not earn tenure (or, in some cases, retention) unless they finished and published more writing.

The question, then, was what newcomers would do in response to suddenly increased pressures for scholarly productivity. Consistent with the literature on procrastination (see Boice, 1989a), the new faculty members who were getting the least writing done responded with inaction. Usual verbal reactions, once unproductive new faculty got past expressing indignancies about the retention and tenure process, resembled this one:

> I don't want to think about it. I'm afraid, more
> than I can ever remember, of failing. I feel immo-

> bilized. I don't think that I'll feel ready to deal
> with this until I've been here longer. But by then
> it may be too late. I'm not sure they will renew
> me again [campus 2, returning].

With writing, as with other demands, the modal stance during this often depressing spring semester was to establish distance from pressures. Distancing had at least one constructive aspect: in regard to collegiality, new faculty, at this point more than any other, actively decided to ignore colleagues who showed little promise of useful support. In regard to writing, the general decision was to put it off until conditions were more propitious.

Both workweeks and productivity continued unchanged, even in the midst of increasing concerns about having to catch up on writing. Consistent, perhaps, with newfound tendencies to take pressures off themselves in the face of the strongest pressures yet experienced on campus, new faculty made modest plans for their third summers. Where they planned to write, their imagined habits seemed more realistic than before; for instance, new faculty saw themselves writing for a few hours per day, not for entire days. And for the first time they talked about using summers to pamper themselves (for example, traveling; joining choral groups).

Seventh Semester: A Critical Period?

When they returned for their fourth years on campus, the cohorts still under study showed remarkable transformations from the prior years on campus. Notably, they expressed less need for collegial and intellectual stimulation; they were resigned to filling these needs with more independent and off-campus resources. Casual comments from senior colleagues, especially chairs, at all three campuses confirmed this transformation. They expressed relief that the first of these large cohorts of new hires were finally operating independently and confidently.

At last, typical workweeks began to approach the original plans of new faculty. While teaching continued to dominate other activities, it no longer occupied half or more of new faculty's professional time. Overall, inexperienced and returning new faculty were spending a mean of 11.5 hours per week (13.8 at campus 2, where the teaching load was higher) in teaching preparation. Writing time had increased slightly but significantly, to an overall mean of 1.7 hours per week (compared to 1.1 hours at campus 2). And by year 4 on campus 1, the mean rate of submitting manuscripts for publication in refereed outlets was 0.9 (contrasted to 1.1 at campus 2) for the same groups.

Year 4 also brought a change in work habits. Teaching preparation, although it still commanded more time than new faculty claimed they wanted to spend, elicited fewer comments about fatigue. Moreover, participants felt somewhat settled as teachers and ready to devote energy to other activities, especially writing:

> Finally, I can think about something else. I'm finding time to write, sometimes by staying home for a day, sometimes by working on Saturdays. I hope I'm not too late to get things finished [regarding tenure committees] [campus 1, returning].

So even though participants (who, by year 4, objected to being labeled as new faculty) claimed that they were taking time for writing from what had been lecture preparation time, their actual writing habits belied that claim, for three reasons.

First, the time no longer spent on teaching was spent mostly on other nonwriting activities, such as committees. Writing occupied little more than an hour a week on average. Second, when most writing occurred, it was confined to the periphery of workweeks; it was still something to be done after more immediately pressing tasks were taken care of. Third, the average of time and page output for participants in year 4 is a bit misleading. Many were still unproductive: 39 percent (compared to 45 percent at campus 2) of inexperienced hires and 31 percent (compared to 60 percent at campus 2) of returning hires were still unproductive during year 4. Participants who were unproductive through four years began to vocalize a "local" (as opposed to "cosmopolitan") orientation to campus by year 4, one that usually included disparagement of scholarly writing:

> This is what I've learned: I can make far more contribution as a teacher and in committees working on [some other activity] than I could by adding more articles to the piles of trivia being published by people in my field. What I'm doing makes me happy. Writing, even the thought of it, makes me miserable [campus 2, inexperienced].

Curiously, the growing majority who got at least one manuscript done by year 4 also reported a general dislike of writing:

> I do it. But I hate it. Can I be any clearer than that? I'll do it until I get my tenure and promotions, but I can't imagine doing it after that. I hate to sit down and write; it's torture [campus 2, inexperienced].

Eighth Semester: Characteristics of Producers

Semester 8 marked the clear end of what developmental theorists might call the entry period for establishing writing productivity. All the new faculty except returning hires at campus 2 felt a part of campus; at all three campuses, the "negative spillover" (Sorcinelli & Near, 1989) from their work into their social and family lives was no longer so much of a problem. Interview comments routinely included mentions of having found time for social life and community activity. The end of the fourth year also was an ideal time for me to sort out differences between the individuals who were clearly headed for tenure and those who seemed in peril as producers. Those faring best offered promise for further study, particularly for answers about what corresponds to finding success as productive writers.

Exemplary New Faculty

These individuals were judged to be quick starters on a series of criteria: (1) ratings from my classroom observations and from student and self-evaluations that indicated comfort, enthusiasm, organization, rapport, and active student involvement related to teaching (Chapter Three); (2) collegial involvement that included collaboration with at least one campus colleague and at least one informal mentoring relationship on campus; and (3) scholarly productivity of at least three manuscripts initiated, completed, and submitted since arrival on campus. Only 13 percent of inexperienced hires met these criteria; the rate was essentially similar across the three study campuses. A comparison of my notes for these individuals versus their counterparts in years 2-4 produced this list of relatively unique characteristics for quick starters:

1. Generally positive attitudes about students, colleagues, and writing that dated back at least to year 2
2. Comparatively balanced work habits dating from years 2-3, including no more than 1.5 hours of lecture preparation per hour of classroom presentation and at least 2 hours a week of collaboration and of writing
3. Preliminary involvement in mentoring newer faculty

Unproductive New Faculty

Criterion success at teaching and at scholarly productivity correlated positively. Hires who remained unproductive as writers during their first four years on campus generally taught in content-only fashion and did little to involve students as active learners (see Chapter Three). Using the same general procedure described earlier, I derived the following list of commonalities that distinguished silent writers among new faculty:

1. Strong vocal negativism toward the act of writing, pressures for writing, and publishing. This negativism was typically accompanied by stated preferences for investing campus energies in local activities, especially teaching.
2. High levels of stated perfectionism that often merged with elitism; conversations about writing would drift into recountings of credentials ("I'm from Michigan, you know").
3. Prior delays in finishing dissertations beyond two years' effort in graduate school and few or no publications prior to arrival on campus. These characteristics accord with other studies of academic productivity (Creswell, 1985).
4. Disproportionate representation of women (61 percent of the unproductive group) and of members of minorities (75 percent) met the criteria for inclusion here).

Similar patterns held for new faculty cohorts studied for less than four years.

Reflections on the Development of Productivity

New faculty in these longitudinal samples from three campuses showed remarkably uniform patterns of coping with pressures to write. In general, writing was given the highest verbal priority. And in plans for future workweeks, time to be spent on scholarly writing was invariably greatest. Even in plans for careers, hopes for success at writing and publishing remained dominant. (Planned priorities for writing were the same for new faculty at the teaching campus as for those at the research campuses.)

Weick (1976), an authority on organizational cultures, supposes that academe is nearly singular for its custom of making plans that rarely see action. Perhaps for this reason, the new faculty studied here typically did not meet their own or their campuses' plans for writing output. Except for a remarkable small group of new faculty who found some balance between the demands of teaching and writing, new faculty did almost no writing for at least the first two to four years.

Should we conclude, as others have done (Taylor & Martin, 1987), that new faculty must accept their first years as unproductive? Certainly, campuses could do a better job of setting clear and realistic goals for writers during their initial semesters; the new faculty in this study reported being highly distressed by the ambivalent expectations that they faced as writers. In the view of new faculty studied here, campuses gave mixed messages. On the one hand, they seemed to say that new faculty are expected to founder for several years. On the other hand, once evaluations for retention and tenure came into focus, campuses clearly demanded productivity of around 1.0 to 1.5 manuscripts per year across almost all disciplines. The evident result of this ambiguous communication was demoralization and delayed productivity.

To make the argument somewhat differently, should we conclude that new faculty simply need time to settle in as teachers? Teaching is, after all, a far greater challenge and consumer of time than most new faculty members anticipate. These are the conclusions that most senior colleagues at study campuses drew when presented these data. But arguments to the contrary may be even more compelling. Consider three reasons why new faculty should be helped to manage more comfort and productivity as writers: First, new faculty, even when they were told about low campus norms for productivity among peers, still wanted to manage more writing. They wanted, more than anything else, to express ideas that they had developed and to make them visible and influential in their fields. And when faced with the data about the slow beginnings that most colleagues made, new faculty expressed even stronger resolve to manage writing well in advance of deadlines. In other words, they recognized the perils of waiting until the last moment to do their best writing. Second, the most positive, most collegial, and best teachers among the new faculty studied here were generally productive as writers. Their enthusiasm, which they saw as essentially rooted in writing fluently, was general across activities. Third, the individuals most at peril because of their silence as writers were women and members of minorities.

If we are to progress beyond our usual unhelpful stance in dealing with new faculty as writers, we might ask why new faculty typically refuse to devote even small amounts of time to writing when it so obviously counts more than anything else they do. The following brief answer provides one suggestion of a conceptual framework for understanding faculty's priorities.

The Hard-Easy Rule

This theoretical notion derives from Kerr's (1988) study of productive and unproductive conditions for work. Specifically, it addresses two related facts: First, supposedly easy tasks (that is, typically untrained and unevaluated activities) such as teaching are far more likely to be associated with punishment than with reward; failing an easy task brings a loss of face. Second, hard tasks (at which workers are commonly expected to fail) are more likely to occasion rewards than punishment, at least in the short run.

In the case of new faculty, the hard-easy rule predicts that teaching, because of its "easiness" and potential for punishment, will take precedence over writing. It follows, then, that avoidance of punishment in an activity that must be faced almost daily (teaching) will supplant a hard activity that can be procrastinated (scholarly writing). The data from all three study campuses support this explanation; that is, new faculty gave almost exclusive urgency to teaching, an activity that few of them initially claimed to value over writing. And consistent with this prediction, they typically explained this priority as a strategy to avoid the punishments that can accompany teaching.

The hard-easy rule also hints at what will have to precede changes in the usual, paradoxical arrangement of rewards for writing and teaching. Stated simply, we cannot expect new faculty to display a fondness for writing, no matter how obviously important it is, until they model what their most productive colleagues do (that is, work in regular moderation at writing, teaching, and collegiality). Nor, to continue the point, can we expect new faculty to thrive as teachers when classroom preparation becomes aversively time-consuming and when classroom performances become prospects for punishments.

The question that remains, in my experience, is where campuses should begin to understand and communicate the hindrances that their own new faculty experience as writers. Once again, I rely on IRSS notions to help provide a sense of how to begin.

IRSS Theory and Productivity

First, I encourage practitioners who are getting to know new faculty as writers to begin by asking about *involvement.* In the three campuses studied here, it was the primary key to productivity. While the connection seems obvious, it is worth confirming with writers who typically operate with limited awareness of their maladaptive habits: where new faculty are not immersed in the regular practice of writing, they are not productive. Waiting for ideal times such as binges induces more than mere uninvolvement. It can also bring procrastination and dissatisfaction.

Second, I urge practitioners and others planning support programs for new faculty to pay close attention to *regimen.* As just implied, involvement alone can be insufficient. Where new faculty on the study campuses did not establish a regimen of writing regularly, they did not establish productivity. Those new faculty who managed the most writing did so via moderation in regimen; that is, instead of trying to find more time before undertaking writing, they restructured the task representation of writing to write in brief daily sessions.

Third, we would do well to take more notice of knowledge usually untaught in open, systematic ways about survival, including *self-management.* In the samples of new faculty reported here, those new faculty members who remained unproductive were almost invariably observed to be solving the wrong problems, notably supposing that they could not write until they found large blocks of undisrupted time. In like fashion, the same new hires also expressed ready negativity about their campuses and colleagues as resources and evaluators in regard to writing.

Fourth, we would do well to note the links between writing productivity and *collegial networking*. The quick starters depicted here, unlike their counterparts, were proactive in soliciting collegial advice. They were quick to dismiss the idea that they had to figure out the subtle rules of productivity on their own. Their counterparts, conversely, kept writing a painfully private and perfectionistic act.

So the moral of this story of getting to know new faculty as new writers is much like that for learning about their experiences as teachers and as colleagues. Until we take the time to discover what hinders and what helps them, we can all too easily get off on the wrong track. (We might even, heaven forbid, be trying to solve the wrong problems.) The vital act in setting up new support programs is paying attention to the most basic of skills and attitudes that new faculty must master.

❧ Part 2

Helping New Faculty
Overcome Obstacles

Part One of this book (Chapters Two through Four) portrayed newcomers struggling to overcome obstacles as colleagues, as teachers, and as writers. Part Two describes support programs that help new hires overcome those three obstacles. Here, at last, we move from insight to action. Chapter Five, first of all, revolves around a traditional scheme for mentoring new faculty with more experienced colleagues. Chapter Six conceptualizes help for new faculty as teachers in terms of traditional support (for example, formative evaluations of teaching) and even more basic practices, including the development of classroom comfort and rapport. Chapter Seven continues the theme of balance and moderation as a means of helping newcomers thrive as productive writers. Finally, Chapter Eight addresses the critical step of helping new faculty help themselves on these and related dimensions. Throughout, these interventions focus on balance between teaching, collegiality, and productivity and on making usually tacit information explicit. Each chapter relies on IRSS (involvement, regimen, self-management, and social networking) theory as a means of identifying the steps for nurturing the most fundamental survival skills.

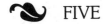 FIVE

Mentoring to Build Collegiality

Along with orientations and release time, mentoring is a common goal of campuses with programs for new hires (Kurfiss & Boice, 1990). Mentoring is, moreover, a customary request of new faculty who report feeling isolated and understimulated (Turner & Boice, 1987). With its associations with activities such as teaching and parenting, mentoring seems a minimally necessary component of support programs for new faculty. Yet clouds loom on the horizon for mentoring as a programmatic component. As a rule, mentoring programs are neither well developed nor widely used. A survey of the literature on mentoring indicates that few campuses conduct mentoring in any systematic and demonstrably effective way (Lavery, Boice, Thompson, & Turner, 1988); moreover, studies of new faculty suggest that only a minority find mentoring of any significance on their own (Boice, 1991a; contrast with Sands, Parson, & Duane, 1991).

There are other, even more common reservations about instituting mentoring programs. Practitioners often imply that it demands too much time (Kram & Isabella, 1985), that some newcomers neither want nor need it (Relch, 1986), that pairings afford too many chances for exploitation (Feinstein, 1988) or dependency (Busch, 1985), and that most mentor-protégé pairs will quit meeting (Wylie, 1985). And to complete the list of contemporary reservations, an even more powerful one is emerging. Some leaders in faculty development dismiss mentoring projects as faddish and mentoring as something best left to occur on its own (Weimer, 1990).

Then, with the horizon darkening, weigh yet another cloud over mentoring programs: most advice about establishing programs is conjecture. But even in the midst of a perspective sullied by lore and skepticism, there is hope for better skies. They apparently await approaches that begin with observations of what kinds of pairings and activities seem to optimize mentoring. Once again, we resort to basics. Even in this fifth chapter, we will find background studies a valuable resource.

The FIPSE Project

Campus 2 from Chapter Four is a comprehensive university with a traditional emphasis on teaching, a new push for publishing, and large cohorts of new faculty trying to meet the conflicting demands for mastering both activities. After a couple of years of observing the loneliness and stress of new faculty at that campus, I applied for funds from a federal agency, the Fund for the Improvement of Post Secondary Education (FIPSE), that commonly supports faculty development projects. I hoped to promote two things. One was the involvement of mentors who would meet weekly with their new faculty protégés for at least a year. The other was a study of mentoring in process to see what mentoring pairs did that corresponded to eventual successes and failures of mentoring. Its submission, curiously, came at a time when other practitioners were already getting involved in similarly comprehensive programs for mentoring (Freudenthal & DiGiorgio, 1989).

Pairings

During the two project years that were funded by FIPSE, I was able to study twenty-five pairs of mentors and protégés (details appear in Boice, 1990c). Briefly, twenty-six new faculty members (fourteen in project year 1 and twelve in year 2) volunteered to participate for at least a year. One protégé quit the program shortly after a preliminary lunch with her mentor; the other twenty-five stayed with the program for the duration.

Protégés. The completion rate was impressive. Still, at least half of those mentored were initially reluctant to volunteer; despite having indicated interests in obtaining mentoring, they felt too busy to take part in any projects once faced with an answer to their wish. To get past this resistance, I resorted to personal visits to the offices of potential protégés. My ploy didn't always work. Nonetheless, the twenty-two inexperienced and returning new faculty members who refused to participate were probably little different from the twenty-six who accepted. When I asked chairpeople to rate the need of their new faculty for mentoring, their ratings were similar for participants and nonparticipants.

To some extent, all the nonparticipants became controls against whom I could measure the progress of project participants. I paid special attention to four inexperienced new faculty members who refused participation because they had already found mentors but did not want to be part of a structured project.

Mentors. Mentors were easier to recruit. Indeed, the struggle was to pick only the most appropriate prospects from a wealth of volunteers. I decided to choose mentors (all of whom got small summer stipends after an academic year of participation) on the basis of demonstrated effectiveness as teachers, scholars, and colleagues.

The big question was how to pair mentors and protégés. The literature on mentoring offers little proof about what kinds of pairings are optimal; Alleman, Cochran, Doverspike, and Newman (1984) provide a compelling refutation of the assumption that pairs should be arranged on the basis of personality indices. Thus, my colleagues and I decided on two kinds of simple arrangements. In half the pairings, mentors were asked to find someone, usually from their own departments, with whom they wanted to form a mentoring pair. In the other half of pairings, mentors were assigned to protégés in a way that distributed them across departments, genders, and ethnicities. On the whole, then, we began by assuming that a variety of pairings would teach us the most about the mentoring process.

Pair Obligations

Most of the structure in this project took the form of obligations; because we wanted to learn as much as possible about how pairs developed bonds, supports, and styles, we asked them to meet each week and to keep records of their activities and reactions. And because we wanted to compare mentoring pairs, we assembled the group of pairs monthly for discussions about what was working and what wasn't. Both formats, of meeting in pairs and in groups of pairs, proved practical in terms of time demands and information yields. And each format had serendipitous qualities of ensuring the success of pairs. As we will see, the act of prodding pairs to meet regularly led to the quick establishment of bonds that persisted. Moreover, assembling pairs for discussions helped educate them, more than anything else, about what mentors and protégés can do.

In my weekly data collections, I asked pairs to complete brief checklists after each interaction. Each time I called or visited them, I asked for ratings of pair compatibility and helpfulness. At the ends of semesters, I collected their notes on weekly meetings to get another sense of the tone and content of meetings from the perspective of each pair member. While pairs initially reported annoyance at my weekly visits and calls, they invariably came to delineate those meetings as the single most powerful factor in ensuring involvement when they feel busy. Once pairs were in the habit of meeting, incidentally, they no longer needed my goads to continue meeting and had grown receptive to reporting what they were doing.

During monthly meetings of all mentoring pairs, I focused on getting all participants involved. These groups essentially ran themselves, because mentoring was a fascinating activity to discuss and because pairs were eager to learn from each other. At the end of each year, the single complaint about these meetings was that there were too few of them.

Pairs' Involvement

My greatest concern, given the usual failures of mentoring projects to induce pairs to meet regularly, was with involvement. After all, I was asking already overscheduled new faculty to submit to a demanding regimen of meetings and data collection. I also began with another apprehension. I had received a federal grant for the mentoring project that came with publicity and expectations. I worried, given what I had read about mentoring projects, that I might be embarrassed by colleagues who would take the money but do little else. And I knew that if the project didn't work, it would be no secret on campus (or with the granting agency, which later sent an observer to campus).

To my surprise, all twenty-five pairs met the stringent requirements for participation, and all but three met them happily and productively. My first impressions, however, confirmed at least some of my worst fears. Protégés paired with strangers from different departments began by reporting that they did not like their mentors and that they were sure that a mentor from a different discipline would be of minimal help. I asked them to try it for a while longer (the involvement component of IRSS theory).

Even mentors started with reservations. Specifically, the label of "mentor" seemed presumptuous; who were they, they asked, to act as if they had all the answers? In addition, the title reminded them that they weren't too sure what mentors were supposed to do beyond being supportive listeners with some expertise to offer. Only when they learned, in monthly group meetings of all pairs, that their protégés attached no stipulations or objections did they stop worrying about the label.

The four pairs of mentors and protégés who met on their own outside the project and who submitted occasional accounts of their progress to me fared less well than expected; they succumbed to the busyness that project pairs had mentioned. None of these pairs met more than twice a semester, but all of them expressed somewhat apologetic plans to meet more often when they were less busy.

Styles of Mentoring

Once I got past concerns about whether pairs would cooperate and report satisfaction with the project, I was able to concentrate more on the process of mentoring. One thing was almost immediately apparent: I had been lucky in my decision to form a diversity of pairs. By their own admission, pairs showed a medley of mentoring styles; the more I saw of mentoring, the less confident I felt in prescribing how it should be done. Evidently, there would have been a problem in how most pairs might have worked together if they had followed a preset plan. By their own estimates, they learned broader styles of interacting after listening to what other pairs did during group meetings, more so as they grew used to describing their experiences. This comment from my weekly notes of contacts with mentors and protégés illustrates the point:

> We just didn't think beyond the obvious. The obvious was getting my R/T/P [retention, tenure, and promotion] materials together—that's about all we ever talked about. But when we heard what other pairs are doing, like going together to the faculty computer center and to the special collections room in the library, we realized that we could do more. Now, it seems to me, we're having more fun—we're more relaxed together.

Another surprise emerged as pairs persisted; this one, however, offered no immediate solutions (although it was an opportunity for me to feel valuable). Eight of the twenty-five pairs, by about the midpoint of their first semester of interaction, suddenly declared that they no longer needed to meet. They had, much as portrayed in this excerpt from my notes, decided that they had run out of things to discuss:

> We probably won't need to meet anymore. We have covered everything that [my protégé] needs help with. There isn't anything else to talk about. If you want us to keep meeting, we'll just have to get together for some pretty short sessions. I think I've given her all the help she needs.

Even group meetings of mentoring pairs provided no ready solutions; if pairs had finished their work, someone asked, why force them to continue? After all, someone else added, who is to say how long mentoring should last? But I had doubts about the wisdom of cutting off mentoring after only a month or two, given my observations of the new faculty involved in those pairs. Protégés might have run out of questions to ask, and their mentors might have exhausted their ready store of advice, but these pairs had not yet mastered the problems that we saw in earlier chapters.

For a clue, I turned to my observations of pairs who had not reported this impasse; they were, to resort to an already familiar concept, quick starters in mentoring. The answer was that pairs progressing most impressively easily were spending far more time on small talk. They knew that some meetings should carry no demands for immediate problem solving; in those instances, the substance of conversation needed to be little more than exchanging pleasantries. What other pairs needed to learn (and did with a minimum of coaching) was that small talk helps build friendships, helps alleviate the ordinary loneliness of professorial lives, and keeps pairs meeting until inevitable problems emerge.

The third lesson about styles of mentoring was the most fascinating. Although the number of pairs who did not function happily and productively was small, they had something in common. All three failed pairs began with preestablished friendships. The evident reason for the discomfort was that mentoring required occasional differences in status; that is, once mentors assumed the roles of adviser and evaluator, protégés bristled and complained (usually only to me). The telling result was their general avoidance of mentors. The greater comfort of pair members who began as relative strangers was augmented by pairings across departments. Evidently, mentoring benefits when the protégé fears no loss of face or of confidentiality from a mentor who works in the same department.

A final aspect of looking at the nature of pairs deserves a brief mention. At the urging of the FIPSE project advisers, I subjected all fifty pair members to a popular personality test, the MBTI. This index of personality showed no connection between personality type and compatibility or effectiveness (both these latter measures are described anon).

Content of Mentoring

In a preliminary way, questions had been answered about how to pair mentors with protégés (avoid preexisting friendships; favor cross-departmental pairings; ensure regular meetings) and about how to train mentors (get pairs to learn from other pairs, especially about broadening their scope of activities; coach pairs to use small talk when they feel stymied). Still, I wanted to learn more about what pairs did that helped new faculty.

One way of getting a sense of what pairs did came from analyzing their notes and ratings of weekly interactions. A few topics, each of them consisting mostly of "how-to" discussions, dominated the mentoring conversations of these twenty-five pairs: (1) scholarly productivity, (2) managing classrooms and students, (3) conflicts and politics with colleagues, (4) and retention and tenure. Curiously, many of the topics that both mentors and protégés predicted would be common before the project began (notably, ethics and time management–balance) never gained much currency. Pairs themselves supposed, in retrospect, that topics such as these might assume more immediacy once protégés were better established. They also recognized an emphasis that had been unforeseen: where pairs functioned best and those mentored were making the most apparent progress, balance and moderation were being actively addressed.

An example of the limitations of pairs in developing expertise comes from the stage of the project where I asked mentors to conduct two visits to their protégés' classrooms. The usual result was only a pair of brief conversations about the teaching that had been observed. Actual plans for changing teaching were vague; conversation about teaching drifted to more general cases. Mentors' reasons for these generally displaced discussions about teaching were enlightening. This excerpt typifies those responses:

> When you described the rating scales and feedback styles in the meeting, it all seemed doable. It was not all that easy when it came down to it, though. Maybe you can give advice because you know a lot about teaching. Not everyone else, including me, feels ready to take on that role of expert.

The same reluctance held, incidentally, when mentors gave advice about writing productivity.

Because mentors often resisted moving beyond the mode of patient listening and general advice, I devised structured exercises, including cataloguing assignments, where mentors and protégés prepared a plan of, say, course designs and teaching innovations that they shared with the departmental colleagues of those being mentored. (Later in this chapter I describe some of the results of this elaboration of usual mentoring activities.) I don't want to leave the impression, though, that the mentors in this study failed their protégés. In fact, they were rated highly as a rule, by their partners and by me. What they may have done best was to provide socioemotional support for new faculty who otherwise would have experienced the lonely and stressful year that their unmentored peers reported. Those who received mentoring concluded that their mentors excelled in four categories: listening, informing, acting as advocates for their protégés, and prodding protégés to meet during busy weeks.

Mentoring Index

In my enthusiasm to measure the effectiveness of mentoring pairs, I devised a mentoring index—a scoring scheme based on ten dimensions (including enthusiasm, reciprocity of caring, and specific advice about teaching) where a score of seven out of ten points was calibrated to indicate an acceptable performance and five points a passable rating. (Details appear in Boice, 1990c.)

Pairs from different departments rated higher (mean = 73.9) than did pairs from the same departments (mean = 67.8). Pairs with senior mentors scored only slightly better than those with relatively junior, untenured mentors. And pairs with differing ethnicity and/or genders rated as highly similar. Thus, some common assumptions about mentoring, including the belief that similar pairs work best, may deserve rethinking. Certainly, campuses faced with the realities of finding effective mentors for increasingly large and diverse groups of new hires may want to consider pairing them with the best mentors, regardless of similarity.

While the sample size was small (twenty-five pairs), the suggestions of relationships between the mentoring index and other signs of success for new faculty were promising. Put simply, the new faculty in pairs rated most highly evidenced two relatively unique traits. First, they showed high levels of reciprocity, with protégés expressing caring about the welfare of their mentors much as their mentors did about theirs. Second, they addressed problems of balance. Clearly, it seemed, good mentoring contributed to the success of the new faculty members fortunate enough to get it. And just as clearly, the protégés in the most highly rated pairs were the easiest and most rewarding to mentor (because, for example, they were more patient, optimistic listeners who were more willing to try alternative ways of doing things).

In the final analysis, incidentally, mentors reported more benefits from participation than did those they mentored. This normative comment from a final interview helps explain why:

> I think I got far more out of this than [my protégé] did. For one thing, I needed a new friend; this is not a very friendly campus. And I had to do a lot of thinking about my career, about my teaching and writing—all this came at a good time. I have been taking my own advice to [my protégé]. Sometimes I feel like I'm starting over again with the benefit of knowing what I should have known back when I came here. I'll tell you this: I surely could have benefited from a program like this twenty-one years ago.

Group Meetings

What mentors and protégés liked almost as much as having a supportive friend was feeling a part of campus through the project, particularly by way of the monthly group meetings. One reward of participation often mentioned was getting to know people who greeted them enthusiastically around campus. The other advantage of the group meetings, already mentioned, was learning how better to conduct a mentoring relationship. As an inveterate data collector, I was interested in identifying the content of these group meetings. The first datum was predictable. Mentors did most of the talking, at a ratio of 3:1. I had, I realized, recruited them for their expertise and their readiness to help. And they had assumed roles where they were expected to teach and nurture.

During the monthly group meetings, mentors typically commented on the problems that their protégés had in adjusting to the campus and on the progress of their pairings. Protégés, by contrast, complimented their mentors and shared some of the most trying of their problems in adjusting to campus. The group was ready with support and advice, but what new faculty reported liking even more was confirmation that their struggles were not unique.

Reflections on the FIPSE Project

One of the most interesting findings was that payments to mentors were necessary only in establishing involvement. Once participation was under way, mentors found that it carries its own rewards. Protégés learned that participation actually saved time and distress. Of all the learning that occurred in the FIPSE project, however, the most may have occurred with the project director. For one thing, I was reminded of the value of letting other people do some of the work. The mentoring project, once in motion, needed little help from me. More often, I have been able to satisfy my need to nurture in helping other practitioners set up new programs.

In the course of my consultations with other campuses planning mentoring projects, I have been asked to summarize my advice in view of the mentoring literature. I generally offer the kind of listing that follows.

1. While the literature on mentoring relies almost exclusively on speculative and anecdotal advice (Cronin-Hillix, Cronin-Hillix, Gensheimer, & Davidson, 1986; Noller, 1982), this study suggests that we can determine what makes mentoring effective. Moreover, it suggests that this information can be collected and shared by practitioners in the course of implementing their programs. This is the use I see for the data outlined above: that other practitioners confirm and/or modify what I have found.
2. A critical step in this project, one overlooked in the literature, was beginning with clear demonstrations of need for a mentoring program on campus. Specifically, I showed that most new hires suffered through initial years of loneliness and inefficiency, that only a handful of them found useful mentoring on their own, and that the few

new faculty members who did find good mentors were prospering. As obvious as the need for a mentoring program may seem, many of our colleagues in central positions on campus and on grants panels may not agree until they are reassured with facts. I find that many of the most reluctant new faculty members were won over to participation by my emphasis on data collection.

3. Another key element in mentoring programs not mentioned in the literature, perhaps because of the neglect of the mentoring process, is the importance of prompting pairs to meet regularly until meetings become habitual. Accomplishing this simple act by calling or visiting pair members for their brief ratings and comments was, again, seen by participants as the single most important intervention in the program. Without it, they assured me, they would have put off meetings (as did the control pairs) so long as they felt overscheduled.

4. The practice of examining and reexamining mentoring as it occurs raises interesting questions about customary practices. The findings here, on the one hand, contradicted assumptions that mentors need do little more than act as "sounding boards" (Bakker & Lacey, 1980) or that mentoring works best when pair members pick each other (Wylie, 1985), preferably on the basis of similarity (Blackburn, 1981). On the other hand, this study confirmed some generally overlooked conclusions of research suggesting that personality types predict little about the success of mentoring (Alleman et al., 1984). Moreover, these results corroborate the view that new faculty themselves must be active in seeking out help and in making relationships rewarding (Menges, 1986). The upshot of this reexamination, at least at first glance, is that we will fare better with mentoring programs if we break the traditional bounds of pairing protégés only with senior mentors from the same department. Evidently, junior mentors work just as well. And pairings across departments can work even better than those within departments.

5. Examination of mentoring in process suggests even more

things not yet emphasized in the literature. While a diversity of styles seem to work well to provide new faculty with needed support, project directors can add simple elements that help ensure optimal interactions: group meetings of mentoring pairs that show alternatives to the typically narrow styles in which mentors and their protégés begin (see Freudenthal & DiGiorgio, 1989, for a variation of the format used here) and coaching some pairs in the lost art (for many faculty) of making small talk to help them maintain continuity during lulls.

6. Analysis of the content of mentoring interactions confirms some expectations (for example, pairs worry together about whether the protégé will gain tenure), disconfirms some others (for example, the expectation that only campuses with rewards for teaching will elicit much conversation about classroom management; see Holmes, 1988), and points out deficiencies in an otherwise promising project (for instance, mentors in this study were reluctant to give specific advice in the areas where new faculty needed the most help—teaching, scholarly productivity, and time management). Thus, content analysis was the spur to thinking beyond an already successful project, one that garnered publicity on and off campus, to ways of making mentoring and related practices even more effective.

Extensions of the FIPSE Project

In the wake of that successful project, in attempting to transport it to another campus where I am helping to build a new faculty development program, I have learned as much as I did in the FIPSE project. Specifically, I have paid more attention to three shortcomings of mentoring that provides little more than socioemotional support. For one thing, mentoring limited to socioemotional supports may not get mentors actively involved as interventionists in activities such as teaching. The lack of more active involvement by mentors, in my experience, owes mostly to their not knowing how to help protégés change their basic styles as teachers.

The second limitation in most mentoring projects, including the FIPSE program, is that they do little or nothing to extend social networks of new faculty to students. While the idea of making classroom researchers of teachers who communicate with students about what they are learning is relatively new among mentoring ideas (for example, Cross & Angelo, 1988), it holds promise for helping new faculty find comfort and success at teaching. Specifically, it makes teachers and students less anonymous to each other. The result of helping new faculty find closer links to students is a lessened strain in teaching and an equally valued feeling of acceptance on campus. To be effective, social networking for new faculty must go beyond the individual senior colleagues who share their expertise and reassurances.

The third limitation to traditional mentoring is its narrowness and passivity. It consists, as we have seen, of agendas that often stop at help with only one specific activity. (Mentoring by most faculty is, after all, modeled after the roles of graduate school advisers, who typically coach protégés on a single task—research leading to a dissertation.) And it commonly waits for people to take the initiative in mutually agreeable ways.

In the remainder of this section, I summarize four extension projects that are helping new faculty build collegial supports and communications. Each of these projects can be implemented to include the systematic pairings and chartings of the FIPSE project already summarized.

Collaborating with Colleagues as Teachers

In my experience, an effective strategy for getting mentors and protégés beyond the level of exchanging advice and reassurance is coteaching. When mentors and protégés coteach, especially if they meet regularly to discuss collegial and student feedback, both can get past usual barriers of talking about teaching in specific, applied ways. And when that interaction is supplemented with advice and modeling from a campus expert on instructional development, the results include increased comfort and innovation in the classroom (see Chapter Six). With security comes a willingness to take risks.

This general strategy of arranging mentoring as coteaching where pairs jointly plan and present classroom materials is a great elicitor of "yet, buts." Consider some of the usual reservations. One concerns teaching loads: "If pairs coteach," I am usually asked, "what happens to their teaching loads?" I suggest giving each pair member a half-course reduction. After all, many campuses already give new faculty release time, usually for activities, such as course planning or increased scholarly productivity, that can be augmented by mentoring.

The most vocal objection concerns coteachers who have different styles or, worse yet, different disciplines. How can I expect, I was recently asked, to pair a new sociologist and a senior mathematician in the same classroom, even in an introductory course? I begin my response by reminding audiences that dissimilar mentoring pairs often work to advantage in ways such as learning from partners with dramatically different teaching styles. Then I speak about Tobias's (1990) book on social scientists visiting classrooms in science and mathematics. The implication of her intriguing study is that science professors might profit by adopting some of the style of social scientists who provide clear rationales and perspectives for what they teach. The allied message, one that she neglects, is that learning will probably occur in both directions.

My own pilot studies in a Lilly Foundation program of mentoring for new faculty as teachers are evolving into coteaching projects. The plan is to pair new and more senior faculty from strikingly different disciplines. Where, say, the coteacher foreign to a course is worked into classroom participation via a gradual, structured plan, he or she makes the transition to teaching the new subject with surprising ease. One reason for this is that the new faculty member feels little need to know the course material perfectly. And by the time the "home court advantage" is reversed in the second semester of coteaching, both mentor and mentored have changed their initial teaching styles in some fundamental ways.

Not all new faculty members or their prospective mentors will want to coteach; successful campus programs must offer flexibility. I like the format for communicating about the teaching experience popularized by my predecessor at Stony Brook, Joseph Katz (1985). The essence of Katz's approach is having a colleague monitor the course of a colleague from the perspective of a student who discusses the experience with the monitoring colleague and, occasionally, with a faculty development practitioner. In the variation I use, the new faculty member monitors his or her mentor's classroom in the role of a student during semester 1. In semester 2, the roles of visitor and host are reversed. Other elements of the Katz approach, such as my presence during discussions on some occasions, are maintained. The result, not surprisingly, is a far greater involvement in attending to and changing teaching by both the mentor and the mentored than occurs in customary mentoring.

Collaborating with Students

This suggestion for enhancing the social networks of new faculty, unlike promoting coteaching, often elicits no initial reaction from other campuses. Campus leaders may not consider rapport with students an important part of socialization to campus. New faculty, however, list gaining acceptance with students as one of their highest priorities (Boice, 1991c). So it is, presumably, that the idea of coaching faculty to communicate closely with students is gaining favor, particularly in the form of classroom research (Cross & Angelo, 1988; Angelo, 1990). In its extreme form, classroom research joins students and teachers as collaborators who investigate what fosters learning. We will examine classroom research in more detail in Chapter Six.

One application of classroom research to new faculty can be explained simply. It relies on the discovery (Chapter Three) that the most successful new faculty members tend to find rewards for teaching by enlisting undergraduates as teaching and research assistants. While these quick starters do not necessarily teach with more enthusiasm than do other new faculty members, they direct some excitement about teaching to incorporating their own interests as creators, scholars, and researchers into classes. One concomitant is the optimistic assumption by quick starters that undergraduates will be eager recruits for service as assistants (usually with credits for independent study). Another result is the experience of finding a reward for teaching well in a cultural context where most new faculty members report that they discern no payoffs.

What has this form of classroom research to do with mentoring? Most critically, it puts new faculty in the role of mentors to the assistants they recruit from their classes. Where new faculty members also have mentors of their own, the related results are interesting. Having to act as mentors makes new faculty members more appreciative of the mentoring they get. And they are more likely to ask their mentors for advice about managing undergraduate assistants.

Collaborating with Colleagues as Writers

What traditional mentoring for new faculty accomplishes least often, in my observations, is surprising: while new hires express concern about productivity from the day they arrive on campus, they are rarely helped by mentors to achieve productivity. This norm is all the more curious considering that we already know the value of collaboration in faculty careers (Creswell, 1985).

Why do senior colleagues offer little more than occasional admonishments to publish or perish? For one thing, seniors may already be invested in collaborations with teams of graduate students. For another, new faculty may have been hired in specialties not already represented on campus; thus, there may be no ready collaborators with kindred interests. But a third reason is most telling: new faculty and their seniors typically engage in a kind of standoff where neither side makes the first move to help or to ask for help. New faculty in this predicament often make comments like this one:

> Sure, I might do better if I collaborated, but the
> fact that no help is offered indicates to me that I
> am expected to survive on my own. That's what
> they probably did, and that's what I can do.

Senior faculty, in turn, say things like this about having
approached newcomers with intentions to offer help and
encouragement:

> I wasn't sure what to make of our interaction. I
> hope I'm wrong, but it felt like a brush-off. I got
> the impression that I was considered a bit out of
> touch with the profession and that the advice that
> I tried to give about getting by on campus was
> considered inconsequential. I didn't feel like
> going back to his office.

So, like other aspects of faculty development often left to
occur spontaneously, mentoring profits from prearrangement
and coaching. The kind of structure depicted in the FIPSE
project typifies the level of coaxing that shy and reticent faculty often need to establish effective mentoring bonds. But we
can do even more. New faculty can profit by being hired with
plans for collaboration that begin before they arrive on campus for interviews. It makes sense to bring new faculty, especially from underrepresented categories, to campus with
specific plans for collaboration in teaching, research, writing,
and applying for grants.

What about cases where newcomers have interests dissimilar to those of senior faculty? Even there, in my experience, mentors can help in all the steps of setting up and
carrying through on projects. In a typical scenario, campuses
can arrange local supports as just described and off-campus
visits for more direct collaborations. In my view, campuses
have no business hiring new faculty, especially women and
members of minorities, for whom they cannot provide this
sort of mentoring and collaboration.

Facilitating Direction and Support with Catalogues

This is the most effective strategy for ensuring the success of new faculty that I know of. It consists of having a new faculty member, usually with the initial guidance of a mentor, compile a catalogue of brief, readable accounts of his or her past accomplishments, ongoing projects, and planned projects. Catalogues have these primary purposes:

1. Ensuring that new faculty will generate specific plans for progress as writers, teachers, and colleagues.
2. Getting the senior colleagues of new faculty, especially those involved in retention and tenure decisions, to provide early indications about whether new faculty members' efforts are likely to be on track and enough.
3. Eliciting advice and collaboration from the senior colleagues who give feedback to new faculty—and eliciting compromise as well, in the sense that experienced faculty should help moderate newcomers' expectations (for scholarly productivity, for example). Ideally, the committee that will make the decision about retention and tenure for a new faculty member should be formed as early as the decision to hire him or her is made. And, ideally, that committee will act as a mentoring group whose members remind each other to provide the advice and supports that new faculty members need.
4. Involving new faculty in ongoing adjustments of expectations and plans. Consider the usual hindrances to writing productivity among new faculty (Chapter Four): rumors abound about how much is enough, few new faculty members get useful information about how to plan productivity, and most new hires produce distressingly little writing. Obviously, this situation could be improved by more open and direct communication.

In my own ongoing research on cataloguing, the results are promising. For example, as new faculty get more specific direction, they report feeling more secure and confident about their careers (Boice, forthcoming). And as senior faculty get more involved in this communication process, they are more likely to become supporters and collaborators. What may begin as a mentoring effort involving one mentor (perhaps from another department) often expands to include several mentors. And what may begin as a set of unrealistic and mysterious expectations for a new faculty member can be tempered and clarified in the process of ongoing discussions as mentors and those mentored monitor accomplishments. This is, I believe, a humane process for communicating expectations about careers early enough for new faculty to make necessary adjustments. It is, evidently, an especially effective way of ensuring fair and helpful treatment of underrepresented new faculty who might otherwise be left out of traditional supports, such as old-boy networks.

In the chapters ahead, especially in my coverage of support for women and members of minorities as new faculty (Chapter Eleven), I address the practicalities of cataloguing (for example, who should take responsibility for cataloguing) and present instances of catalogues (including attendant feedback). Like other aspects of mentoring, cataloguing works easily once under way; involvement is always the crucial first step.

IRSS Theory and Mentoring

Think back to the outset of this chapter and the usual reservations about mentoring programs (for example, about time commitments; about newcomers who may neither want nor need it). The same arguments may still hold; in my experience, few campuses are immediately willing to take on obligations for programs that include weekly checks on mentoring pairs and monthly meetings of program participants. Fewer still see themselves as ready to change the traditional retention and tenure committees into mentoring groups.

When I visit campuses setting up support programs for new faculty, I emphasize beginning with smaller-scale projects, such as coteaching or the Katz paradigm. But I argue

that any campus trying to help its new faculty to more efficient starts should eventually implement something like
cataloguing. Without ongoing communication about what
campuses expect and without more obvious attempts to collaborate with the new faculty in meeting these expectations,
we may have missed the most vital step in mentoring. Then,
of course, I remind colleagues about IRSS notions as an effective way of planning a mentoring project.

Involvement

At its essence, mentoring ensures involvement. It builds acculturation and success by means of shared experience and
encouragement, especially by involving new faculty in the
everyday activity of mentors who know and profit by the local
culture. When, as in the model study of mentoring presented
earlier, protégés are made part of cataloguing groups, the
benefits multiply. And when mentoring programs can become
nontraditional enough to include students as protégés in the
whole process of socializing new faculty to campus, we will
at last maximize mentoring.

Regimen

The caution here is to guard against well-intentioned desires
to keep mentoring entirely spontaneous. Even when, as in the
FIPSE project, the content of mentoring interactions is left to
the pairs and groups of pairs, the success of mentoring
depends on discipline. Pairs that do not meet regularly are
unlikely to bond or accomplish much.

Self-Control

Part of the challenge, again, is to solve the right problem.
The problem to be solved by new faculty is more than finding
one supporter who can transmit one paradigm for doing
research or socializing to campus; we must move beyond the
vision of mentoring that we acquired as graduate students.

Part of it is proceeding with balance and moderation: by starting small and by ensuring that projects provide more than help in a single dimension (for example, teaching or socio-emotional support), we increase the chances that practitioners and other colleagues will stay involved and succeed.

Social Networking

To some extent, this last of the IRSS components has been preempted by what we have just considered. Whatever else it may be, mentoring is a matter of social support. But what may not be so apparent until we consider the most fundamental and tacit of survival skills is this: when we think of fostering the success of new faculty, we might overlook their need to spend as much time in networking (some of it arranged by mentors) as in other activities.

In the next chapter, we will see another example of the power of balance and social networks. In mastering teaching, new faculty evidently fare best at spontaneity and student involvement when they prepare less, at least to the point of moderation. When they manage this counterintuitive skill of teaching well, they do something else interesting. As a rule, they rush to tell colleagues, at least a friend or two, of the value of learning to "get more from less."

∾ SIX

Establishing Basic
Teaching Skills

Earlier, in Chapter Three, we examined the generally disappointing experiences of new faculty as teachers. Typically, they overprepared lectures and presented too much material too rapidly, they taught defensively so as to avoid public criticism, and they had few plans to improve their teaching beyond improving the content of their lectures. But there was a glimmering of hope in Chapter Three; quick starters, far more than their peers, found comfort, rapport, and acceptance in classrooms. This chapter resumes a focus on quick starters. In so doing, it strikes a theme quite different from what is found in the myriad books and articles on instructional development.

The premise here is that new faculty most need help with basics that are usually ignored. Those first-order basics are classroom comfort and rapport, balance between teaching and other academic activities, and rewards in teaching. Without this foundation in knowledge usually kept tacit, new faculty seem to postpone involvement in higher-order teaching skills, perhaps indefinitely.

In some ways, this approach is not novel. Most faculty development programs already stress teaching. Well they should. And most campuses, after considering the issue carefully, end up taking a simple approach. This too makes sense. But despite these sensible traditions, problems still arise. As a result of wanting to correct a problem overdue for attention, we may decide prematurely on what kind of help is best. And in the view taken here, we may not offer help at a level basic enough to be of much use for most new faculty.

Traditional Resources

I begin with a consideration of why usual resources for instructional development can fall short of transforming new faculty into thriving teachers.

Self-Help Books

When they decide to improve their teaching beyond perfecting its content, new faculty turn to predictable sources. McKeachie's (1986) *Teaching Tips* is a perennial best seller for a good reason: faculty like it. This excerpt from the subsection "Should Students Take Notes?" illustrates its informational style: "Hartley and Davies (1978) reviewed the research on note taking and student information processing during lectures. They report that students believe there are two purposes for taking notes: One is that the process of taking notes will in itself help later recall; the other is that the notes provide external storage of concepts which may be reviewed when needed. The research results indicate some support for both beliefs (p. 74)." Another book with potential attractiveness for new faculty is Eble's (1988) *The Craft of Teaching*. It covers the mechanics of managing classrooms ("grubby stuff and dirty work") and encourages reticent faculty to find rapport by treating teaching as conversation with students.

But as we saw in Chapter Three, new faculty too rarely take the initiative in improving their teaching. Thus, self-help books such as McKeachie's and Eble's probably play only a minor role in improving the teaching of new faculty. My own continued surveys with new faculty suggest that the small numbers who read books such as *Teaching Tips* rarely translate their insights into action.

Instructional Development

While we may not yet be able to expect many new faculty members to take effective initiative in improving their teaching, most campuses have a ready resource that can help. As a rule, the mission of presenting ideas and consultation about teaching lies in the hands of instructional development specialists. The field of instructional development (ID) has produced an assortment of readable and practical books about facilitating teaching. Menges and Mathis (1988) summarize this literature in helpful and realistic fashion.

To some extent, ID relies on the self-help books that faculty themselves prefer. The tradition of self-help books goes back at least to William James's (1899) *Talks to Teachers* and includes classics such as Highet's (1950) *The Art of Teaching.* Menges and Mathis note a mixture of pluses and minuses for this literature: On the one hand, it emphasizes common themes with apparent significance, including the value of evocative teaching, intellectual excitement, interpersonal rapport, and involvement. But, on the other, it is a literature without a grand theory of instruction or a credible base in generalizable, research-based principles.

The literature on teaching improvement that aims to surmount the limitations of self-help books more properly represents the ideals and aims of instructional development. We have already seen some of its classics, such as Katz's (1985) *Teaching as Though Students Mattered* and Eble and McKeachie's (1985) report on programs funded by the Bush Foundation, *Improving Undergraduate Education Through Faculty Development.* These are books with a foundation in systematic investigation. Other examples of resources from this rich area of advice and insight based on inquiry address communication skills, abilities to make judgments, and capacities for thinking. Readers unfamiliar with this literature are directed to the summaries and overviews provided by Menges and Mathis (1988). In the main, the ID literature plays a role beyond the scope of this book; only rarely do its prescriptions deal with the special plights of novice teachers.

Still, we can benefit from an acquaintance with the decades of systematic knowledge amassed by instructional developers. Weimer's (1990) *Improving College Teaching* is a good example of accumulated progress in ID. Consider two examples of her clear thinking and expertise, typical of ID writing. One is the concept of instructional awareness; most faculty benefit from beginning with overdue reflections on how they teach as an initial step in becoming better teachers. Another is a stepwise plan for improving teaching. It begins with instructional awareness and includes informal feedback and setting goals for change.

Weimer, however, insists on maintaining the practical realism that characterizes ID and thus highlights cautions about the shortcomings of ID programs (that is, she promotes a kind of "ID awareness" by warning readers about the limitations of the ID literature): "levels of instructional quality have not yet made the dramatic upturn that one might expect as a result of the attention focused on faculty and instructional development during the last twenty years . . . much work remains to be done" (p. xi).

A preliminary goal of this chapter, then, is to suggest ways of moving beyond this traditional shortage of proven and lasting results. A related goal, again, is to focus on even more fundamental beginnings in nurturing teaching than ID experts have advocated. The idea isn't mine; it came from the exemplary new faculty to whom I keep referring. Ultimately, then, my goal is both to enhance the teaching of new faculty and to broaden ID.

Starting with Quick Starters

We launch our inquiry into improving the teaching of new faculty on a positive note by returning to the quick starters we first met in Chapter Three. What makes quick starters worth studying and emulating? The following review list pro-

vides a reminder of the characteristics of the twenty-two individuals undergoing extensive study.

1. They teach with obvious comfort. Their presentations
   are unhurried and encourage active student involvement;
   within their first year on campus, these new faculty make
   observable strides in terms of relaxing in class and leaving classrooms without feeling fatigued. By their second
   semesters on campus, they find clear approval from
   students.
2. They verbalize general optimism about their students,
   their colleagues, and their campus. Within a year, they
   feel a welcome part of campus.
3. They proactively seek advice from colleagues, especially
   about teaching. They commonly visit colleagues' classes
   for ideas and modeling of alternative ways of teaching;
   some quick starters sit in on whole semesters of stimulating classes. Their successes in social networking include
   forming links with students in ways such as enlisting
   them as teaching and research assistants; quick starters
   integrate their scholarly and research interests into enthusiastic classroom presentations and so elicit student assistance as a reward for teaching well.
4. They establish balance between time spent on teaching
   preparation and on collegiality and scholarly productivity. By semesters 2-3 on campus, they spend enough time
   at writing and at social networking to generate about 1.5
   manuscripts per year, a level sufficient for routine tenuring criteria. And by year 2 on campus, quick starters moderate teaching preparation to the extent that it no longer
   undermines the enjoyment of teaching.

Messages from Quick Starters

Two points stand out in this list. The first is that these keys
to success at teaching bear little resemblance to what campuses usually offer new faculty. We may, for example, overlook nonteaching activities such as collegial networking as

part of helping novices acquire teaching skills. And, second, campus programs for new faculty seldom promote balance among all academic activities, especially balance that depends on moderating time spent at teaching preparation. Why have we been remiss in helping new faculty as teachers? We may assume that our faculty, new or not, have already mastered these first-order skills and attitudes (Peterson, Kromrey, Borg, & Lewis, 1990). And in our own defense, we may be reluctant to teach colleagues things that seem too easy to offer without stigmatizing them as incompetent (Langer & Park, 1990).

Coaching Comfort, Balance, and Rewards

The most pressing question about the unique practices of quick starters is whether other new faculty can mimic and benefit from them. Is it true, as Sternberg (1988) might contend, that these characteristics are as readily mastered as the other academic skills traditionally left untaught but essential to thriving in school? Or, as skeptics might claim, are these characteristics coincidental to teaching well?

In one test of the notion that the basic skills of quick starters can be transferred with profit to other new faculty members (Boice, 1992), I studied a sample of fifteen new faculty members who clearly were not exemplars of success. These volunteers came from two very different campuses (campuses 1 and 2 from Chapter Three) but shared the commonality of difficult starts as teachers, including mediocre teaching ratings, overpreparation, and a growing dislike for teaching. A key component in understanding and helping these new hires was enlisting quick starters as observers and advisers.

Beginning with Advice from Quick Starters. Quick starters, consistent with their generally proactive and collegial styles, were ready with advice about how to initiate a program for facilitating the teaching of new faculty. It was quick starters who labeled the venture as the "balance program." So it was that they insisted on finding ways to help colleagues equalize time expenditures as the first step (not the step with which I would have begun, at least for teaching); in their view, the other two essentials, establishing classroom comfort and ensuring rewards for teaching, should follow the first step of balance. With their consultation, we devised a regimen for the fifteen participants who had agreed to spend an academic year or more in the balance program. The resulting paradigm is listed as follows (I indicate in brackets how each step relates to the IRSS theory discussed throughout this book):

1.   Keep daily, verifiable records of how they spent their work days (see Boice, 1987b, for details). [This pertains to the IRSS component of involvement.]
2.   Limit classroom preparation time in a maximum of two hours per classroom hour. [This is akin to the IRSS components of establishing regimen and of solving the right problem—that is, of reshaping tasks to fit into busy days.]
3.   Spend at least two hours per workweek on social networking related to teaching and scholarly productivity. [This is the IRSS principle of social networking.]
4.   Find brief daily times for scholarly writing, at least thirty to sixty minutes. [Learning how much time is optimal is an example of mastering the IRSS notion of self-management.]
5.   Integrate scholarly and research interests into lectures, where appropriate, with a goal of interesting students in eventual involvement as teaching and research assistants. [This, too, is a matter of learning things usually kept tacit and of building social networks. And it induces involvement for students.]

While the plan emphasized balance, it included considerations of comfort and reward. Balance, by definition, included a mix of those basic practices; as defined here, it is necessarily a matter of moderation.

Initial Reactions of Participants. First responses of new faculty given this five-step assignment confirmed our fears that this might be an unrealistic program. This comment from an inexperienced new hire at a research campus typifies initial misgivings:

> I definitely do not think I can do all that. I don't have time now. And I don't know that I've ever been more tired than I am now. I am absolutely positive that I cannot prepare properly for class in the time you've allotted; I need more time than that just to do the readings that I assign to my classes. You don't understand what I have to do.

Given such responses, I asked participants to consider two things. First, I reminded them that some of their most successful colleagues were already following the plan, usually with the result of more free time than displayed by other new faculty members. In some cases, I asked quick starters to model and describe their success at finding balance. As a rule, these interactions were undemanding and brief; quick starters dropped in on my consultations with new faculty for brief confirmations that they were getting "more from less" and then invited project participants to visit them during lecture preparation times. Second, I reminded participants in the balance program of the results-first approach (Peters & Waterman, 1984); that is, they would be more likely to find benefits by leaping in and trying this method than by expecting to find solace in talking about their reservations.

Indeed, involvement is evidently the critical element in improvements. Once involved in the five steps of the balance program, participants reported being most surprised about finding more time:

> Amazing! That's what it is. I was certain that I would have too little time for all this, but I already have far more time to take care of myself than I imagined. I feel less harried, and I feel more confident because I am getting more done in less time.

Then, still within the first five weeks of participation, new
faculty began to report benefits in teaching:

> My lectures are less hurried, just as you predicted.
> I almost hate to admit it. I have finally slowed
> down—to my relief and to my students' relief.
> That was the hardest part, going to class without
> so much material, wondering if there would be
> enough to say and if the class would get out of
> control. But it hasn't. It's much better letting stu-
> dents do some of the work.

Longer-Term Reactions of Participants. As participants ap-
proximated the standards set out in the balance plan, two
essential things happened. First, these new faculty members
continued to find more efficiency in working at professorial
activities. Second, they started to find comfort in carrying out
the plan, even its regimen:

> I have *never* liked to be on any kind of schedule,
> mostly, I think, because I believed it would stifle
> my creativity and enjoyment in doing things. But
> when I realized that I was not finding creativity
> and enjoyment as a teacher as it was, I could see no
> real harm in trying the balance thing. And, to my
> surprise, I actually like being regimented in this
> way. I have more time and energy, and I have more
> interest in doing better at things like teaching.

Another surprise has already been hinted at. As new
faculty found more time for reflection about teaching, they
expressed a spontaneous interest in mastering more aspects of
teaching. First they requested coaching to help them make
their teaching even more effective; then they asked for regular
meetings where we could discuss the literature on teaching
excellence. Predictably, quick starters joined them in discussion groups that share the tacit and explicit knowledge

of teaching. One of the first observations about this group was its novelty on a research campus where faculty rarely talked about teaching improvement.

Intermediate Steps: Comfort and Rewards

Simply by virtue of practicing balance, the fifteen new faculty members in the initial study group are reporting remarkable increase in comfort and rewards as teachers. And like their peer advisers (that is, quick starters), they are becoming primed to see possibilities for doing better, especially at finding more comfort and rewards in teaching.

Classroom Comfort and Communication

In all my studies of new faculty who were not new to teaching (that is, who fit the experienced category of Chapters One through Three), I have found that the thing they mastered more quickly than their inexperienced counterparts on the same campus was a noticeable increase in classroom comfort. As a rule, they felt more at ease by semester 3, in part because they had learned what to expect from their students and to worry less about their disapproval. When I asked experienced new faculty how they managed this sort of improvement, however, they were almost invariably unable to verbalize the processes. Clearly, what knowledge they had was tacit; they had learned it on their own and without examining how or how well they had done it. And when I observed them before, during, and after classes, they displayed variable and admittedly incomplete patterns of having established comfort and communication. Still, the value of having managed even partial success at comfort and communication was so obvious that it reinforced my plans to implement this aspect of what quick starters did well.

The TSED. I began my systematic efforts with more classroom observations. But unlike most of the observational approaches I have described so far, I eventually relied on teachers themselves to do the essential observing. I anticipated at least three advantages of emphasizing self-ratings. One was the likelihood that new faculty can be the best judges of their discomfort. Another was that monitoring their anxiety would provide chances for getting in touch with its patterns and effects, as part of establishing greater teaching awareness. And the third was that the habit of monitoring discomfort as it happens provides the best occasion for modifying it.

I developed an uncomplicated and fast instrument for these self-ratings, the Teacher's Self-Evaluation of Discomfort (TSED). The TSED scale is employed before, during, and after classes. Its format is shown in Exhibit 6.1. Regular experience with the TSED shows new faculty, first of all, that its practice is neither intrusive nor time-consuming. The TSED takes a minute for completion and reflection (usually after class, when students have gone). Second, practice with the TSED is in itself sufficient to help some new faculty members enhance their comfort; that is, simply seeing the prevalence and counterproductivity of discomfort is often sufficient to instigate searches for alternatives.

Exhibit 6.1. The Teacher's Self-Evaluation of Discomfort.

Give Subjective Discomfort Scale (SUDS) ratings for the following items (1 = no discomfort; 100 = maximum discomfort):

1. Entering the classroom _____
2. Talking to students before class starts _____
3. Beginning the lecture _____
4. Answering initial questions from students _____
5. Dealing with signs of student disapproval or lack of interest _____
6. The pace of presentation _____
7. Ending the class on time _____
8. Talking to students after class _____

The TSEIC. The Teacher's Self-Evaluation of Improvements in Comfort (TSEIC) indexes changes in both classroom comfort and communication (see Exhibit 6.2.). As I use it, the TSEIC is eventually administered in place of the TSED and

Exhibit 6.2. The Teacher's Self-Evaluation of Improvement in Comfort.

Rate your effectiveness in today's class for the following activities
(1 = ineffective; 7 = highly effective):

1. Ignoring the anxiety that accompanies beginnings of class _____
2. Putting myself at ease once the class is under way _____
3. Making myself slow down while lecturing or presenting _____
4. Listening and reflecting patiently _____
5. Displaying obvious enjoyment of the class _____
6. Taking unhurried time for previewing and reviewing _____
7. Letting moments of classroom silence pass with comfort _____

---

sets the stage for evaluating progress in carrying out relaxation exercises that help facilitate classroom comfort.

Relaxation Workshops. Relaxation, as a rule, requires more
than insight. It demands the involvement of practice. I have
a long-standing investment in leading workshops on classroom comfort and communication with colleagues, one that
predates my awareness of quick starters. This, as much as
anything else I have evaluated, brings about lasting improvements in students' evaluations and in teachers' self-rated satisfaction with their classroom performances.

As a rule, I present the TSED and the TSEIC in brief,
informal workshops where participants do most of the work.
I begin with an informal demonstration of putting myself
and them at ease by seeking them out and chatting with them
as they arrive and take seats. I even do some of the same with
colleagues who invariably arrive late (that is, I pause to welcome them, to give them a brief review of what we have been
doing, and to establish preliminary rapport with them). We
start meetings, though, by taking the focus off the individuals
in attendance, with a discussion about ways of taking the
anonymity away from students as a means of ensuring comfortable beginnings.

For example, I ask why most new faculty don't arrive
at their classes early to chat informally with their students,
away from the podium. The groups know the answers all too
well: they simply hadn't thought of it; they had come to class

after rushing to complete even more materials for presentation and so were too busy for informal chats; and, most troublesome, they were not sure how students would respond. I then remind them of their response to my informal chats before the workshop. Next, groups come to agree that most students, even those sitting on the periphery, appreciate a friendly display of interest. As we continue, groups of this sort invariably raise the same concern and the same solution. The problem is that students who generate the most tension in teachers (and in classmates) may discourage early, informal chats. Nonetheless, we come to agree that the best corrective for disruptive students is undoubtedly a reduction in their anonymity. "Joining" them by means of casual chats is easier than the alternatives. (The same tactic works with disruptive faculty in workshops.)

Step two in these workshops usually focuses on learning to loosen up as teachers by practicing common relaxation techniques. Most campuses have resident experts who can help teach the techniques. I advocate an unusually simple, almost comical strategy for relaxing; keeping one's tongue at the bottom of one's mouth where it belongs except when speaking. Tense people keep their tongues at the roofs of their mouths, ready to speak at a millisecond's notice. Moreover, while they tense their tongues, they strain their jaws and necks. So it is that simply relaxing and lowering our tongues helps calm our jaws and necks and, in turn, calms our ongoing performance. In practice, it is so unobtrusive that it can be invoked (perhaps with a self-statement to "relax") while walking to the lectern, while pausing for questions, even while preparing for class.

What difference does classroom comfort make? This comment from a new faculty member who had only recently mastered its rudiments is illustrative:

> It can make all the difference in the world. It has meant not steaming my way into class at the last minute, not steeling myself against the questions that will at last expose me as a fraud. It has

meant slowing down and enjoying myself and
my students. I find myself actually looking more
at them; they notice my attention and composure
and seem to enjoy it; I notice subtleties, including occasions for humor. Learning to relax, to
find classroom comfort, has meant that teaching
is not the hard, grueling work it used to be.

Communication with Students. Once new faculty are comfortable with their classes, and not before, they are ideally
ready to benefit from student feedback such as comments on
lectures and course evaluations. Like the self-evaluations of
comfort and improvement we saw earlier, estimates of success
at establishing rapport work best when kept private from colleagues and administrators, at least in the short run.

My workshops on communication, then, come to focus
on more than evaluations, on ratings that go beyond the relative comfort of self-assessments to student ratings. Even so,
the sticking point in these workshops on rapport is a powerful one that precedes usual reluctance to be evaluated; new
faculty commonly suppose that they already do a good job at
communicating with students:

> I do that. I know what students are thinking and
> how they are doing because I occasionally ask for
> comments during class. Not only that, but stu-
> dents come by after class and tell me what they
> aren't getting or what about my course they don't
> like. [In response to my question about how
> many students provide this feedback] Well, yeah,
> it is only a handful. Most of the students keep
> things to themselves.

Initially, at least, my queries about rapport annoy new faculty;
they seem to be taken to mean that I doubt their social skills
in general. But then, to demonstrate the point about how
much usually fails to get communicated in classes and similar
contexts, I interrupt the workshop for an early, informal eval-

uation of how things are going. The format of the feedback instrument is the same as the one that I advocate for use in their classrooms: the Early, Informal Evaluation (EIE).

The EIE (Boice, 1990a) solicits a brief sample of participants' reactions that I (and they) can use to improve things well before the workshop comes to an end. It also plays a similar role in classrooms (see Exhibit 6.3.). When I demonstrate the EIE in the workshops, I also model some of its unusual aspects of application. For one thing, it is collected, summarized, and distributed by one or a few class (or workshop) members. This helps ensure that written comments will remain confidential, and it involves group members in the process. (One or two group members calculate mean values for the rating items and select normative but not extreme comments for listing on the summary page; all this can be conducted during a break in the session or after a class). Immediate analysis also sets the stage for immediate discussion of the results.

As I review the results of the EIE with the group, I usually begin by reflecting on what I think are helpful and what unhelpful suggestions about how I can make the workshop better. In my own workshops, there are often problems of some members not feeling involved or worrying that the workshop will not cover topics of interest to them. In the

---

Exhibit 6.3. The Early, Informal Evaluation.

A. Open-ended questions:
  1. Indicate what the instructor does well (please be specific and generous):

  2. Indicate what the instructor could do differently and/or better (please be specific and constructive):

B. Rating items (use a scale of 1–7 where 1 = disagree strongly and 7 = agree strongly):
  1. The instructor is approachable and helpful _____
  2. I am learning a lot in this class _____
  3. I would recommend this class to a friend _____

---

classes of new faculty, the EIE generally reveals problems of pacing and involvement; new teachers, as we saw in Chapter Three, often prepare too much to say and say it too rapidly. The point, ultimately, is this: the kinds of deficits or misunderstandings uncovered by the EIE almost always demand little more than simple solutions; where changes consist of, say, slowing one's pace, students are employed as friendly monitors; where requested changes represent only minority interests or demands incompatible with course objectives, the ensuing discussion helps inform the requestors about the reasons why changes may not be forthcoming.

So, shortly after I begin reviewing the EIE, I pause to reexplain the rationale for doing things the way I do (evaluations are prime opportunities for clarifying one's rationales). Then I ask the group to speculate about what the evaluation means, especially the written comments from disgruntled workshop members (typically by getting group members to role play what peers meant by certain ratings or comments). Finally, I use the occasion to rate the group as a whole in terms of qualities of involvement and supportiveness. I let them know where I think the evaluation has been most helpful, where and why I disagree, and how I think they could be more helpful, both as evaluators and as workshop participants. Done well, evaluations are bidirectional.

Then, in the aftermath of the EIE interactions, I point out the parallels in what we are doing to what would happen with an EIE administered in their classes. And I note again how little effective communication there had been about what was happening in the workshop before we did the EIE exercise. Unspoken feedback was mostly remaining just that.

Two things generally impress workshop participants most about this exercise. First, it takes only five to ten minutes. Second, it demonstrates how easy it can be for the leader or teacher to deal with feedback, even some barbs from disgruntled participants, while listening to what can be learned from the group. Three usual qualms from faculty considering the EIE merit mention here. First, new faculty usually suppose that students will object to taking time out of busy lecture schedules and that they will see requests to collect and summarize the evaluations as an imposition. Instead, students welcome being asked what they think of the class, especially in a format where the instructor will pay attention; at least some students in class will welcome the opportunity to collect and analyze the evaluations. The second usual qualm is that new faculty imagine that the result could be an outpouring of hostility and a public embarrassment. In fact, students are generally kind. In practice, the instructor's feedback to the class on the evaluation is an opportunity to educate students about what makes for useful and appropriate comments; in almost every EIE situation that I know about, asking the compilers to edit out obviously extreme comments, positive and negative, makes sense. Third, new faculty commonly worry that students' complaints will be aimed largely at receiving easier tests and assignments or at changing courses in ways so drastic that no conscientious professor could comply. Part of what many new faculty members need to do is to clarify rationales for why the course is taught the way it is, including reasonable demands for accountability for student involvement. In actual practice with the EIE, students rarely ask for more than slower-paced lectures, clearer expectations about what they are supposed to learn and how they will be graded, more signs of approachability and openness from the instructor, and a demonstrated willingness to coach students in ways that will help them meet the demanding standards set for the class (see Elbow, 1983).

As new faculty and their classes get used to early evaluations, one result is a marked increase in communication and comfort. Just as happens in the workshops just described, classes become more relaxed, more participative, and more collaborative. As new faculty encourage more feedback and as they show promise of listening to and acting on those interactions, the most important change begins to occur: students do more of the work.

Rewards for Teaching

With balance, comfort, and communication established, have we and our new faculty done enough in establishing basics?

We might suppose so if we hadn't collected the kind of systematic feedback just advocated for communicating with students about how to improve classes. New faculty themselves initially react to the kinds of changes just described by supposing that comfort and rapport will make teaching rewarding enough to sustain their newly found enthusiasm. My longer-term contacts with new faculty, however, suggest that the individuals who maintain their enthusiasm eventually make a priority of finding additional rewards for teaching. As a rule, these rewards involve interactions with students outside classrooms, a context where programs for improving teaching may ordinarily fall short.

Comments from forty-four new faculty members following up on programmatic EIE exercises indicate that the most powerful rewards center around a single configuration: those who integrate information about their interests into class and who encourage students to become involved in those interests find by far the most satisfaction as teachers. Evidently, their students also find these classes the most enjoyable and instructive, even more so than classes taught in more refined and entertaining fashion. It is, in my experience, vitally important to show new faculty ways to find student acceptance without being classroom entertainers.

There are a great many ways to get new faculty to integrate their interests into classes in appropriate ways. One is as modest as telling new faculty about how it can work; oddly, most new faculty members either haven't thought of it or else have dismissed it as an overly selfish act. A second way builds on a preexisting tradition to integrate rewards into teaching. While new faculty had not been encouraged to excel at teaching by their campus, they had been urged to compete for small grants that provide summer salaries. When I was able to get some funds that had been used for small grants to use for my own support programs, I started a project that explicitly gives money to new faculty members who can use large, lower-level classes to promote their research.

Briefly, here is the plan: At the beginning of their first or second year on campus, new faculty can apply for grants that will fund their summer salaries and those of the under-graduate research assistants they recruit as part of the project. In a way, the application period lasts through the first and second semesters as new faculty, aided by my coaching and written materials, practice the balance and comfort programs already described as part of qualifying for consideration. The key dimensions on which they can win summer salaries are judged on these activities: (1) success in demonstrating enthusiasm for their research and scholarly interests while meeting the preestablished learning goals of the class; (2) success in recruiting undergraduate students as research assistants for the subsequent semesters; and (3) success in extending the teaching experience to the research or creative project and back again to the classroom (for example, having former class members return to a subsequent class to share their experiences).

The dramatic enthusiasm of undergraduates for these projects has led to some related projects. The first sort involves students as returning teaching assistants who actually get experience at coteaching and other classroom leadership skills. The second sort involves undergraduate assistants as classroom researchers who help collect and facilitate discussions about the kinds of EIE information reviewed earlier. Both these recruitment procedures have the advantage of making teaching more rewarding; both also have the potential to help remedy the growing shortage of prospective teachers among certain categories of undergraduates in areas such as the sciences, mathematics, and engineering. In our pilot efforts, at least, a brief and well-supported exposure to assisting in a class can apparently engage students in plans for a teaching career.

Advanced Steps: Investigating Complex Aspects of Teaching

When, as we saw earlier, new faculty find balance, comfort, and rewards, they spontaneously show interest in moving beyond the basics. At last, they are primed to enjoy the subtleties of excelling at teaching. Again, I portray how my own support groups have developed interests in teaching. I suspect that there may be some generality in these patterns, but I encourage readers to consider these as mere suggestions of how a program might proceed after meeting the basics.

Discussion Groups

Scholars that we all are, we can find some appeal in meeting regularly with groups of new faculty to discuss the literature on teaching. This is an occasion for involving some of the more senior faculty, especially those with expertise and enthusiasm to share. I find it easy to recruit members for my discussion groups by way of the contacts I establish in interviewing new faculty each semester and in surveying the senior colleagues who are participants in mentoring projects. There is a lot to be discussed in such groups; they function as much as anything to winnow out the chaff and bring in the substance. In the best of these groups, in which I have been involved, we proceeded in the following general fashion.

First, the group looked for a common base of agreement; we agreed to begin with McKeachie's (1986) *Teaching Tips*, the most practical of books of advice about teaching. As a group, we decided that four of his points could be shared with other colleagues as representative and instructive:

1. Outstanding lecturers have only a few points to make, but they use a wealth of examples in the process.
2. We can learn a lot about how students are processing our lectures by watching them take notes; poorer students often need redundancy.
3. An ideal time to capture students' interest is during introductions to lectures, usually by pointing out gaps in their knowledge.
4. The best time to clarify goals for learning is at the beginning of courses.

Second, we found especially useful excerpts such as this one from annotated bibliographies about the importance of expanding usual practices with teaching evaluations: "End-of-course ratings of the average teacher who receives feedback at midterm are at about the 59th percentile (the average teacher receiving no feedback would be at the 50th percentile). When ratings information is accompanied by consultation and/or other types of feedback, the effect is considerably larger, about the 85th percentile. Effects on the achievement and affect of students are less clear from available research but appear to be positive" (Menges & Brinko, 1986, annotated in Menges & Mathis, 1988, pp. 105–106).

Third, in a mood to look at more systematic approaches to ID, we examined books such as Weimer's (1990) *Improving College Teaching*. We selected her stepwise advice on setting programs for formative evaluations as exemplary:

1. Get faculty involved in the choices about what feedback to collect; giving faculty a sense of control helps reduce their defensiveness about evaluations.
2. Show faculty the advantages of collecting feedback in a variety of ways. They will learn more (and be better buffered against single bad ratings) by seeking input from more than one course, from more than one kind of evaluation (for example, open-ended questions and checklists provide different kinds of information), and about different classroom activities (for example, getting brief evaluations of the fairness and comprehensiveness of tests).
3. Use evaluation formats that balance positive and negative feedback.
4. Elicit feedback about the feedback from colleagues, consultants, even students.
5. Emphasize the potential of formative feedback for specifying different ways of teaching; otherwise, faculty may see only one, aversive alternative (for example, lowering standards) in response to criticism.

Fourth, feeling ready for more difficult materials, we moved to the research literature on teaching effectiveness; in a way, the ID literature left us longing for more facts. In one rather demanding investigation, we read and discussed a series of analyses by Feldman (1986, 1988, 1989a, 1989b) and summarized his findings in provocative fashion (we also compared them to my own findings with new faculty, as shown below in brackets):

1. Experience in teaching brings perceived improvement in knowledge of the subject matter and in intellectual expansiveness. [These are precisely the two areas in which new faculty say they want to excel.]

2. Personality correlates of effective teaching include positive self-esteem, cultural and aesthetic sensitivity, sophistication, and orderliness. [While new faculty rarely show explicit awareness of the first and second factors, they pay close attention to orderliness.]

3. Faculty suspicions that students want to be entertained and pampered may be correct; certainly, students do not share faculty's values of making teaching challenging and making learning self-initiated. [New faculty routinely use this dilemma to argue against abandoning lecturing because they suppose that they know better than students what should be taught and how to teach it.]

4. Faculty are poor judges of how well they clarify course objectives, give feedback on student performance, sense class levels of comprehension, and express friendliness and helpfulness. [When confronted with these facts, new faculty respond by concluding that these patterns hold only for poorer students; one presumption of the lecture method, as in much scholarly writing, is that the audience must bring a willingness to work at involvement and understanding.]

5. Instructional dimensions that show the clearest and broadest impact are preparation and organization, clarity and understandability, sensitivity to class progress, and stimulation of student interest. [Actually, new faculty are generally on target in aspiring to these goals; in practice, as indicated in item 4, they may not know how to effect them.]

In the long term, though, interest waned in meeting and discussing these practical and theoretical bits of information about teaching excellence. It may be that such groups run a course where members need a change in emphasis, especially from insight to action. At least that is what has happened with the new faculty with whom I have conducted this and similar discussion groups. Indeed, both groups with whom I have managed a long run of interactions in this fashion spontaneously chose the same direction after an immersion in the ID literature.

Classroom Research Groups

Discussion groups can set the stage for an interest in classroom research. So can other activities, including the programs for enlisting undergraduates as research and teaching assistants mentioned earlier. In my experience, classroom research has a broader and more enduring appeal than other group projects. Classroom research (that is, learning from one's students about how to make teaching more effective) is not new. But its systematization and popularization are. Weimer, whose advocacy of a stepwise approach for learning from student evaluations we have seen, and other leaders of ID are actively promoting accountability in the classroom. Two of the leaders of this revolution, Cross and Angelo (1988), not only involve faculty in the collection of feedback about their classes but engage them as collaborators with students in learning how certain aspects of teaching affect learning. The appeal of Cross and Angelo's classroom research for new faculty is at least twofold: they like its emphasis on data-based changes in teaching approaches, and they approve of its practical, flexible strategies for learning from small-sample experiments on only one or two classes at a time.

Cross and Angelo note a third advantage in their approach: the research most likely to influence how professors teach is research that they themselves conduct. When faculty carry out classroom research, they get information about how to change and experience a powerful source of motivation for change. The single most attractive component of classroom research, though, may be its readiness for successful application. Consider some examples from Cross and Angelo's (1988) handbook on *Classroom Assessment Techniques* that have proved especially effective with the new faculty groups at my own campus. The first is the project notion of melding evaluation instruments with teaching tips. In one application, students are taught to observe themselves in the process of learning with exercises such as compiling autobiographies as learners. Both they and their teachers learn from the recountings of experiences considered failures and successes. In another application, students are directed to identify and role play the skills that they must have to succeed in planned careers. As a result, students learn how to assess their performance, how specific skills are coached, and how to demonstrate their expert knowledge more readily.

Many of Cross and Angelo's strategies, as the name of their handbook suggests, deal with collecting student feedback. They suggest a variety of innovative techniques, including electronic mail, whereby students can convey anonymous messages to their professors throughout the semester. A related exercise, one not original to Cross and Angelo, has students concoct chain letters to professors; in this way, students can adapt what they write to what their peers are writing.

A Test of Classroom Research

Of all the classroom research approaches, one that I have found of particular value, uses focused evaluations to collect experimental information about the success of a particular innovation. I offer an example from my own classes because it revolves around criticisms of the courses that I teach. Even faculty developers are subject to criticism.

In one recent instance, I taught a graduate course in organizational psychology with a writing-intensive format. In each weekly meeting of this class, students were required to write about what they were learning, and each assignment for the next class meeting required them to work outside class in a regimen of brief writing projects. These demands, coupled with experiences of reading and evaluating each other's prose each week, surprised students in a course that traditionally puts little emphasis on teaching writing as a professional skill; some made angry comments about the inappropriateness of this emphasis in a course preparing them for applied work. Moreover, almost all students felt that I was expecting too much of them and that I did not appreciate how busy they were outside class.

To keep feedback simple but systematic, I used a variation of the focused evaluations format from classroom research: I collected these evaluations each week. Ratings and written comments about the value of writing experiences started at rock bottom; students began with a low opinion of me and of my class. But over the fifteen weeks of the semester, as students also indicated that they had gained confidence and fluency as writers, ratings of usefulness increased to near maximum. Moreover, students' ratings of the usefulness of the evaluation exercise and of its related discussions went up dramatically over the semester.

Was there any value in this instance beyond proving that I had done the right things in assigning regular writing and student evaluations? I concluded, as a classroom researcher, that the focused evaluations revealed things about my style of teaching writing that led me to make changes I otherwise would not have made. Here is an example of a specific: I had assumed that things I demonstrated in class and then had students mimic (with coaching) would work as easily outside class. I had expected a ready transfer of what I demonstrated to what I wanted them to accomplish outside class as writers. I was quite wrong.

I learned, for example, that I had presented the exercises in finding fluency as writers with such enthusiasm and conviction that my students felt remiss in failing. They hesitated in telling me, at least to my face, that they were letting me down. When the class and I worked out more gradual plans for out-of-class assignments and for readier acceptance of my coaching during office hours, things proceeded more smoothly.

Later, when I described this experience to colleagues, the same question usually came up: Is this research? My response came to be this: It is in an elementary way. Only when I subjected myself and my class to routine measurement of students' learning processes did I learn much about the effects of how I taught. Having done it, I felt motivated to check on the generality of that test. In a similar class, I checked to see whether students objected to focused weekly evaluations even though we were experiencing no controversy (and no regular pressure to write). They came to welcome the evaluations, mostly because they liked being consulted and because it helped make them aware of how they could discover what their peers were learning. (After all, classroom research focuses on what students are learning.)

Where will my new colleagues and I go next? I anticipate that as we persist in building our interests in teaching, we will move in two divergent but mutually rewarding directions. One, already in progress, involves supporting other new faculty as teachers. Without question, the single best motivator for self-improvement of new faculty as teachers that I have seen is getting them involved as mentors for other new faculty. The second direction is one that is less appropriate for detailing in a book on new faculty; it is more a matter of what new faculty who are teaching well will tackle when they are no longer new. From what I can see in the groups of new faculty traced into their fifth and sixth years, the most involved teachers will pursue ways to impart critical thinking to their classes. This may be a major step in a developmental series of attempting to master the stepwise tasks of teaching. And it may be that, in a brief examination of how faculty learn to teach critical thinking, we will encounter a valuable last lesson in making ID work.

A Final Step: Critical Thinking

Here again, those who began as quick starters have taken the strongest initiative. As they have become confident in their mastery of the basics, they have started to read the literature on teaching for themselves. One area of strong interest is teaching critical thinking (a goal that they have held in common with most new faculty since my first interviews with them). One book that they like for its succinct and research-based style is Kurfiss's (1988) *Critical Thinking*. Among the points that stand out when we discuss it is that critical thinking, as Kurfiss notes, is rarely taught, despite the value that educators claim to place on it. (Recall Sternberg's conclusion—for example, in Sternberg et al., 1990—about the importance of tacit knowledge as traditionally unmentioned but vital to thriving.) What makes the teaching of critical thinking similar to the problems in supporting new faculty is that both need a basis in knowledge usually left untaught in systematic ways.

Among the techniques that Kurfiss outlines for teachers are modeling critical thinking, coaching and scaffolding it, and coexploring it. Her most recent work (now under the name of Gainen, 1991) may be the most useful guide for translating insight into customs that foster critical thinking. In her view of the research literature, two strategies seem most promising: arranging opportunities for collaborative inquiry among students (for a similar approach in cooperative learning, see Cooper, 1990) and teaching cognitive strategies for problem solving (for example, talking aloud while solving a problem so as to articulate the usually tacit procedures that make up higher-level thinking).

Reflections on Helping New Faculty Establish Basic Skills

Any endeavor in instructional development may, if we are not careful, be marked most obviously by how few colleagues we help. We may too often be tempted to go with support programs that work well with the minority of faculty members who readily accept them. When we fail to attract and help the majority of the faculty members we serve, we weaken the chances for long-term survival of our programs and of our new colleagues. So it is that I close this chapter with a reminder of what can keep many new faculty members from participating in even so basic a program as this and with variations on the IRSS theory of what new faculty need to benefit from support programs. As we come full circle, to considering what we can learn about supporting new faculty as teachers from recent research on teaching students, we move to areas that remain to be developed.

We have already seen some compelling factors that keep new faculty from participating in instructional support programs. Beyond the ambivalent messages that they get from their campuses about the value of teaching, three more reasons merit close attention.

Support may not help with the necessities. First, most traditional campus programs do not help new hires with the root problem of success on a new campus—finding time to work on teaching and other tasks in effective ways. The balance program advocated here is a tested way of helping new faculty past that obstacle. That is, newcomers need to begin by making teaching preparation a task of moderation, one that does not exclude other important professorial activities, one that does not discourage active student participation in class.

Moreover, most new faculty need to learn tacit knowledge about teaching at a level as basic as finding comfort and rewards before they are ready to proceed to the more complex skills usually emphasized in ID programs. But balance and first-order basics of teaching as we have described them do not complete the picture. Other components that may play vital roles in first-order competencies still need study in faculty development.

New faculty may lack resilience. One such component is the resilience with which new faculty recover from frustrations and disappointments. In my experience with new faculty, those who persist in self-doubts about their capabilities undermine their efficiency and expose themselves to experiences of vulnerability and stress. Bandura (1990), the leading researcher on what he calls "self-efficacy," outlines four steps for building this antidote for cognitions associated with self-doubting: (1) mastery experiences; (2) modeling; (3) social persuasion and support; and (4) building physical status. The first three of these resemble IRSS notions. Mastery is akin to involvement, modeling to solving the right problems and to learning tacit knowledge, and social persuasion and support to social networking. What Bandura adds to first-fact theory, building physical status, resembles regimen, but from a perspective that we too often overlook in nurturing the teaching of new faculty. Teaching can be, after all, an emotionally and physically demanding task.

New faculty may need to engage in critical thinking about problems or teaching as part of learning to teach. The third factor that seems to inhibit the participation of new faculty in instructional development is also neglected as a rule. It may be that we need to employ the same kinds of coaching that we employ for students learning to think critically as part of teaching colleagues how to teach. Learning to teach effectively is, after all, far more than rote memorization. Consider the parallels between the two situations: the critical step in effecting critical thinking among students is getting them to internalize the critical thinking processes that they have seen demonstrated (Gainen, 1991). The same problem seems to hold for new faculty considering instructional development strategies; often, they do not translate insights into action. The solution, at least with students, is a form of involvement: simply immersing students in a clear explanation of procedural knowledge and then coaching them in ways of discussing the procedural knowledge with classmates is sufficient to induce evidence of learning to think critically (King, 1990). The same procedure—combining involvement in procedural knowledge and in shared comprehension with peers—may be a critical first step in getting new faculty to attempt the transition to internalization and action.

The second step, according to research on teaching students to think critically, is coaching them in the cognitive strategies of learning and applying the tacit knowledge of problem solving. For students, at least, an effective cognitive strategy is problem-based learning (Schmidt, 1983). To start with, effective teachers operationally define the target skill as something usually left tacit, as something done unthinkingly by experts. Students begin their efforts by analyzing the problem task to discover the components of that tacit knowledge, usually with assistance in small-group tutorials. Then, with coaching from teachers and peers, they practice those skills. In a similar approach, called guided design, students work in teams without supervision. The result is a real increase in objective knowledge and in problem-solving ability.

Here, too, faculty developers, many of whom already rely on procedures established for student development, can extend established strategies to new faculty. Our programs for new faculty can be strengthened only by simulating collaborative, problem-based approaches that help induce critical thinking. Modest but promising evidence already exists for the efficacy of teaching students critical thinking with the strategies just reviewed (Gainen, 1991). The next step is a matter of transferring what we know about critical thinking to what we are learning about new faculty. After all, effective approaches to teaching critical thinking include the same components that we have been considering in a broader sense—that is, involvement, regimen, self-management, and social networking.

 SEVEN

Encouraging
Scholarly
Productivity

Consider a paradox about scholarly writing, one that I have confirmed repeatedly in my studies of new faculty and their evaluators. We want our new hires to show proficiency at it; yet we expect them to fail in most of their experiences as writers trying to publish in the highest-status outlets, many boasting of rejection rates in excess of 90 percent. And we expect them to suffer as writers. Nowhere else in professorial life do we expect new faculty to tolerate the severity of criticism, some of it capricious and cruel, that can come from editors and anonymous reviewers (Boice & Jones, 1984). But the dilemma facing those of us who might help colleagues improve their productivity as writers goes beyond the difficulty and exclusivity of writing. Writing is also a typically private, self-mastered activity, one that is rarely discussed. Indeed, as I have discovered in two decades of writing about writing, there is a taboo about encouraging the silent majority of academicians to take up writing. We have, I am frequently reminded by critics, too many writers already.

While almost no one questions the propriety of conducting programs for instructional development, many faculty developers shun support for writing. Thus, this chapter presents a plan for encouraging reconsideration of support for writing. First, I briefly review the costs of not writing, for new faculty in general and for underrepresented new hires in particular. Next, I overview the little-known literature about what keeps most of us from fluency and enjoyment as writers. Then I integrate emerging facts about the potential for mutual facilitation among teaching, collegiality, and writing productivity. Next, having set a rationale for supporting writing, I present a stepwise plan for implementing that support in workshops and related projects for new faculty. Finally, I consider the factors that hinder campuses from adopting such a plan and suggest how IRSS theory can help overcome common resistances.

Costs of Silence

Obvious costs of nonproductivity are failures to gain degrees, promotions, and other rewards. Some estimates of the number of dissertation-level students who do not finish are as high as 50 percent (Sternberg, 1981). Oddly, with the growing concern about finding enough applicants for professorial jobs (Bowen & Schuster, 1986), this problem of curtailing our supply is never mentioned.

The price of silence for those who make it to professorial careers is all too clear. No other shortcoming comes close in denying visibility, portability, and satisfaction (Boice & Jones, 1984). Moreover, silence may occur at the expense of an important kind of self-education that encourages clarity of thinking and expression. When we don't write, we exclude ourselves from the core of our profession in a critical way: nonwriters have little say in shaping the policies, the funding, and the core educational materials of their disciplines. And when we are not heard, we may stop listening.

Silence is, at the least, a powerful form of disenfranchisement, one that extracts especially costly penalties from underrepresented groups of academicians. My own surveys of new faculty as publishers (see Chapter Four) suggest that black new faculty members are particularly likely to remain silent for their first three years on campus. The reasons seem clear. These new faculty members face greater demands for participation in committee and other service activities. Their students demand far more of their time. They feel isolated from their most productive colleagues. Yet, in my experience, expectations from tenure and promotion committees for publishing are no less for these new faculty members than for white males. One clear result of relative silence for blacks as new faculty is a reported feeling of being excluded from the process that allows new faculty to become credible professionals.

Another result for black faculty resembles that of women facing up to demands for publication (Boice & Kelly, 1987; Boice, Shaughnessy, and Pecker, 1985). Both groups perceive the experience of trying to manage productivity as one where subtle discouragements work in surprisingly powerful ways. As a consequence, women and blacks are among new faculty members who feel pressured to pursue careers emphasizing service over productivity. The stated chagrin of women and blacks in accepting this role concerns relegation to second-class citizenship.

Four Insights About Writing Fluency

The costs of silence go beyond underrepresented newcomers. A normative lack of fluency in writing affects the majority of new faculty in their first few years in ways that imperil their confidence and enjoyment of writing.

Writing Fluency Is Enhanced by Automaticity

Most of what we know about productivity and unproductivity in writers comes from the long-standing and scattered literature on writing blocks. Writing blocks occur when we cannot begin or finish writing in fluent, timely, and comfortable fashion. Much of the writing about writing blocks is nothing more than lore, consisting of superstitions and idiosyncratic solutions to dysfluency. So it is that the best-known remedies for blocking include sharpening pencils, putting one's work aside, and consuming alcohol (Boice, 1991g).

More useful and systematic information about support for writers appeared as early as the mid 1800s, when spiritualists and other observers of "automatic" writers ostensibly transmitting messages from the spirit world noticed that a lack of self-consciousness enhances fluency. Similarly, Freud's style of conducting therapy whereby patients said whatever came to mind had its roots in a popular self-help book that prescribed a similar kind of "automaticity" for helping writers write in rapid-fire, unthinking fashion (Ellenberger, 1970). The clearest explanation of the value of automaticity in writing fluently came from Hilgard (1977) and his students. Bowers (1979), for example, showed that the most fluent writers are the most hypnotizable and, it follows, the most readily absorbed into writing. That is, they write with only a casual awareness of the words that they use, relying more on images than on consciously selected words. In contrast, dysfluent writers have difficulty in proceeding by trusting vague images; instead, they work in the presence of a salient and disruptive background editor.

Writing Fluency Has No Magical Source

The second major lesson from the study of blocking came when early psychologists debunked the magical properties of fluency (Ribot, 1906; Royce, 1898). Nixon (1928) put it simply: fluent writing is far more the result of hard work and borrowing than of inspiration. Nixon's related point is also worth another look. Good writing, because it grows effortless with careful preparation and intense concentration, is too easily misperceived as having supernatural origins. Extension of the notion that fluency awaits hard and regular work came with the behavioral revolution in psychotherapy during the 1960s and 1970s. When writers agreed to write in order to gain access to other, more desirable events, they wrote more productively, regardless of how inspired they felt (for example, Nurnberger & Zimmerman, 1970). Proof for the validity of such "forced" methods of inducing fluency gets a special boost from the long tradition of successful novelists who recorded observations such as this: "I started keeping a more detailed chart which also showed how many pages I had written by the end of every working day. I am not sure why I started keeping such records. I suspect that it was because, as a free-lance writer, entirely on my own, without employer or deadline, I wanted to create disciplines for myself, ones that were guilt-making when ignored. A chart on the wall served as such a discipline, its figures scolding me or encouraging me" (Wallace, 1968, p. 77).

As public interest in discipline and regimen accumulated, so did disproofs of traditional arguments against "produced" writing, especially the misbelief that it must be superficial and uncreative (for example, Boice, 1982).

Writing Fluency Depends on Effective Cognitive Strategies

The third lesson about fluency awaited the resurgence of cognitive studies in psychology and in composition. One of the best known of these is Flower and Hayes's (1984) use of "talking-aloud" protocols, whereby students vocalize their writing processes as they compose. These studies indicate, among other things, that fluent writers develop repertoires of problem-solving strategies for figuring out ways to compose their writing.

With another cognitive approach to distinguishing productive from unproductive writers, blocked and fluent academicians list their self-talk at scheduled writing times (Boice, 1985a). Blocked writers were far more likely to report cognitions that were maladaptive (for example, perfectionism, impatience) and far less likely to use positive self-talk (for instance, "The sooner I get started, the sooner I finish") than were fluent writers.

Writing Fluency Depends on Social Fluency

The fourth insight about what keeps many of us from writing came recently, most obviously from the current feminist revolution. It addresses the likelihood that the minority of faculty members who already write successfully have had access to tacit knowledge usually obtained through old-boy networks (Scarr, 1982). And it helps teach the usually disenfranchised the traditionally unwritten information about habits and social skills that correspond to writing productively and successfully (Bem, 1987; Boice, 1990d). So, for instance, strategies for helping writers include writing ways of meeting the expectations of editors, of coping with rejection, of finding adaptive attitudes about collaboration, and of improving writing skills with a sense of audience in mind.

Taken together, then, these four historical insights about what helps writers to fluency also imply causes of silence. When, first of all, writers try to write self-consciously, in the presence of noisome internal editors, fluency is undermined. And when, to continue the points just listed above, writers write without regular discipline, without the advantage of constructive self-talk, and without knowledge of how best to deal with the gatekeepers of publishing, their fluency is almost necessarily constrained. Another way of appreciating the four insights listed above is likening them to the IRSS theory developed throughout this book: helping writers find unself-consciousness and automaticity is akin to effecting involvement. Arranging schedules of hard, regular work for writers is like assisting them in establishing regimen (contrasted to the usual attempts to await inspiration or binges). Learning the cognitive strategies behind fluency is a good example of mastering self-management. And the fourth component of IRSS theory, social networking, includes skills in dealing with audiences of editors and reviewers.

Mutual Facilitation of Writing, Collegiality, and Teaching

The curious thing about the four insights into what makes writers fluent is that they are little known and rarely implemented. They are, to refer to a concept introduced earlier in this book, exemplars of tacit knowledge. One prediction of notions about tacit knowledge is that when information is presented, it will typically be ineffective.

As a rule, help given to faculty as writers is limited to style guides, publication manuals, and release time from teaching. Actual studies of both these traditional forms of faculty development suggest that neither is very helpful, especially for faculty who already show tendencies to remain silent (Boice, 1987b). Specifically, style guides tend to reinforce the perfectionism that already blocks many writers. Release time, because it rarely includes useful supports or accountability, simply perpetuates the preexisting habits of unproductive writers.

What works better? Extensive research indicates that the four lessons of fluency just reviewed offer immediate and lasting help for faculty as writers (Boice, 1990b). What keeps campuses, despite their obvious concerns for productivity, from embracing these demonstrated principles? My own surveys at a variety of colleges and universities suggest that we approach such methods with ambivalence in part because we suppose that productivity must come at the expense of collegiality and teaching. Here again, as with traditional lore about ways to ensure fluency, beliefs about the costs of writing productivity are often mistaken.

In fact, the findings about the concomitants of productivity are clearly established and can be stated quickly. First, the most productive and oft-cited authors in academe exhibit a striking quality: they spend as much time on networking with colleagues as they do writing (Creswell, 1985). That is, productive writers contradict their stereotypes as isolates and curmudgeons. Second, the widely assumed interference between teaching and productivity does not exist (Feldman, 1987). While lore holds that excellence in teaching and productivity in writing grow at the expense of each other the valid studies of this relationship show either no correlation or a slight positive correlation between the two activities. More importantly, when studies have actually been done where faculty had meaningful incentives to excel at both teaching and writing, the two activities have been positively correlated (Boice, 1984). Similarly, the new faculty who find the quickest success as productive writers show balance among teaching, writing, and collegiality. They also tend to show higher student ratings than do their unproductive peers (Chapters Two and Three).

Thus, the key correlate of writing from this perspective is balance. In the stepwise scheme for supporting writers that follows, the keys to effective implementation are symmetry, moderation, and balance; that is, no one step seems to work well in the absence of the others, and writing is most productive and enjoyable when practiced in regular moderation. When either writing or teaching occurs at the expense of the other, both may suffer.

A Four-Step Plan for Nurturing Productivity

These four steps for supporting new faculty as writers come from the historical insights about writing productivity: (1) establishing momentum via unself-consciousness, (2) creating regimen amid busy work schedules, (3) abandoning negative self-talk and impatience when writing, and (4) making writing a socially skilled activity. The preliminary step, having writers reexamine their beliefs about writing, is implicit in this chapter. In some workshop series, this act of reexamination constitutes an entire session.

Step 1: Establishing Ideas and Momentum for Writing

Once under way, writing builds its own momentum; the biggest difficulty for most writers is getting started. As we have already seen, a primary obstacle to momentum is self-consciousness. The most effective solution to self-consciousness may be the oldest—simply beginning by writing quickly and without stopping to edit. Doing so helps quiet the internal editor and helps writers discover what they have to say. As William James might have put it, "How can I know what I think until I see what I write?" Elbow's (1973) instructions for free writing are the clearest: "The idea is simply to write for ten minutes. . . . Don't stop for anything. Go quickly without rushing. Never stop to look back, to cross something out

. . . to wonder what word or thought to use, or to think about what you are doing. If you can't think of a word or a spelling, just use a squiggle or else write 'I can't think of it.' Just put down something" (p. 1).

Recall a kindred idea from the previous chapter: in the business literature, this sort of tactic for getting things done is known as the results-first approach. Peters and Waterman (1984), authors of the best-selling *In Search of Excellence,* explain it this way: "The *results-first* approach changes the whole psychology of performance improvement. . . . People must ask different kinds of questions . . . not, 'what is standing in the way?' but rather, 'what are some things we can accomplish in the next little while?' . . . Instead of trying to overcome resistance to what people are *not* ready to do, find out what they *are* ready to do" (p. 149).

In my own workshops for new faculty, I like to list the rationales for free writing; this well-known variation on automaticity brings a surprising variety of benefits, including (1) momentum (impressively so for writers who had been unable to get started); (2) simple and direct writing, often in short sentences (a rare commodity for academic writers); (3) ideas for writing, often in forms that can be transposed into manuscripts; (4) invaluable practice in starting writing before feeling ready to write and in combatting impatience in writing (for many writers, spending even five minutes on free writing relieves the impatience that they feel to catch up on an enormous backlog of writing tasks); and (5) fun.

Free writing can be the basis for an easy workshop. I recommend that the group facilitator begin by reviewing the rationale for automaticity. Then, before the participants are given much chance to think about it, the group is launched into the task (using the instructions from Elbow or directives to write about a more specific topic, such as plans for an unstarted manuscript; see Boice, 1990d). Curiously, no matter how blocked participants are, they invariably plunge into writing with only a few seconds' delay. The reason seems to be social pressure; everyone else writes with little apparent trouble, so even the most reluctant individuals join in.

Done properly, the group experience consists of much more than showing faculty that they can write on demand and produce useful copy. It is also an occasion to make writing, especially imperfect writing, public. I ask writers in my workshops to read aloud from their free writing. To ease the process of sharing, I begin by reading what I have written—and then I immodestly list what I like about it (for example, its directness, its promise in generating ideas for a new manuscript), despite its imperfections. Next, I ask a few brave souls to read aloud from their free writing. In the course of this sharing, I appeal for three rules. First, no one is allowed to read perfect material; imperfect material is far more likely to benefit from criticism and revision. Second, no one is allowed to apologize for writing read aloud. Third, commentors on what is read must preface their remarks with specific compliments about what was done well by the writer (despite well-practiced habits of leaping immediately into criticism).

The advantages that accrue to this sharing of free writing include experience in making the formative stages of writing less private and less self-conscious (and thus less susceptible to blocking), appreciation that writing before feeling ready produces copy that is surprisingly clear and on task in the view of listeners, and recognition that colleagues will act as ready sources of support and even collaboration for ideas that are not yet completed. Beyond the workshop, participants are encouraged to continue free writing as a prelude for writing sessions where more traditional prose is generated. I also state a strong caution here about limiting free writing to no more than five to ten minutes at a time: if carried on extensively, free writing poses dangers of becoming an end in itself, keeping writers from getting to manuscripts and eventually inducing gloomy, frightening copy that, among other problems, will discourage productive writing (Boice, 1985c).

Step 2: Establishing Regimen

For all its advantages, free writing has a crucial limitation. It does not ensure regular writing. It does not help writers deal with busyness and procrastination, the common maladies of new faculty depicted in Chapter Four. And it can create a false sense of productivity, one that in fact results in only occasional writing.

When they put off writing, new faculty members typically suppose that doing so will result in better writing, especially if it can be done at ideal times. For most new faculty members, as we saw in Chapter Four, "ideal" means awaiting big blocks of undisrupted time. And for most new faculty members, writing is seen as something that must be delayed in the face of more pressing tasks (such as mastering teaching). In a way, the philosophy of new faculty can be summed up in this half-facetious rule:

> *The Law of Delay:* That which can be delayed will be.

A related rule speaks to new faculty's typical rationale for delaying writing:

> *The Perfectionist's Law of Time Management:* The best writing is done in big blocks of undisrupted time and only after the writer is fully prepared, highly motivated, and in possession of a clever idea. Done properly, such binges of writing require substantial amounts of warm-up time. The best times for writing are vacations, sabbaticals, and, better yet, retirements.

There are two main problems with delaying and bingeing writing. First, this pattern corresponds to low productivity among new faculty (Boice, 1989a). Second, this maladaptive pattern is not self-correcting. Productivity and satisfaction with writing generally depend on a very different rule:

> *The Rule of Balance and Moderation:* At most, writing deserves to be a moderate priority, one that can be handled in brief daily sessions amid

other, more important tasks. When practiced daily, writing stays freshly in mind and requires little or no warm-up time. Perfectionism in writing is best indulged in final revisions, not in initial drafts. Productive writing is best undertaken as a leap of faith, before one feels ready. The most productive and cited writers, surprisingly, balance time spent on writing with that for collegiality and teaching.

In fact, research on writing productivity supports the productivity rule. New faculty, among others, write far more productively in a regimen of brief daily sessions than in binges (Boice, 1989a). Moreover, new faculty who find only an hour per weekday to write generally manage to submit about 1.5 manuscripts per year, an output level consistent with the expectations of tenure and promotion committees at their campuses (Boice, 1987b). And to complete the picture, new faculty who adopt the schedule of brief daily periods for writing typically experience less busyness and stressfulness during their first few years on campus.

Moreover, practice at balance and moderation often generalizes. By learning to resist the temptation to binge at writing, new faculty also move away from bingeing at other activities, especially lecture preparation (an endeavor depicted in Chapter Four as routinely taking twenty-five or more hours a week for new faculty). The result is a generalized sense of feeling less rushed at any particular task, of being more caught up with the varied demands for making it as a new faculty member, and of feeling more in control. And these new faculty eschew busyness displays.

In implementing regimen, the workshop format for getting new faculty to try the productivity rule is again uncomplicated. It can be effectively carried out by project directors who themselves have no special expertise in teaching writing or in publishing. Often, the most effective facilitators are colleagues who work along with participants in mastering better habits and attitudes of productivity. When

I conduct these workshops, they take on a structure such as the following.

I often begin with a brief lecture on the *rationale* for brief daily sessions. Sometimes, depending on whether the faculty are mostly from the sciences and related areas with an emphasis on data, I make a case for the proven superiority of brief daily sessions by presenting the tables from studies of new faculty (see Boice, 1989a). In any case, I emphasize the logical appeal of making writing a medium priority. Then I state yet another rule:

> *Minsky's Law:* The highest-order intentions (say, New Year's resolutions) have the lowest behavioral probabilities.

In other words, when we identify writing as our highest-ranking priority (despite the distaste that many of us feel for it), we place unrealistic demands on ourselves to do it under perfect conditions and in novel, significant fashion. The predictable result of making writing (or almost any activity) an unrealistically high priority is procrastination.

Then, to complete the rationale for brief daily sessions, I explain some of the reasons why this regimen works so well:

1. It helps limit writing to durations where tension and fatigue are minimized.
2. It helps keep writing freshly in mind from day to day and thus minimizes warm-up time.
3. It coaxes writers to begin writing before feeling ready and thus helps teach them to proceed before literature searches and data analyses are complete. As they do this, writers learn to feel comfortable about moving beyond holes in their manuscripts and about finishing first drafts that are truly imperfect.
4. It helps writers finish more quickly, because when they write with holes in their manuscripts, they feel compelled to finish the analyses, literature reviews, and rethinking

left by those holes, often in the other brief openings in workdays.

5. It encourages more revision and thus better and more patient writing.

6. It permits new faculty the rare luxury of feeling that they have done enough for a day, at least in terms of writing. A leading cause of the burnout that can afflict faculty is the feeling when leaving campus that they have never done enough (Boice & Myers, 1987). One of the real advantages of brief daily sessions is that they help set moderate limits on writing output. This, again, helps ensure that writing remains nonfatiguing (see Rabinbach, 1990) and that writers do not invoke implicit, unexamined goals that can be met only during days with little else to do.

7. It affords the comforting feeling that one's scholarship is not being neglected; progress is clearly being made in steady and conscientious fashion.

8. Finally, it promotes conversations about ongoing writing, with colleagues and in classes; this means that writing becomes more public. It also means that writing becomes less isolated from and less competitive with other, more valued activities, such as collegiality.

The second phase in workshops about regimen aims at *commitment*. New faculty are asked to find brief openings in busy workdays for prewriting and writing activities. And they are asked to give the regimen a try, despite their reservations. In effect, this step reminds new faculty to make writing a moderate priority, one that does not have to await ideal conditions. One way to get colleagues to pursue this plan relies on social contracts. When writers agree to meet for mutually quiet writing sessions at locations such as the library or to chat briefly by phone with the project director after writing sessions, their outputs rise dramatically.

The third phase coincides with the second and emphasizes basic *behavioral principles* of making writing more likely once scheduled. Its essence can be conveyed in lists:

Rearranging the Writing Environment

1. Establish one or a few regular places where you will do
    almost all scholarly writing; make these locations places
    where you do nothing but serious writing. That is, writ-
    ing and prewriting (taking notes on reading, planning
    manuscripts, outlining) are done here; all other activities
    are done elsewhere.
2. Make these sacred writing sites free of temptations such
    as magazines, newspapers, and correspondence—keep non-
    essential reading elsewhere.
3. Avoid the urge to begin writing sessions by first cleaning
    the writing site. Instead, organize the work site (and pre-
    pare materials for the next session) at the end of writing
    sessions. Doing so helps reduce time needed for warm-
    ups.
4. Limit social interruptions during your brief daily sessions
    by closing the door to your office or writing area; posting
    a writing schedule on the door and asking others to help
    you keep it; notifying interlopers that interruptions must
    be limited to urgent matters and to very short durations;
    unplugging the phone or turning on the answering
    machine; and recruiting significant others, colleagues,
    and secretaries as enforcers who agree to remind you and
    potential disruptors that this is your brief period for
    writing.
5. Make your writing site comfortable. For example, try sit-
    ting in a recliner chair with good back and neck support
    as you work on a word processor, holding the keyboard
    on your lap or a lapboard.

Rearranging Writing Habits

1. Make writing a moderate priority, one that deserves no
    more or less than a brief session during weekdays; this
    means that writing is rarely done during evenings, week-
    ends, or vacations. Produce something, even prewriting
    such as notes on relevant literature, regardless of mood or
    readiness; once you have it under way (like an unmoti-

vated exerciser who has just forced herself to run only a single lap), writing may develop its own momentum.

2. Make writing something you do before you give yourself access to something you prefer to do (for example, newspapers, phone calls, correspondence), but don't make essentials, such as eating, contingent on writing.

3. Keep a chart on the wall that shows when you are scheduled to write and what you actually did. Begin with easy goals, as little as fifteen-minute sessions, and build up to perhaps an hour or even two when workdays permit it.

4. Write while you are fresh, preferably in the morning. Save other, less demanding tasks (such as correspondence) for times of the day when you are less energetic and alert.

5. Set firm limits on the length of writing sessions. Most full-time professional writers set limits such as three to four hours per day; academics often find that one or two hours are maximally effective. Research shows that when academic writers exceed these limits by substantial amounts (that is, when they binge), they are unlikely to write during subsequent days (Boice, 1982) or to be productive in the long run (Creswell, 1985). In other words, learn to recognize the irrational element in continuing beyond preset limits once writing comes easily. And remind yourself of this fact: momentum can always be reinstituted the next day. Moreover, ideas for writing that flow readily as writing sessions end can be jotted down. Indeed, many writers who follow schedules of brief daily sessions routinely use the last five minutes of each sitting to make such notes, to plan the next day's writing, and to clean up their writing sites.

6. Set reasonable, specific goals for writing sessions. For example, plan to rewrite the last page written during the preceding day and to write one new page per session. Equally important, learn to compliment yourself when you have met your daily goals. Once under way, make longer-range plans that project your progress over a completed manuscript. Doing so helps writers see ends to the

tasks they pursue in patient fashion and can encourage the planning of concurrent manuscripts.

7. Try working on two or three manuscripts concurrently, especially once you are able to manage at least an hour of writing per workday. The majority of academic writers who do so report benefits in cross-fertilization of ideas and in reduced boredom with any single project. Especially productive writers often make a point of intermixing occasional short and enjoyable manuscripts into their schedules.

Even where these suggestions immediately strike new faculty as sensible, they are easily postponed and forgotten. Thus, a critical function of support programs is redundancy. New hires need reminders about principles of productivity and balance in repeated workshops and in repeated personal contacts. I generally preface such reminders by joking about my role as a nuisance; new faculty, though, are usually quick to express their appreciation for such reminders. Occasions for repeated reminders include preliminary materials sent to new hires before they settle on campus, miniworkshops during new faculty orientations, biennial interviews in the offices of new faculty, and workshops offered each semester.

The fourth phase of supporting new faculty in establishing regimen focuses on *accountability*. Workshop exercises include practice at keeping charts of productivity arrayed against goals (Boice, 1990d) and at building social contracts for writing collaboratively. A postworkshop exercise, one with even greater lasting value, consists of follow-ups. In some contexts, new faculty form their own support groups. In any situation, however, there is no substitute for occasional visits and calls from project directors to determine the progress made by new faculty as writers. Where new faculty exhibit special difficulties at establishing regimen, I routinely contact them (after they have voluntarily agreed) on a weekly basis. This simple act of staying in touch (one that typically requires no more than five or ten minutes per contact) makes a major difference in the likelihood that new faculty will establish and maintain productivity (Boice, 1990d): without follow-ups, all but 10–20 percent of new faculty cease being productive within a year; with follow-ups, stable productivity typically persists in more than 80 percent of participants.

Step 3: Establishing Comfort

Like automaticity, regimen works only to a point. While it almost invariably induces regular and productive writing, it does not ensure comfort and enjoyment in writing. In a study with sixty faculty members who kept records of who they felt and what they said to themselves at scheduled writing times (Boice, 1985a), the aversiveness of writing was made surprisingly clear. Nearly two-thirds of what blocked writers said to themselves was maladaptive (for example, "This will probably be rejected"). And more than a third of what already fluent writers said to themselves helped make the process less difficult (for example, "Once I'm writing, I'll enjoy it"). The relevance of this finding goes beyond comfort. Writers who find writing aversive are more likely to founder when inevitable disappointments, such as editorial rejections, occur (Boice, 1990d). Fortunately, solutions for discomfort with writing, as with discomfort with teaching, are easily arranged.

I typically address comfort in the third or fourth workshop about writing. In these groups, my colleagues and I practice three exercises. First, we revisit free writing as a reminder of how to cope with impatience by enjoying the process of writing as much as the product. Second, we practice simple relaxation exercises much like those described in Chapter Six for establishing classroom comfort. The point of rehearsing exercises such as keeping our tongues at the bottoms of our mouths is that writing practiced in its usual form induces tension. Working in tense, hurried fashion contributes to the fatigue that helps make writing a hurried and aversive task for most academicians (Boice, 1985a). Third, we practice the most difficult but crucial element in establishing comfort by role playing how we talk to ourselves about writing in negative and undermining ways. The demonstration is made specific to writing times and to the maladaptive self-talk that makes writing more difficult than it needs to be.

The strategy for coping with this self-talk comes from cognitive psychotherapies and has three components. Writers begin by actually noticing the usually unobtrusive self-talk that accompanies attempts to begin writing. Despite assumptions that we have little or no cognition of this sort, we often do, unless we are in the minority of fluent writers who simply get on with writing with no self-consciousness at all. Then workshop participants are encouraged to practice recognizing maladaptive self-talk and stopping it. Curiously, one of the most effective tactics consists of authoritatively saying "STOP" to ourselves. Finally, group members rehearse the maneuver of supplanting negative self-talk with more helpful self-statements (for example, "I might as well get started; the sooner I start, the sooner I'll finish"). In all these exercises, the group helps generate examples for negative and positive self-statements.

One strategy in cognitive self-management particularly helps ensure that these workshops will have lasting effects. When participants learn to make "thought lists" of ongoing self-talk that they fill out at the beginning of each scheduled writing session, they are more likely to combat this source of discomfort (Boice, 1985a, 1990d). The role of the project directors here is much like that in ensuring follow-up results in the step for regimen; regular calls and visits to new faculty who plan to carry out this exercise greatly increase the likelihood that it will persist.

Step 4: Making Writing a Socially Skilled Act

Like momentum and regimen, comfort works only to a point. In two decades of work with writers, I have learned that newly fluent writers are likely to reblock if they have not mastered the skills of making writing public and more publicly acceptable. The workshop format for supporting new faculty in these related endeavors shows how elementary they are.

In the social skills workshop, groups share expertise on how to cope with the editorial process and, along with that, the inevitable disappointment of writing—rejection. To help ensure that useful information is shared, I typically invite senior faculty members who have had clear successes in writing for publication (but I try to avoid individuals who will use the occasion to show off). Then I distribute a handout that contains at least a modicum of presolicited advice on how to deal with rejection:

1. Making writing more public and less private. Practice sharing it in its most formative stages; when readers can see conceptual outlines, for example, they are much more likely to make useful suggestions for changes in direction and sources that you will actually incorporate than if they are given finished drafts. A remarkably effective strategy for seeing whether you are on track with a manuscript idea is to share a conceptual outline (an organizational scheme of brief statements of what sections of the manuscript will be about) with the members of the editorial board for the journal to which you are planning to submit it.

2. Anticipate criticisms. Ask colleagues who read your drafts to help you foresee where reviewers will criticize your manuscript (without such specific requests for criticisms, most colleagues resort to vague feedback such as "Interesting!"; that is, they may not be sure that you really want criticism, and they may not know how to give the most functional advice). This drill helps anticipate editorial criticism in two ways. First, it may suggest corrections that will head off criticisms (the most common form of such advice addresses unstated assumptions made by the manuscript writer). Second, it will prepare you for what reviewers will criticize. Forewarned writers are less devastated by rejections.

3. Make your whole plan for research and writing public. An oft-observed tragedy among new faculty occurs when they work at writing over the five or six years until tenure decisions are made only to discover that they were off track in terms of what their colleagues expected. In my

experience, most new faculty members who fail to get tenure, despite the obviousness of their shortcomings to their colleagues, were surprised to discover that they had not done enough or that their work was considered irrelevant in light of departmental values. In fact, departmental and campus expectations are rarely communicated in clear, concrete fashion to new faculty.

The solution to the usual dilemma of not understanding expectations about writing is simple. New faculty can be shown how to compile catalogues (see also Chapter Five) that list their already completed projects, ongoing projects, and planned projects (including probable journals) in a brief and readable format. Then new faculty share these catalogues, first with a mentor and then with colleagues, including chairs who will be involved in tenure and promotion decisions. In all cases, the question that accompanies the catalogue is this: "Do I seem to be headed in the right direction? Do I seem to be doing enough?" In all cases, the new faculty member soliciting this feedback ideally adds a proviso, preferably in writing, that he or she expects or wants no guarantees, only guidance. Moreover, new faculty should discourage colleagues from giving the early feedback in writing; this advice flows much more freely when colleagues do not worry about it being held against them later.

What should new faculty do when their requests are denied by a key colleague such as their chairperson? In my experience, the best strategy is to continue to submit catalogues of plans and progress each semester, with or without feedback. Some resistant chairs come around to seeing the value in such exercises; in any case, the mere act of planning one's productivity carries rewards for the planner.

4.   Find ways to agree with and to learn from criticism. Doing this requires a method of defusing the emotionality of criticism, especially the defensiveness that it reflexively elicits. The strategy is as basic and counterintuitive as finding something in any criticism, even the most

insulting, with which you can honestly agree. This will force you to listen to the criticism and to stay calm while doing so. And it will encourage you to put yourself in the role of the critic in an attempt to understand why he or she reacts in a certain way to your writing. Thus, in the most annoying instances of critical feedback (for instance, when a reviewer doesn't seem to have read your manuscript), you can begin by asking yourself what about your presentation helped cause that reaction. Once that process is under way, the next step, calmly asking the critic for clarification and for suggestions as to how you can improve your paper, comes with surprising ease. By asking for specification of feedback, we stay calm and learn from criticism. We also save ourselves a lot of wear and tear while sometimes winning over our critics.

5. Stated briefly, the principles for coping with criticism can be written as three interrelated rules: (1) let others do some of the work in anticipating criticism, (2) welcome and learn from criticism, and (3) resist the temptation to indulge in scripts of victimization. In other words, learn to make writing a more socially skilled process, one where your work is more public and more publicly acceptable.

IRSS Theory and Writing Productivity

Does the four-step plan work? It has produced solid evidence for lasting success on a variety of campuses (Boice, 1983b, 1989a) and under the direction of a variety of faculty developers (for example, Lucas & Harrington, 1990). Equally importantly, my own ongoing programs of support for new faculty suggest the practicality of "balance programs" where new faculty find simultaneous success as teachers, writers, and colleagues.

I close this chapter by considering what factors would keep campuses from adopting a plan such as this. In my experience, four factors conspire to keep us from giving new faculty this vital kind of support. The first is the reluctance

of practitioners devoted to instructional development to
devote energies to an activity that seems oppositional to excellence in teaching. Second is the feeling of project leaders that
they cannot lead a program for writing facilitation if they
have not already established themselves as productive writers
and composition teachers. The third inhibition is inertia.
Project directors, like many new faculty members, await perfect conditions before beginning. The fourth is skepticism
about a plan that seems to imply that no other approach will
work.

I typically respond by reminding resisters that I am
merely sharing the details of a strategy that has worked for
many faculty members. And I find a way to agree with their
implied criticism: yes, it is probably true that other approaches help induce productivity. Whatever works, especially while
maintaining balance and moderation, is fine with me. Then,
as a way of moving past skepticism about a single solution
and other resistances, I suggest the value of considering
another way of seeing the challenge of helping new faculty
establish productivity. The IRSS theory of components can
provide a convincing sense of direction to our actions and
effectiveness as practitioners.

First, I ask what would be the harm in merely getting
involved in writing workshops, even if they are run by colleagues? *Involvement* generates momentum, confidence, and
ideas. It even facilitates the writing productivity of the practitioners supporting it among new hires.

Second, I suggest that practitioners experiment with the
potential power of working at tasks such as writing in brief
daily sessions. Managed correctly, I add, *regimen* does not have
to engender feelings of working under pressure; it can even
help generate more free time. And then, with practitioners
perhaps considering my suggestion, I calmly ask them whether
their current approach to productivity is working well.

Third, I encourage practitioners to pay attention to the
problems that they try to solve. If, I argue, they wait until
feeling fully qualified and convinced before attempting to
arrange help with writing, support programs for productivity,

like much of planned writing, may never happen. And as part of the IRSS component of *self-management*, I suggest that they observe and question already fluent writers (including already experienced presenters of writing workshops) to learn the tacit knowledge about what helps new faculty as writers. Some of the tacit knowledge about enhancing productivity is as simple as helping writers find collaborators.

Fourth, I mention the fun of getting faculty together to work on productivity and writing skills; setting up *social networks* for writing, like other support, works best when we let others do some of the work.

Finally, nearing the point of having worked harder than I would like, I finish with an observation that helps end the discussion on a mutually satisfactory note: In my experience, most practitioners and new faculty react at first with strong doubts and disinclination. Only later, sometimes after a year or two, do many of them begin to give the strategy a try. I gladly settle for that.

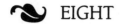 EIGHT

Helping New Faculty
Help Themselves

To this point, we have seen the kinds of obstacles facing new
faculty as colleagues, teachers, and writers, and we have
reviewed strategies for supporting their development in those
three domains. Now, having defined the problem and some of
the solutions, we pause for reflection. We may need more
reminders about probable shortcomings in what might have
seemed a thoroughgoing approach. One clue comes from leaders in faculty development who have reviewed the field. In
*Key Resources on Teaching, Learning, Curriculum, and Faculty
Development,* Menges and Mathis (1988) conclude with a bit
of alarm that the most neglected theme in faculty development is the development of the individual faculty member.
Schuster (1990b), in the latest of a series of influential analyses, makes a related point: despite our efforts at faculty development, things are getting worse for new faculty.

What the broad view of faculty development suggests,
then, is the need for support programs that effectively reach
more individual faculty members. The era of accountability
now dawning may mark the end of faculty development programs that reach only the few faculty members who least
need it (Finkelstein, 1984). To extend our reach and to improve
what we already do, we may need to concentrate more on a
new approach to self-help programs.

A second clue about the need to do more with self-help programs came when I shared early versions of my programs with fellow practitioners. They expressed concerns such as this one:

> I honestly am enthusiastic about trying the support programs you set out for new faculty at [this university]. But [a colleague] and I have an apprehension we want to share. We worry about whether we will be able to do as well as you seem to assume we should with our new faculty. It isn't that [this university] hires dolts. We have lots of responsibilities besides shepherding new faculty. We don't even expect to be able to spend much time with all our new faculty. Where we think we need help most is something missing in your book. We want help in coming up with effective self-help materials that we can distribute to our new faculty and that will accomplish a whole lot more than the handouts of rules and advice that we already disburse at orientations. We mean materials that can accomplish what you outline in helping new faculty find mentors, comfort at teaching, and so on, largely on their *own*, with minimal assistance from us. Do you have any ideas for managing this bit of magic?

My immediate response was a qualified no. But I promised her that I would think about it, investigate it, and seek advice. The result is this chapter. Because of the freshness of its discovery process for me, I have arranged the chapter as a series of insights.

Insight 1: Effective First Steps Concern Motivation

I began my search with a realization that many new faculty members need help first and foremost with motivation. Without it, they cannot find the resources to benefit from support programs. So it is, apparently, that reluctant individuals are left out of most faculty development programs (Lucas, 1990b); these colleagues ordinarily do little to reward their own or a program's efforts. Inevitably, because effective motivation in academe is an intrinsic matter (Eble & McKeachie, 1985), many faculty members must be helped to help themselves in building it. An allied lesson I learned was that faculty, reluctant or not, want to work on some kinds of development on their own. As I developed self-help programs (Boice, 1990d), I discovered a related benefit: it made my task of trying to serve so large a constituency more practical. I did not have time to work at length with every colleague who needed help.

Still, as I reflect on these lessons, I recognize that what helped most in building effective programs was a readiness to evaluate and then modify self-help components according to what worked. The result was a set of procedures that address usually unaddressed needs of new faculty. When I assembled my reflections on providing self-help, I found (perhaps all too conveniently) that they fit the IRSS theory that I have been relating to new faculty throughout this book.

IRSS Theory Likenesses

As we will see, what makes self-help programs especially effective is starting with the most rudimentary of skills needed to thrive as a new faculty member. Without them, new faculty are unlikely to find the motivation to sustain involvement. We have already seen examples of this rule. In Chapter Six, we saw new faculty faring best as developing teachers when they were first helped to develop classroom comfort and rapport, to establish balance in time spent preparing for class, and to find social rewards for teaching enthusiastically. These are elementary skills of thriving that usually remain tacit. It may be that we do not teach them because they are unthinking habits for those of us who have already mastered them (Sternberg et al., 1990).

Consider another example of the power of beginning with usually untaught basics. Chapter Seven showed that new faculty can be helped to gain productivity as writers via modest strategies for personal management (for instance, finding momentum and ideas for writing), for task management (finding time for writing during busy schedules), and for social management (arranging useful collaboration for writing). Once productive and confident, academic writers initiate these more complex kinds of learning on their own; motivation may come in the wake of involvement.

So it is that I emphasize the teaching of usually untaught knowledge in my efforts with new faculty. The significance of this move away from conventional practices can be seen in an analogy to what teachers of writing commonly do. Traditionally, they have focused on the *product* of writing. They taught, more or less, by having students model finished products and by giving feedback about students' own efforts on final drafts. But a revolution in the teaching of writing has brought a change of emphasis to the *process* of writing (Boice, 1985b). Teachers of writing nowadays concentrate on getting students to be aware of their composing processes and to learn from critiques of how, more than what, they write (Flower, 1990). Still, the revolution in the teaching of writing is apparently not over; usual classroom strategies for teaching better ways of writing have yet to demonstrate lasting improvements for average students. As a result, some teachers are moving to the basics of *productivity*. These include coaching students to establish regular habits of writing, habits of the sort that already successful writers display.

The results of one demonstration of the benefits of having students learn the elementary skills of writing productively are worth listing here (Tremmel, 1989):

1. It brought discussions about process (that is, learning how to write) to an effective, intrinsically motivated center of attention in the classroom; once they are writing, writers develop a natural and realistic interest in doing it better.
2. Students quickly learned, despite initial misgivings, that they could manage productive writing every day.

3. Students noticed that growth as writers went hand in hand with increases in confidence about writing. With confidence came a sense of power as writers.
4. Students developed a "writing awareness"; they became sensitive to what successful writers experience, including the rhythms of writing, such as occasional slumps.

What impressed students most about this approach, once past their initial reservations, was that it built self-discipline and a fondness for writing. They realized, Tremmel notes, that the experience of writing on a schedule was very different from their original expectations of feeling punished; instead, it seemed to stimulate the kinds of self-discipline and fondness for writing usually left unpublicized by thriving writers. What Tremmel and other teachers of writing have confirmed, then, is the importance of first-factor components (involvement, task representation, and tacit knowledge) in coaching students to adopt self-management skills in mastering the difficult task of writing. Tremmel's work may remind us of the importance of coaching the basics for effective self-help.

Do we need similar changes in how we help new faculty with, say, writing? Traditionally, we offer new faculty information about little more than product (for example, publication guides that show correct formats for submitting manuscripts and style guides that illustrate exemplary sentences) and only rarely offer them information about process (the nearly exclusive emphasis of traditional advice on fluency as induced via automaticity: see Chapter Seven). Neither approach has been shown effective in any lasting way. Success at mastering process and product, again, apparently depends on a prior step, on first learning the IRSS components of involvement, regimen, and, with them, confidence and motivation as preludes to production. That is, before most of us can become skilled at product and process, we must practice at productivity (the "results-first" approach to finding motivation that we have seen throughout this book). This practice is an overlooked variety of the practical intelligence essential to survive in academe.

Practical Intelligence

Notions of the primacy of confidence and motivation are not new. One survey of 7,534 faculty members, for instance, suggests that their success and satisfaction depended largely on establishing trust and control in their work (Cares & Blackburn, 1978). Another instance comes from an eminent faculty development program in the Great Lakes Colleges Association. It eschews the teaching of specific classroom skills in favor of enhancing student attention and motivation (Wylie, 1990).

Sternberg (1990), whom we met in the introductory chapter, has brought credibility to the notion of teaching the usually tacit skills of thriving in school; in so doing, he takes self-help a step beyond giving opportunities for success to active coaching. His research on teaching is most relevant here (Sternberg et al., 1990). Again, what poor students have not learned, he and his colleagues have discovered, is the tacit knowledge necessary to succeed. What has proved effective in helping convey the requisite skills for thriving is a program that teaches three kinds of tacit skills: (1) self-management (accepting responsibility, knowing how one works best, learning by doing); (2) task management (breaking habits, getting organized, getting it done on time); and (3) cooperating with others (tuning one's conversation, understanding social networks, figuring out the rules).

After documenting the successes of this program (the Yale Practical Intelligence-for-School curriculum), Sternberg and his colleagues offered a conclusion and a caveat: "The usually unspoken knowledge that is crucial to practical intelligence for school is teachable. Rather than merely hope that students have learned survival skills in their previous grades, we can directly teach these skills to all students. But teaching practical intelligence for schools is anything but easy: For many teachers, successfully teaching it requires a fundamental reorientation of attitudes and teaching style. In particular, teachers need to come to value a kind of knowledge they usually do not teach, despite expecting students somehow to learn it" (Sternberg et al., 1990, p. 38).

Those of us nurturing the developing of new faculty can substitute the labels of "new faculty" and "practitioners" for the "students" and "teachers" mentioned in Sternberg's studies. Evidence exists to show, for instance, that the three kinds of tacit knowledge listed above have been found critical to adaptation in any kind of environment (Wagner & Sternberg, 1985). With this view of the IRSS theory in mind, we have a fresh perspective for examining the contributions of traditional resources to supporting new faculty.

Insight 2: Customary Self-Help Tends Toward Social Darwinism

On the whole, academe subscribes, however unwittingly, to social Darwinism. We expect people with the right stuff to succeed and those without it to fail. In general, the help we offer is no exception to this implicit attitude; most programs include generous lengths of rope with which new faculty can hang themselves. Consider, first of all, the form of self-help that campuses prefer to offer, release time (Kurfiss & Boice, 1990).

Release Time as a Form of Self-Help

Release time, the practice of awarding time off from teaching assignments for faculty development, has gained in popularity for some good reasons. It is a response to faculty complaints about overloads (Fink, 1984; Pellino, Blackburn, & Boberg, 1984). It helps make amends for inequities in support programs; while some campuses provide obvious help with teaching, almost none do so for research and writing (Brookes & German, 1983). Its practice coincides with what faculty themselves say they want most in support programs (Centra, 1978; Cross, 1977; Sorcinelli, 1985). And it offers a seemingly effective means of helping faculty help themselves, with a minimum of investment beyond paying someone else to teach their courses.

So it is that release time is cited as a presumed aid to faculty development (Braskamp, 1980), preventing burnout

(Dailey & Jeffries, 1983), motivating research (Ciampa, 1978), and meeting the vital needs of faculty not yet hired (Eble & McKeachie, 1985). But for all this buildup, release time has rarely been held accountable, except in limited cases where it was used to encourage course redesign (Kozma, 1978) or simply as a short-term means of reducing the stress of a heavy work load (Pearson & Seiler, 1983). Until recently, we knew little about the cost-effectiveness of this oft-used practice for helping new faculty acquire effective beginnings.

Proof, where it has been presented at all, has often consisted of nothing more than participation as an index of program success (for example, Fuller & Evans, 1985). Some proponents have concluded that the only justification necessary for offering release time is that it constitutes a statement about proper campus values. And even where evaluations of the effects of release time on the productivity of faculty have actually been conducted, data have been confined to satisfaction measures (Eble & McKeachie, 1985). Studies in a variety of organizational settings indicate that satisfaction measures are not correlated with productivity (Baron, 1983). Why, then, does release time continue to command so much respect and budget?

Hidden Agendas and Growing Doubts. One problem with usual practices of supplying release time is somewhat paradoxical. At best, it may be a nice way to reward colleagues already doing well, not those who need self-help the most. This is exactly what Eble and McKeachie (1985), in their landmark study of midwestern campuses supported by the Bush Foundation, concluded: grants went to faculty members already performing at high levels, to faculty members who would probably have carried out faculty development activities without the external incentives (pp. 96–97).

But even for the faculty members who get release time, the effects are doubtful. Consider these variations on a point made in the previous chapter: Free time may not be as critical to faculty success as we suppose. In fact, productive faculty make time for writing throughout their careers, regardless of distractions (Creswell, 1985). Productivity does not drop off after tenure is achieved (McKeachie, 1983) or even when faculty members become chairs (Smart & McLaughlin, 1978). Perhaps the belief in the need for more time comes from the perception of busyness in faculty's workweeks, usually self-estimated as upward of fifty to sixty hours (Boice & Johnson, 1984). It also, no doubt, has roots in traditional notions that teaching and writing are mutually incompatible (Boice, 1984); this mistaken notion implies that faculty must take irreplaceable time from one to do the other.

A final qualm about release time from its infrequent critics is this: if it is given as reward for prowess in research and publishing, doesn't its practice convey a negative message about the value of teaching? Faculty are rarely given time off from research as a reward for teaching well; no wonder that the value of research is often rated above that of teaching (Astin & Bayer, 1979).

A Study of Release Time and New Faculty. In one study of release-time programs for new faculty (Boice, 1987b), I collected field-based data from four campuses. Two were comprehensive universities, one a doctorate-granting campus, and one a four-year college. All four campuses required new faculty to publish for tenure; all had instituted release-time program (one-course reductions for one or two semesters) to encourage productivity. Thirty-nine new faculty members agreed to my unannounced weekly visits to their offices. They also kept daily charts of how they spent their workdays. Visits during their workdays helped ensure the reliability of new faculty's record keeping.

The results of tracking these new faculty for at least two academic years showed that workweeks were surprisingly similar at the four campuses. Time spent on scholarly writing, for example, was rarely more than two hours per week. Especially surprising was the total of actual time spent working during workweeks. The range for campus averages was twenty-four to thirty hours a week (these new faculty made preparticipation estimates of workweeks of at least twice the amount verified). Not only does this finding show the importance of verifying faculty's self-estimates of workweeks, but it makes another point, one readily seconded by the new faculty involved: they clearly had time for writing, despite initial claims of being too busy. Another revelation came in comparing the writing output of these thirty-nine new faculty members before, during, and after their semester or two of release time. There were no general increases in outputs during or after the release time, despite the universal goal of using it to increase productivity. The majority of these new faculty members simply persisted in a pattern that they described as busyness, one marked by rushing to complete one overdue task after another. Most of the rest of the new faculty did find time for alternative activities but invested it in activities unrelated to writing (for example, committees, home repairs, and errands).

Faculty members' own reasons for patterns of continuing unproductiveness during release time proved interesting. First, they steadfastly claimed that they deserved the release time despite not having used it as planned. One reason was that they should have been rewarded for hard work done prior to the program, amid heavy teaching loads. A second reason was that, while they recognized available time to do more writing, they were waiting for more optimal writing conditions. Time available for writing during most workdays typically came in periods of thirty to sixty minutes. As a rule, new faculty members opted to use these for more immediately demanding tasks, such as answering correspondence or running errands. Ideal writing times, they felt, would consist of far longer and undisrupted times of at least a day or two.

On reflection, new faculty readily admitted that existing programs for release time did not accomplish their stated goals; they invariably ended the release time period feeling even further in arrears as writers. When I met with two of these groups for a shared reprise, we reached some consistent conclusions. One was that new faculty might do better to learn to utilize the brief times available for writing more effectively—ideally before entering the period of release time. This was corroborated, in seemingly effective fashion, when the few new faculty members who were writing productively noted that this was part of what they had done during release time. Another consensus was that present programs of release time suffered from a lack of clear goals, of supervision and support, and of accountability. Once administrators awarded release time, it seemed, they did not care what new faculty did with it. (Indeed, some administrators with whom I discussed this scenario said that it was up to new faculty to take advantage of opportunities such as release time; those who did not deserved no compassion.)

What do the results of this study of release time as self-help mean? They do not mean, as some critics conclude, that I oppose the awarding of release time. Nor do they mean, as some other critics assume, that I suppose faculty's existing teaching loads are ideal. Instead, I conclude that these data speak to the necessity of goals, supports, learning task management, and accountability as vital parts of release-time programs. Indeed, this is what my own subsequent (as yet unpublished) studies have shown. That is, the simple combination of clear goals, regular checks on progress, establishing the habit of writing in brief daily sessions, and awards (public recognition and opportunities for further release time) made contingent on meeting goals leads to reliable increases in writing output during and after release time.

New Faculty Handbooks as Self-Help

The second most common kind of self-help provided for new faculty is written guidance. It ranges from handouts to handbooks of advice and rules; we previewed some of these in the introductory chapter. Curiously, although many campuses have put together elaborate handbooks for new teaching assistants (see Eckstein, Boice, & Chua-Yap, 1991, for a review), few have produced anything comparable for new faculty (see Stice, Svinicki, & Lewis, 1990). Teaching assistant (TA) handbooks typically contain articles on the specifics of teaching (for example, the discussion method) and on coping in general (for example, services available at the counseling and career centers). But campus-based materials for new faculty are brief and directed at more mundane matters, such as parking and health insurance plans. Apparently, we suppose that new TAs are more in need of help or amenable to it than are new faculty.

The most widely used written materials for new faculty are pamphlets such as the National Education Association's *Entering the Profession: Advice for the Untenured* (Bledsoe, 1988). But their scope is typically as narrow as Bledsoe's emphasis on protecting readers' legal rights in the tenure process. More comprehensive books include *The Academic's Handbook* (Deneef, Goodwin, & McCrate, 1988) put out by Duke University. This is a collection of articles by distinguished scholars who decipher the common varieties of campuses (such as private versus public) and of faculty (for example, "humanist intellectuals"); the special problems faced by women and members of minorities in academe; tenure and salary systems; and suggestions for teaching ("Why I teach by discussion"). All in all, this handbook does a nice job of offering useful information about the culture of academe. Its limitation, however, may be general to such handbooks; when I canvassed a campus where *The Academic's Handbook* has been distributed to all new hires, fewer than 20 percent admitted to having read at least some of it, and fewer than 8 percent could cite a useful specific after a year on campus. Like release time, handbooks are provided with the attitude that self-help consists of little more than offering resources.

But what about handbooks generally acknowledged as exemplary? A good example is *The Compleat Academic* (Zanna & Darley, 1987), a book that has received glowing reviews and widespread adoption. Because it includes chapters that offer advice regarding research, power and politics in academic departments (Salancik, 1987), and tips on teaching (McKeachie, 1987), it tends more toward practical knowledge and thus may be more useful for survival. And even where chapters are based more on the individual experiences of their authors, they aim at practicality. Baron's (1987) chapter on writing research grants is a good example. His section on submitting proposals includes advice such as this: "At many universities, the statement 'rules are made to be broken' is at least partially true. Where the federal government is concerned, however, it rarely applies. Thus, when you prepare a research proposal for submission to a federal granting agency, it is *absolutely, positively, unconditionally* essential that you pay attention to the mechanics of the process. That is, you must devote careful attention to following the rules for submission established by the particular agency or agencies with which you wish to deal. To make life more complicated, each agency often insists on slightly different things" (p. 161).

Overall, however, *The Compleat Academic* assumes that readers already have practical knowledge. Consider this product-oriented directive from the chapter on writing (Bem, 1987, p. 200): "*That* versus *Which*. *That* clauses (called restrictive) are essential to the meaning of a sentence; *which* clauses (called nonrestrictive) merely add further information." There is nothing mistaken in Bem's advice; it merely assumes that new faculty are already functioning beyond the level of managing to find the time, the confidence, and the ideas for writing. It may be solving the wrong problem.

Materials on Wellness as Self-Help

As we move away from traditional advice, the literature for newcomers becomes more basic, more related to adeptness in self-management and task management. The best examples concern stress management, fitness, and wellness; recall from Chapter Two that the first few years on campus are incredibly stressful. Add to that a related fact: recent surveys indicate that academic careers are becoming more stressful and that this stress interferes with job functioning (Schuster, 1990b; Seldin, 1987).

The growing array of books and articles on wellness bears examination as we gather materials for distribution to our new faculty. For example, Schwartz (1983) offers a useful list of the most troublesome stresses: overloads; ambiguity of roles; negative competition; social isolation; colleagues who act as "stress carriers"; and a campus culture that makes reactivity to stress unacceptable. Naditch (1983) describes "stay-well" programs that include educational courses, life-style change lessons, and social support groups. She concludes that effective programs include a) a focus on behavior change, not just on information dissemination; b) a focus on long-term changes; c) efforts to change the cultural context; and d) rigorous evaluations as the basis for constant reformulation of programs. We would, of course, do well to adopt similar criteria for all our support programs.

Another example of such works includes a reminder for practitioners to take care of themselves as well as their colleagues. The kinds of people who come to academe, especially in helping roles, stress themselves in two particular ways. First, they routinely perceive and dwell on shortages of time. Second, they tend toward perfectionism and fear of failure (Scott & Hawk, 1986). What can help? Practitioners are admonished to let others do some of the work in setting up self-help offerings: Simpson and Jackson (1990) specify ways of recruiting faculty experts to put on workshops about topics such as fitness. Hill (1990) speaks to workshop formats that include family growth, self-management, and other critical topics for new hires.

Self-Assessment and Self-Help

The least common type of self-help is based in self-assessments of new faculty. Classroom research, with its emphasis on getting faculty to assess their own and their students' progress in the classroom (Chapter Six), approximates self-assessment. But there are surprisingly few systematic indices by which new faculty can judge their own progress. One example is the Blocking Questionnaire, a self-assessment of tendencies toward problematic habits and attitudes as scholarly writers. This experimentally developed scale is the basis for a series of self-help exercises aimed at remedying the problems of faculty as writers. In the course of its development and extensions into a published book, *Professors as Writers* (Boice, 1990d), this self-assessment has proved effective in facilitating productivity, enjoyment, and success among scholarly writers.

Insight 3: Self-Help Needs Help

We know with a fair amount of confidence what undermines the acculturation and survival of new faculty on our campuses. We have already seen examples, including social isolation, a perceived lack of time, and unrealistic or unclear expectations. And at least in terms of those programs requiring the direct involvement of new faculty, we have some ideas about what kinds of support can help overcome those usual obstacles, such as help in finding social support and basic skills in teaching and writing. How can we translate this information into a focused and practical program of self-help? The most useful scheme, at least in my own efforts, has come from the approach devised by Sternberg and his colleagues for teaching students usually tacit knowledge about how to thrive. Their three categories for the types of help needed for thriving as students are used as organizing strategies for helping new faculty help themselves to thrive (Sternberg et al., 1990).

Self-Management

Managing oneself (Sternberg et al., 1990) is a matter of learning to do usually untaught things, such as setting useful goals, recognizing optimal work styles, and learning by doing. I have chosen to emphasize the aspect of self-management that new faculty themselves say they find most valuable—fostering better control of mood (I would have picked control of time if the choice had been mine alone; perhaps the two come to the same thing in the end).

Worrying. I have three exploratory projects on self-help with control of mood under way. One deals with obsessive worrying, especially about failure, and includes self-helps such as readings on cognitive therapies for self-control (deciding to save worrying for one specific period of the day) and a self-run support group where participants share their experiences. Initial results suggest that this will be an effective intercession for some new faculty members. Still, not everyone feels comfortable with the strategy or with the self-revelation involved in the meetings. To be done well, cognitive self-management requires practice and coaching.

Fitness. The second strategy aims more at Bandura's (1990) component of physical fitness. For more than four years, I have cosponsored a fitness group for faculty that emphasizes participation of new faculty and successful senior faculty. Much of its appeal comes from its basis in sound methods of practicing relaxation, muscular flexibility, cardiovascular fitness, and strength conditioning; the group is led by a physical education professor, who begins each of three brief weekly sessions with a didactic lecture and then leads the group in its exercises. Once under way, the group runs itself.

The fitness class has shown effectiveness in several ways. For one thing, participants report improvements in conditioning (including lowered heart rates and cholesterol counts) and in a self-rated sense of well-being on campus. For another, they make friends in the group and feel that they are a part of campus. Finally, the fitness group is remarkably effective in eliciting the participation of new faculty who would otherwise be unlikely to take part in faculty development. It has been, for example, by far the most effective means of getting colleagues from engineering and the sciences, especially those of Asian backgrounds, to participate in other support projects. These are new faculty members who tell me that they avoid faculty development sessions that seem to consist of little more than talk.

Depression. The third project assists new faculty in self-management of mood, especially depression. In this instance, I administer copies of a simple, self-scored index of depression (the Beck Depression Inventory) and encourage new faculty to chart their levels of depression after specific events. In particular, I ask them to observe the effects of having spent large blocks of time in intensive work. The result of distributing these materials and instructions to new faculty is fascinating. Clearly, bingeing, notably in demanding sessions of writing that took up most of weekends and vacations, is associated with depressive moods. And, to the surprise of participants, assuming a more temperate allocation of time and energy results in drops in depression indices. This simple exercise of charting proved an effective method for demonstrating the value of brief daily sessions for carrying out activities such as writing and lecture preparation, particularly among new faculty who were resisting participation in more public support programs.

Task Management

This second category of management skills deals with breaking habits, getting organized, and getting things done on time (Sternberg et al., 1990). Here, I simply opted to extend an already established format for helping new faculty overcome procrastination as writers (Chapter Seven). But instead of expecting new faculty to take advantage of a self-help strategy that I publicized in, say, a newsletter, I used an old strategy that ensured more exposure. It began in the once-a-semester interviews that I carry out with all new faculty on campus (Chapters Two through Four). At the ends of those sessions, I talked briefly about my interest in new faculty who preferred to carry out vital tasks in large blocks of time. (Initially, at least, I held off using my pejorative label of *bingeing*.)

In one such inquiry (Boice, 1989a), I recruited twenty-one bingers and eight nonbingers as data collectors (I classified them on the basis of how they reported using their time); none in my estimate (or theirs) was likely to have participated in my usual support programs—they preferred to work largely on their own. Table 8.1 shows the results of relating their category as bingers or nonbingers to other observable patterns.

**Table 8.1. Behaviors Claimed by Bingers
and Nonbingers During Weekly Visits.**

	Percentage of Occurrence During Weekly Visits	
Behavior Category	Bingers	Nonbingers
Bingeing on day of visit	92	33
Complaining of busyness	93	33
Claiming writing as highest priority	77	29
Finishing at least one manuscript during year	6	17
Evidencing overpreparation for teaching	88	23

When I stopped by to update their data for time-use patterns, I collected other signs of functioning. Bingers, first of all, confirmed their claims of bingeing; they were almost always in the midst of a binge when I visited them (for example, spending six successive hours, often with minimal breaks, on lecture preparation). Second, their comments to me almost always emphasized how busy they were; nonbingers, in contrast, displayed far fewer signs of busyness. Third, they, much more than nonbingers, made writing their highest priority. (The irony was that the higher the priority for writing, the less likely its timely production—as in Minsky's Law, Chapter Seven.) Fourth, perhaps because they spent the bulk of work-weeks on classroom preparation, bingers reported feeling rushed while teaching. Nonbingers, again, showed a less problem-causing pattern in this regard.

Some of these bingers were asked to participate in loosely organized support programs that left them alone to function as self-helpers. They eventually learned to master their procrastination, busyness, and bingeing by means of the paradigms of brief daily sessions described in Chapter Seven. But, more germane to this chapter, many of the nonpartici-pating new faculty did volunteer an interest in reading my self-help book for writers (Boice, 1990d); I had, as a matter of course, reminded all new faculty of its availability. Nearly

half of those normally reticent colleagues have since mentioned that they have successfully adopted some approximation to brief daily sessions in lieu of bingeing. Moreover, they
often add comments such as these:

> It really does work. I've even tried to sell some of
> my friends on the method. But they're as suspi-
> cious of these self-help things as I was. Usually,
> they fall into disuse. Not this one, though; I can
> tell you that. One other thing: I'm applying the
> general strategy of doing things in brief and daily
> blocks, and it makes things much more efficient
> [inexperienced, year 2].

> No, I'm not doing the things that I know I
> should do yet. But I'm thinking about it, and
> that's not so bad, is it? [returning, year 1].

Social Management

In their applications of teaching practical knowledge to
schoolchildren, Sternberg, Okagaki, and Jackson (1990) call
this category "cooperating with others." It includes understanding social networks, putting oneself in the place of
another, and solving communication problems. In my pilot
projects on social management, I am focusing on what I see
as the single most critical deficit of new faculty in social
networking: they often undermine their progress and success
by failing to discover whether they are on track and doing
enough (Chapter Two).

Mentors can provide some help in provoking inquiries
and feedback about quantities, qualities, and directions (Chapter Five), especially given the usual dearth of such communication. But even mentors often don't know how to effect better
communication of this typically unspoken sort. So it was
that I resorted again to a kind of cataloguing, one that works
with or without a traditional mentor. The plan consists of
having new faculty start by constructing a brief, readable cat-

alogue of planned activities as teachers, as colleagues, and as researchers and writers. Job interviews are an ideal point to begin collecting these documents. Because most new faculty members have had little experience in constructing such documents, they profit in examining model catalogues. And given the trepidation that sharing a first draft of such a document elicits, new faculty respond readily to offers from neutral people (including project directors) for critical readings. Even a quick glance indicates that most first efforts contain activity descriptions that are too esoteric or wordy to expect sustained reading from colleagues; some plans seem obviously too ambitious for practical completion, compared to those of other junior faculty. Once the catalogue has passed initial scrutiny, it may profit from one more round of informal reading by a few trusted colleagues.

Is This Self-Help?

One question that arises is whether all this is self-help. Shouldn't self-help, properly done, consist of letting people do things pretty much on their own? This chapter, as we have seen, extends the concept of self-help to something that works even better with an occasional bit of coaching. Given a few models and chances for practice, new faculty do most of the work on their own. Once in motion, with some more coaching for the colleagues who themselves act as coaches, projects can essentially run themselves. Moreover, new faculty who have done cataloguing enjoy guiding even newer faculty through the process. So, in the final analysis, what makes this approach somewhat different from traditional concepts of self-help is that it typically helps bring new faculty into support networks, often of their own making. Once again, participation precedes motivation.

Insight 4: Participation Often Precedes Attractiveness

By reviewing the preceding three insights, we can make sense of this fourth one. The first said that the most vital skills for new faculty, especially the precedence of involvement over motivation, may be so simple that we usually neglect teaching them. The second insight suggests a reason for our usual reluctance to teach this tacit knowledge: perhaps we unwittingly follow the tradition of social Darwinism in supposing that new hires with the right stuff will benefit from the usual handbooks and release time that we offer them. The third insight restates the obvious: self-help, to be effective and far-reaching, requires minimal help from campus leaders. Indeed, projects such as getting new faculty involved in communicating about their catalogued plans with colleagues confirm the power of adding some structure and networking to self-help paradigms.

The fourth insight completes the picture. It says that we, as practitioners, may not feel motivated to help many of our new hires until they are already participating. The confidence and self-esteem that make some of our new colleagues immediately rewarding participants may not emerge until after we have helped them to help themselves. To operate from any other assumption is to deny many of our new faculty members, including those from underrepresented backgrounds, a meaningful chance for involvement in support programs. Tobias's (1990) findings in an analogous situation help clarify this point.

Tobias's method of finding out why already successful students left science majors was cleverly uncomplicated. She hired social science students who had formerly majored in science to enroll in science classes for grades and to take notes on their impressions of the fields that they had left. The results are fascinating: social science majors were reminded that they disliked science classes because professors all too clearly limited their attention and approval to students who were already motivated to excel and who already had the practical knowledge to thrive in their classes. Science professors, incidentally, confirmed this observation; they wanted students to come to class with their background skills and interest fully developed. Students who did not were deemed unattractive.

When I shared this summary of Tobias's findings with a long-term friend, a faculty developer with a well-established habit of working only with the most successful colleagues, his initial response was encouraging. He recognized at once the need to address the needs of students who required more explanations and other support, especially academically disadvantaged students. But when I prodded him to think about the parallel situation, where some new faculty come to campus without the background and motivation that will make their success easy, his stance shifted in the direction of the science teachers studied by Tobias. He was not sure whether he had the time or energy to deal with colleagues who didn't care enough to solicit help; he also noted that he already had enough to do with colleagues who seek out faculty development programs on their own.

Almost immediately, though, he saw the need to rethink his assumptions. If ways could be found to reach all the new faculty, at first by way of brief coaching in self-help strategies, then he might take more interest in them as a group, even the most rejecting of them. If they would get somewhat involved, he supposed, he would meet them more than halfway. In a sense—and this is something that I especially value in a friend—he echoed my own realizations about helping new faculty who may not welcome help, and then he reminded me of something that I needed to reconsider. He said that at some point, those of us in faculty development who struggle with ambivalent administrators and proudly autonomous colleagues have to set limits. We too need balance and moderation. So it is, he added on a quiet note, that there is no harm in letting self-help programs work, at least some of the time, on their own. I agreed. In the final analysis, he went on, self-help programs for new faculty can serve both sides well. We can help those who like to do some or all of the work alone. And we might even save ourselves from trying to do too much.

 *Part 3*

Building an
Institutional
Support System

This part first addresses the needs of new faculty at special times and the special needs of some new faculty members: Chapters Nine, Ten, and Eleven deal with recruitment and orientation, retention and tenure, and nontraditional faculty, including women and members of minority groups. Chapters Twelve and Thirteen then discuss practical problems of implementing support systems and offer strategies for dealing with them; too many faculty development programs simply disappear for lack of ongoing support.

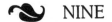 NINE

Recruitment
and Orientation

First impressions are lasting. New faculty have indelible memories of good treatment. And just as they cherish pleasant beginnings, they have particular trouble getting bad beginnings out of mind. However, while new faculty typically see recruitment and orientation experiences as unforgettable, their older colleagues may dismiss them as passing events. Perhaps this is why new faculty are alone in expressing surprise (see Chapters Two through Four) about the lack of continuity between recruitment and orientation. Promises made during recruitment may be dismissed by everyone except the new hire still forming an attachment to campus. This chapter samples what we already know about recruiting and orienting new faculty from the sparse literature and from surveys of various constituencies affected by hiring. It reviews model guidelines for recruiting and formats for orienting new faculty. Finally, it proposes rules for recruiting and orienting based on accumulating knowledge; throughout, I explain ways of assessing and redesigning customary practices in these vital areas.

I begin my overview of what we already know with an irony in a literature that teems with ironies. Bowen and Schuster (1986) note a contradiction in the usual neglect of hiring and socializing new faculty: for any other campus investment of more than a million dollars—say, a small building or major equipment—we would spend far more time and effort on planning and caring. Yet the colleague whom we hire may affect us far more than the remodeling of a building or the purchase of a new computer. Often, a new colleague is destined to stay with us for many decades. With the right choices, we can have enjoyable partners who share the work and inspire us to growth; the million dollars and more that each new hire will earn over the years could seem a bargain. With the wrong decisions, we may face years of discomfort and of unmet promise for stimulating students and each other. But Bowen and Schuster also argue that we may at last be ready for a new perspective on recruiting and orienting. We already know the reasons—the growing shortage of new faculty, the need to find and nurture underrepresented colleagues, and the demand for accountability about new faculty's efforts. To put it simply, we must make every position count.

Although recruitment and orientation intermesh when done well, we can profit by first examining them as separate practices; tradition generally holds them apart.

Recruitment

Little of a systematic sort is known about professorial recruitment. The best relevant studies deal with student recruitment; decreases in student enrollments have hit campuses harder, as least so far, than have shortages of new faculty. Much of what is being learned about student recruitment has application to faculty hiring. Two examples from that literature make the point.

Milo (1986, p. 180) offers a message about the emergence of accountability in student recruiting (academe is demanding a "more business-like approach") and of pressures to enlist more faculty to assist in the process. The latter detail is especially interesting here; while faculty turn out to be naive about the optimal ways of recruiting the best students, they are willing to learn and to participate in ventures such as campus tours and high school visits. Faculty members' usual reason for uninvolvement is telling: no one has ever asked them before.

Rynes and Boudreau (1986) are more critical of college recruiting, because most recruiters diverge from their own, oft-stated ideals: recruiters seldom have training, they seem to disregard techniques known to be effective (for example, pursuing lines of inquiry established as most predictive of success), and they rarely follow up their choices with assessments of how effective they were. To answer the quandary of why recruiters seem so often to work inefficiently, Rynes and Boudreau turn to a political explanation: Tsui (1984) concludes that recruiting choices are more often made to avoid disturbing cultural norms than to add productivity.

While the scattered literature offers some starting points in our examination of recruiting, particularly in reminders that recruiters often operate from a suspect base, we can get more useful information elsewhere. As with instances of getting to know new faculty, we begin with observation. In the following paragraphs, I illustrate three kinds of surveys about recruiting that can be implemented on most campuses and that show promise of offering feedback for reforming and improving our usual practices.

Problems in Recruiting New Faculty

Even colleagues who express ambivalence about support programs for teaching or writing agree that we could do better in selecting new faculty. One way to trigger an awareness of the importance of careful recruitment is to ask for recollections of regrettable choices. Such inquiries do more than provide ventilation. They also offer an ideal format for involving colleagues across campus in efforts to improve recruitment.

Surveys of Recruitment Committees. In one effective format for enlisting both involvement and a wealth of information, campuses convene meetings of their recruitment committees (usually formed within departments) to share concerns and advice. How this can lead to productive thinking was illustrated on a campus where these meetings were followed up by a committee of faculty representatives and administrators. Together, they generated a list of the most salient and common problems expressed at the meetings (Edwards et al., 1986):

1. Departments were often handicapped by delays in administrative authorizations for hiring—when authorizations came late in the academic year, the best candidates had already taken jobs elsewhere.
2. Policies and guidelines for recruiting existed but were scattered and generally unheeded. One difficulty arising from the mystery surrounding how to proceed, beyond having to "reinvent the wheel" each year, was the awkward discovery that particularly attractive candidates, often members of minorities, could not be hired because of campus oversights in filling out requisite forms.
3. Departments differed dramatically in recruiting effectiveness. Some could boast of having competed successfully for leading candidates in their field, evidently because of carefully planned and executed efforts (usually with chairpeople playing key roles). Others could only admit to having fared poorly, in part because of departmental lack of interest and disorganization. These departments were most likely to have hired candidates who ranked low on their lists.
4. Given its importance, recruiting was underfunded. Often, monies were unavailable to bring the most promising candidates to campus from more than a few hundred miles away.

My own involvement in this same campuswide meeting of colleagues involved in recruiting and hiring new faculty left an impression of ambivalence: while the senior faculty, the chairs, and the administrators fretted about other problems, they worried most vocally about the costs of hiring newcomers from the very best universities and with the strongest research credentials. Would these new faculty fit in at a campus with a tradition of valuing teaching above all else? Would they carry their share of teaching responsibilities? Would they show loyalty to their new campus, or would they leave for the first opening at a more prestigious campus? And, finally, should the campus opt for mediocrity?

Later in this chapter, we will return to questions about how to determine which hires will most likely fit in and fare well as teachers, producers, and colleagues. In fact, we know enough about the predictors that we could, like the student recruiters already mentioned, do better-informed jobs of selection.

Surveys of Chairpeople. I routinely interview chairs, much as I do new faculty. Even chairs, with their busy schedules and sometimes skeptical style, come to express an appreciation for these moments of reflection and feedback. They, like other academicians, talk with special fervor about recruiting. In one case, I asked them to explain what led to good choices in hiring. The result is this list from a decade of interviews and a sample of about two hundred chairpeople:

1. The candidate was known to the department beforehand, and there were faculty already in the department with kindred interests.
2. The candidate was obviously interested in joining the department and may have limited efforts to look elsewhere.
3. Once hired, the new colleague fit in quickly and established collaborations with students and other faculty.
4. Throughout the recruitment process, the new hire was positive about coming to campus.

While the concomitants of hiring strong faculty were generated with apparent ease, those for hiring weak, unsatisfactory faculty took longer to formulate. For one thing, the cases and reasons varied; it seemed harder to draw generalities. For another, this sort of contemplation was less fun. Nonetheless, chairs' comments produced some telling uniformities about what events accompanied regrettable decisions:

1. Getting a late authorization for hiring and then having to hire a low-priority candidate rather than risk losing the "slot" back to the administration.
2. Departmental rifts that either limited who could be hired or brought newcomers into a situation where they had to take sides in the dispute.
3. Ignoring signs of impending difficulty, including hints of troubled relationships during graduate school and/or jobs since and of discordant interactions during interviews; often, these people were hired to meet a need about which the department felt ambivalent (for instance, someone who could bring in a large federal grant; someone who could fill a vacant specialty niche).

Of these three most commonly stated concomitants of regrettable hirings, the first was far and away the most serious. Campus budgets, especially those dictated by state legislatures that are always running behind schedule in making allocations, have a far more powerful effect on recruitment than may be generally realized. One obvious solution would be to commit slots to departments until they make the best possible hire, even if doing so takes two or more years. As a rule, however, the uncertainties of budgets and of campus politics (say, of new deans and provosts unwilling to honor the commitments of their predecessors) make this remedy unlikely.

Surveys of New Faculty. New hires definitely see recruiting differently from the way the people who conduct it do. I used nine years of interviews from three strikingly different campuses (Chapters Two through Four) to derive this list of what recruits most often perceive as problems in the hiring process:

1. Long silences after initial acknowledgments of applications (usually via form letters) and a feeling that a cam-

pus did not care enough to keep candidates informed about their status.

2. Seeming lack of interest during the campus visit (such as being abandoned to find their own way around campus between interviews; small, unenthusiastic audiences for "job talks").

3. Lack of clarification during recruitment about campus expectations, resources, and practical knowledge essential to getting ready for campus.

4. Hostile interviewers who acted as though they would never again see the candidate. (New faculty, once hired, typically marveled at the function of these behaviors: "Do they," one newcomer asked me, "expect me to forget that it happened?")

5. Losses of face during recruitment (for instance, telephone inquiries about one's references that suggested that the candidate was suspect; cancellation by faculty of scheduled appointments; breaking of promises made as an enticement for hiring, most commonly promises of moving money, space, and resources such as personnel and equipment).

6. Losses of expected continuity between recruitment and hiring. (Specifically, new faculty expected the senior faculty and administrators who paid such keen attention to persist in it.)

Yet another source of information about how we could do better at recruiting new faculty is the sourcebook or handbook that campuses occasionally compile in the hope of standardizing and improving their practices and policies. I have taken information from six of these assembled since 1985 and combined the most useful advice with that from the survey findings listed above. The result is a set of working rules for recruiting, one that deserves the keenest sort of skepticism, testing, and revision.

Working Rules for the Recruitment of New Faculty

First, plan for each hire with a clear sense of the long-term investment involved (especially the costs of bad choices) and of necessary campus and collegial support to make a sound decision. New hires who are denied tenure cause nearly everyone distress of one sort or another, and replacing them is expensive and time-consuming. For information about better ways to recruit, survey a small sample of departments with evident success at hiring the best candidates about what they do best. In my experience, many chairs and other contact people are open with advice (for instance, many exemplary committees start recruiting the best prospects midway through their graduate work; their advisers can identify them for periodic contacts with faculty at the recruiting campus).

Another source of useful insights is interviews of candidates who were deemed desirable but who dropped out of the process. While some of these "rejecters" make decisions for expected reasons (better offers), some may offer surprising reasons. Earlier in this book, I cited the results of one such survey that focused on underrepresented prospects who opted for nonacademic careers (Boice, 1991e). The gist of their reasons was a fear of trying to survive in contexts where they saw pressures for grants and writing but few campus supports. Where recruiters address such concerns before such decisions are made, the results of recruitment could be quite different.

Second, set clear policies for marketing positions in visible and timely fashion (especially deadlines for getting notices to key media and contacts). Advertisements must be clear, accurate, informative, and enticing; as a rule, committees planning these notices do well to model them after the most impressive advertisements in disciplinary outlets and the more personalized letters of job announcements that come to dissertation supervisors on campus.

Third, plan and execute follow-ups to applications with the same vigor and thoroughness as with any other truly important activity (such as grant applications). That is, write to candidates. Inform them about probable time lines for decisions and encourage them to call if they experience conflicts or concerns. Assign each promising candidate a personal contact on the faculty and have that person initiate contacts with a phone call. Eschew form letters, especially when rejecting applicants; instead, have their contacts inform them by phone if possible. The rule of thumb here is to treat applicants as though we will encounter them later in our careers; often we do.

Fourth, educate selection committees, faculty and administrators who take part as interviewers (even students where they participate), and everyone who votes for acceptance or rejection about the established predictors for success in new hires. There are at least three sources of information about predictors. I summarize each briefly here: (1) The literature on career productivity of faculty (see Creswell, 1985) is replete with empirically based predictors, including the age at which the doctorate is awarded (by age twenty-five is optimal), intrinsic motivation for productivity, confidence, graduation from a prestigious department, and already established patterns of productivity. (2) The literature on quick starters (Chapters Six and Seven; see also Cole, 1986) suggests several qualities that can be discerned during recruitment: a high energy level and broad range of interests, including hobbies; a general positiveness toward students, teaching, and the recruiting campus; a readiness to seek out and use collegial advice; and a disinclination toward bingeing and procrastinating on key tasks such as dissertations. (3) Researchers on teaching effectiveness (see Feldman, 1986, 1989b) have verified a variety of predictors of what kinds of professors induce student learning and favorable teaching ratings: preparedness, orderliness, clarity and understandability, student perceptions of rapport and approachability, enthusiasm, emotional stability, and self-esteem. Harbingers of these may be seen in colloquia and simulated teaching. (4) There is even a literature on preemployment indicators of termination (Inwald, 1988), such as personality tests and psychologists' ratings interviews (none of it, unfortunately, directly about professors) that merits examination.

Fifth, share campus and department procedures, rules, and expectations for hiring with candidates coming for interviews. Keeping these policies cryptic, as is usually done, pays dividends for no one. Encourage prospective interviewees to seek out advice such as Darley and Zanna's (1987) chapter on what to expect and how to behave. Candidates, particularly those from underrepresented backgrounds, may lose jobs over minor faux pas or cultural surprises. It is in the interest of both the campus and the candidate to secure the best impression from each.

Sixth, have finalists prepare brief catalogues (Chapter Five) that clarify their accomplishments and plans as teachers, researchers and writers, and colleagues. Much as with new faculty already on campus, these should be the subject of feedback and revision through interactions with recruiting faculty. Interactions about cataloguing reveal a lot about the styles, expectations, and probable future behaviors of candidates—and their prospective colleagues. Cataloguing can also provide a lasting advantage with candidates; the odds are that few other campuses will have taken such a constructive interest in them.

Seventh, reexamine traditional assumptions about recruiting and hiring (Turner, 1979). Perhaps early recruitment, where prospects are first contacted and nurtured years in advance, will prove worth the effort. And it might be that one tenure-track slot could be devoted to bringing visiting professors with special promise for collaboration to campus as researchers and/or teachers with departmental faculty who would otherwise experience intellectual isolation.

Eighth, find effective rewards for all faculty and administrators whose recruiting teams achieve exemplary results. In my experience, rewards as inexpensive as $50 certificates for redemption at the campus bookstore are sufficient (especially if accompanied by public recognition).

Ninth, assess the results of recruiting, continually and publicly. Note, for example, the procedures most associated with success at recruiting, in the short and the long run (at least to the time when departure or tenure decisions are made). Make the results public. And note where programs have problems, such as histories of conflict over hirings, high rates of rejection by preferred candidates, and high rates of failure of new hires to gain tenure. Use the results of evaluations to revise policies and procedures.

Tenth, put *all* promises in writing and have candidates read and approve the copy. Distribute copies to all interested parties. Warn new faculty that the intensity of interest shown toward candidates does not always carry over to their arrival on campus. Explain, for one thing, that hirings are made, to some extent, on the premise that academicians will be relatively self-sufficient (and that those who need help will seek it). And add a caution about the usual pattern of faculty who participate in hiring committees: once the marathon of activity is finished with a hiring, most committee members want to get back to their own work.

Finally, compile procedures and policies such as these (with the addition of all necessary forms and deadlines) in a guidebook, and distribute it on and off campus for praise and criticism. And in the midst of raising campus consciousness and involvement about recruiting, persist in reminding everyone that when done well, it extends, almost seamlessly, into effective orienting for new faculty.

Orienting

If, indeed, recruiting and other preliminaries were properly carried out, orientations would be mere afterthoughts. So it is that some of the most progressive reformers in faculty development want to take the focus of instructional development off the new faculty experience and put it back on proper graduate training (Diamond & Wilbur, 1990; Schuster, 1990b). In their scenarios, we would choose from applicants for junior faculty positions who are already experienced as teachers, who are versed in basic teaching skills, and who are even certified on the basis of performance.

I like the idea of pretraining and preorienting our new faculty. But in its present manifestation, the idea suffers a serious deficit in logic. Its adherents may suppose that new faculty, as products of research universities, come ready to succeed in all areas but teaching. We have already seen the fallacy of that assumption in Chapters Two through Four. My guess is that, at least for the foreseeable future, campuses that hire must also be prepared to provide many of the other basics of professorial skills. Even the advent of widespread and evaluated training of future professors as teachers may leave room for more training. Learning a new campus culture requires readjustment, even for experienced faculty.

Information About Orienting New Faculty

Orientations appear to be vitally important to new faculty. Fortunately, there is a wealth of information available about orienting new faculty. First impressions, as new faculty regular note (Chapters Two through Four), are lasting.

Surveys of Practitioners. Several surveys (see Kurfiss & Boice, 1990) suggest that new faculty orientations are common. As a rule, though, surveys provide few specifics about orientations. In a recent phone survey of fourteen campuses of diverse sorts, I confirmed the assumption that almost all campuses provide some form of orientation for new faculty. Most typically, these are brief and take the form of a meeting about benefits (insurance and retirement plans) and/or a reception for new faculty. Half of the campuses added one more element, a meeting where new faculty are exposed to a series of (ostensibly) brief talks by administrators (say, the vice president for academic affairs) and service providers (perhaps the director of the counseling center). None of these three most common kinds of orientations was judged adequate by faculty developers reporting them. Nonetheless, all but three of these practitioners planned no immediate changes. The most common reasons were that (1) the campus program for faculty development was still relatively new and had not yet moved beyond its initial focus on TA training or instructional development for faculty; (2) there were too few new hires to justify more effort at orienting; and (3) the new faculty orientation was captive to territorial interests (for instance, the benefits office had been doing the orientation for years and did not want to give it up). Still, all these respondents expressed an interest in doing more; everyone recognized the need to deal with the coming infusion of new faculty.

Published Accounts. The best information about how to orient new hires in academe is not about new faculty; it is about new TAs (see the annotated bibliography in Eckstein, Boice, & Chua-Yap, 1991). Perhaps because we suppose that TAs are still more amenable to training as teachers (or at least more susceptible to obligatory participation), orientations for TAs are common, well funded, supplied with impressive materials, and the subject of several articles and chapters (Chism, 1988) and national meetings (Nyquist, Abbott, Wulff, & Sprague, 1991). One of the most revered and emulated of these is the week-long orientation run by Diamond and his colleagues at Syracuse University. My point in beginning with a mention of TA orientations and materials is that they lend themselves to ready translation for use with new faculty.

Written directives for new faculty orientations, while not as elaborate as those for TAs, are well worth consulting. The first of three categories consists of handbooks for new faculty. The handbook for new faculty at Texas A&M University (Johnson, 1988) is exemplary for its scope of useful reading (for instance, ways to facilitate student and faculty interactions) and for its use of planning guides and self-ratings (including setting course objectives). The package of materials (articles about teaching, pamphlets describing campus resources, a faculty handbook, cultural guides) distributed to new faculty by W. L. Humphreys, director of the Learning Research Center at the University of Tennessee at Knoxville, is also useful. The massive and impressive handbook *Teachers and Students,* published for new faculty at the University of Texas, Austin (Stice et al., 1990), includes readings that cover the nature of effective teaching, getting started with such things as a syllabus, alternative teaching methods, improving specific teaching techniques, teaching large classes, the case-study method, and communication skills.

The second category of information about orientations

for new faculty is the most voluminous. It covers an interesting range of primarily presemester orientations. Eison (1989) portrays a useful array of materials on teaching, grading, and learning. The outstanding value of his article is that it details solutions to the sticky problem of mandatory participation. Two things helped correct what had once been an awkward situation: (1) preparticipation surveys of new faculty about what is expected and wanted and (2) program flexibility. Since Eison's article was published, what began as an impressive week-long orientation for which participants were paid has evolved into an equally effective but shortened and unpaid workshop (Stice et al., 1990). Sometimes less is better.

Noonan (1980) describes a program that many campuses would like to emulate: a three-day retreat involving the new faculty from four colleges in traditional instructional development, including videotapes of practice lectures, and a creative twist—discussions derived from self-disclosures about "critical moments as teachers." An example of blending orientation with mentoring efforts such as attention to scholarly production is depicted by Freudenthal and DiGiorgio (1989). While Wylie (1986) prescribes orientations run within a consortium of colleges, his plan contains a message for all programs. Wylie and his colleagues learned to emphasize the adjustment aspects of orienting (such as managing stress and politics) more than specific teaching skills, much like the first-factor notion emphasized throughout this book.

The third category of information about orientations adds the sensible practice of following initial orientations with periodic orientations. Both Fink (1991) and Sorcinelli (1988) center their continuing meetings around luncheons, part of the reason, probably, for the remarkably high level of attendance that they report.

Assessments. Despite the growing abundance of useful directives for new faculty orientations, one problem remains in current practices. Almost none of these orientations are evaluated beyond measures of participant satisfaction collected as new faculty leave the meetings. A well-established fact from applied and organizational researchers (see Baron, 1983) is that satisfaction measures are useless in predicting long-term results in areas such as job adjustment and productivity. More useful evaluations of orientations might ask new faculty for their assessments on more specific dimensions (what was learned that was new; what from the workshop are they planning to implement or already implementing), both in the short and the long run.

When these kinds of assessments are collected after an orientation, the result can be a major change in assumptions about what an orientation accomplishes. Consider an example from my own experience, one since replicated by fellow practitioners at other campuses. I came to a large, comprehensive university where the format for orientations was already a standing tradition. It began by having new faculty stand and introduce themselves. Then came lunch, with a brief welcoming talk by the campus president. It ended with a series of lengthy talks by administrators and service providers. In all the years of following this format, none of the presenters had thought to assess its value. After all, they said when I first began questioning them, the new faculty almost always attended. Moreover, new hires were being introduced to each other and to campus leaders worth knowing. Administrators were dismayed when I shared the results of my own interviews with the new faculty who had been through the usual orientations. I depict the general message here in terms of the normative responses of a single new hire:

Q: What did you think of the new faculty orientation, now that you've had a semester and a half to reflect on it?

A: I still think it was a dreadful bore, a waste of time.

Q: What did you like best about it?

A: That it ended. Ha! That it showed some interest in us by the administration—although it also showed a lack of sensitivity.

Q: What about the part where you met the other new faculty?

A: That was a joke, too. Waiting my turn to stand up and introduce myself makes me incredibly nervous; my heart was ready to burst by the time the chain came up and down the rows to me. While all that was going on, I was barely noticing who the other people were, unless they were noticeably nervous and making fools of themselves. You see, I didn't really make any real acquaintances there.

Q: What about the part of the orientation where you were introduced to a series of administrators and providers?

A: I hope they got something out of it. I didn't. By about the third or fourth one, I had stopped listening; I couldn't tell you the names of, let's see, more than one of them now— or even recognize them on campus. It was too much at once, a stimulus overload, for one of my first days on campus.

Q: What did you learn from the workshop that you can put into use?

A: Nothing. What I wanted wasn't even covered. I wanted some specific information about what was necessary for tenure. I wanted to meet other new faculty, especially people who might be friends. Most of what the "suits" had to say was no doubt important, but it should have been put into handouts, not into tedious talks.

Q: What that you learned in the workshop might you be applying to your success as a new faculty member?

A: I think I already answered that. But wait a minute. I did meet someone who sat near me. We have since gone to lunch together several times. We might collaborate. What I learned, I guess, was that going to a meeting where I could meet someone like her is useful.

Since that time, I have learned that some campuses with similar formats for orientations receive favorable evaluations from new faculty. Merely subjecting new hires to a series of talks from administrators will not necessarily offend them; a lot seems to depend on how the talks are delivered. And, so far as I can see, the campuses that plan orientations seriously elicit reactions to match. The point is to build orientations on feedback, not on preset expectations.

A Model Orientation Shaped by Evaluations

In what follows, I offer my own orientation plan, which is based on what I have found new faculty to like and benefit from most. While I do not suppose that the specifics will necessarily be most comfortable and effective for other practitioners and campuses, I do suggest emulating the developmental process.

In essence, my own orientations for new faculty have gone from several days of presemester workshops to less than one day; from including a variety of administrators throughout the orientation to including only a handful, who are confined to brief comments after lunch; and from asking for brief self-introductions of new faculty to assembling small groups of new faculty with kindred interests and concerns, who are later introduced to the group by their "guide," an exemplary junior faculty member acting as a sort of mentor. Where I previously held hour-long workshops about teaching and writing, I now offer three miniworkshops of twelve minutes each that preview the workshops that will be presented during the semester.

I now realize that orientations, especially first meetings, should accomplish just what new faculty want them to. So, for instance, I try to maintain an unhurried pace in a process that focuses mostly on meeting kindred colleagues and that provides answers to questions about practical knowledge from pretrained guides in small groups, mercifully brief and reassuring greetings from campus leaders (who are coached to at least indicate when the campus will address concerns about tenure norms), and samples of the kinds of supports for new faculty available from my office. In sum, I have learned to do less in the first orientation. I follow up with more orientations, on an individual basis (interviews and visits to classes after asking permission) and on a group basis (a variety of workshops and projects). The result is a more relaxed and collegial atmosphere, one where, for example, new faculty readily sign up for my interviews, and one that is recommended by former participants to incoming new hires. The participants who claim they benefit most are the guides, the sophomore new faculty adjusting nicely to campus; this is consistent with what we saw about mentoring in Chapter Five. These guides come to the orientation prepared to facilitate the interaction of their groups of three to five new faculty members, to introduce them to the rest of the reassembled group, and to follow up with occasional calls to their group members after the orientation. They report enjoyment in being selected as exemplary new faculty members, in reflecting on what useful advice they can give, in meeting another round of potential friends and collaborators, and, surprisingly, in sitting through the miniworkshops again entirely on their own volition. The plan for the presemester orientation as I now conduct it is shown in Exhibit 9.1.

After consulting about orientations at a variety of campuses and reviewing the literature and surveys on orientations for new faculty and TAs, I have devised the following guidelines:

1. Begin recruiting for attendance as soon as new hires have accepted positions. Ask the higher administrator who writes the letter of offer to include an enthusiastic invitation to attend the orientation for new faculty. Follow up with a letter and phone call of your own.

2. Emphasize welcomes and praise (for instance, what a talented group has been hired) in invitations and during the orientation. With any luck, you will be telling the truth.

3. Include components of practical knowledge about parking, benefits, resources, and so on, preferably in handouts distributed in advance of arrival on campus and again at the orientation. Complement written advice with counsel from exemplary junior faculty members who meet with new faculty members in small groups

Exhibit 9.1. Orientation Schedule.

9:15–9:55   Juice, coffee, rolls, and milling about (please get a name tag and, sooner or later, find your name card at the table, where you can join other new faculty with kindred interests).

10:00–10:15   Welcoming statements from the provost.

10:15–11:00   Small groups meet and exchange background information, advice, and concerns with each other and with guides (exemplary junior faculty who have been on campus for a year or two). During this time, a sign-up sheet for participation in new faculty interviews will be circulated; please volunteer for this important opportunity to document the new faculty experience on campus.

11:00–11:55   Small group representatives report the gist of their discussions and introduce group members to the reassembled company.

12:00–1:00   Lunch at the University Club (please sit with people you haven't yet met).

1:00–1:30   Certificates of appreciation awarded to guides. Brief chats with the president of the Academic Senate, the vice-provost for research, and the vice provost for undergraduate studies.

1:45–2:00   Miniworkshop: Advice to New Faculty as Teachers.

2:00–2:15   Miniworkshop: Advice for New Faculty About Procuring In-House Grants.

2:15–2:30   Miniworkshop: Advice for New Faculty as Scholarly Writers.

2:30–3:30   Campus tour, including a stop at the reference room of the library, where on-line searches of interest-specific literature have been prepared for each new faculty member.

---

during the orientation and with a campus tour (with maps). Include a useful stop such as a visit to reference librarians who have prepared sample on-line searches of the literature for each new faculty members.

4. Emphasize components of collegiality, especially opportunities for new faculty to meet other new hires who may become friends and/or collaborators. Consider including exemplary junior faculty members who can act as mentors of sorts.

5. Include some clear information about when guidelines for campus expectations about retention and tenuring standards will be communicated (perhaps in a scheduled meeting on tenure or in routine meetings with department chairs), preferably presented by a higher administrator.

6. Limit administrative presentations to a few brief comments by individuals whom new faculty express an interest in meeting. Encourage administrators and service providers who do not attend to prepare handouts for distribution at the orientation.

7. Limit workshops for new faculty to brief presentations to elicit interest in attending lengthier workshops to be held regularly during the semester. Take advantage of the compliant ambience at orientation to sign up new faculty for programs such as regular luncheons, workshops, interviews, and mentoring.

8. Follow up with individual contacts (including contacts by exemplary junior faculty members enlisted as guides) and interviews to see how new hires are faring.

9. Evaluate. Collect systematic feedback immediately after the orientation, after follow-up activities, and in the longer run. Expand feedback beyond measures of satisfaction; find out what was done well, what could be done better, what was especially valuable, and what has resulted in actual changes in the practices of new faculty.

10. Encourage higher administrators to meet for lunch with small groups of new faculty during the course of the next semesters. This reinforces the value of orientation as a whole; new faculty members who talk about the orientation as an outstanding experience can help convince administrators of its value. New faculty members also tend, in my experience, to use this occasion to praise the faculty development programs on campus.

Mentoring as Orienting

Done well, orienting includes mentoring, the most thoroughgoing kind of socialization. We have already covered strategies of mentoring for new faculty (Chapter Five). Sometimes, though, campuses separate mentoring and orienting, even supposing that mentoring works best for new faculty who are settled in. In my studies of mentoring, I have found that the best results are achieved when it starts early, even before new faculty arrive on campus.

Where to Begin

There are several common threads in recruiting, orientation, and similar processes, such as mentoring, that exemplify support activities for new faculty. As a rule, campuses have paid little attention to them, assuming, perhaps, that they are matters of common sense. And ordinarily, we have done little to ensure that new faculty get the best kinds of recruiting and orienting; while we readily agree that these are important activities, we may have hoped that the process would take care of itself.

In fact, recruitment and orientation have commonly been conducted in deplorable fashion. The kindest description might be benign neglect. A harsher interpretation assumes that we expect natural and unnatural selection pressures to do the work. But again, with growing pressures for more humane, representative, and cost-effective recruitment, we will inevitably pay more attention to selecting the best prospects for success and then maximizing their growth and our investments. In the course of acting on these changing practices and policies, recruiting and orienting will herald how much and how well we are doing. Nowhere is it easier to begin to collect the information about how best to proceed; nowhere will changes be easier to make; nowhere will the results be more dramatic and more documentable. Here, far more than in programs that try to bring excellence in teaching or productivity in scholarship, support can be shown to pay dividends for campuses. And here, probably more than elsewhere, support programs can affect the survival of our new hires.

How can campuses make decisive beginnings toward reforming their recruitment and orientation practices and policies? I suggest four immediate steps. Again, I have found ways to align closing points with conceptions of IRSS theory.

First, move out of the role of passive observer. Survey recent hires to see what they liked and disliked about their orientations to campus and what they learned from them (or, in the absence of any organized orientations, some indication of what would have helped). Distribute this information, along with information about what other campuses are doing, for collegial consideration. In other words, the place to start is with *involvement*, yours and your colleagues'.

Second, survey departments about recruiting practices and successes and publicize the exemplars, particularly those that lead to retention and success for new faculty. Distribute this information, along with information about how recruiting can be done better, for campus consideration in discussion groups. Whatever else, help the campus begin to solve the right problems—for example, getting beyond the supposition that the problem is attracting the best faculty to the realization that the real problem is exercising carefully planned selection that includes samples of performance and plans and support that begin with the invitation to interview. In other words, help departments establish a *regimen* of collecting and acting on information about hiring and socializing new faculty.

Third, form campus committees to plan improved and uniform practices of recruiting and orienting and to solicit endorsement of their conclusions by key campus leaders. That is, make a point of sharing knowledge that is usually kept tacit, despite its importance. Equally important, coach committees in ways to help them build credibility and confidence in their decisions (and coach administrators to publicly support the intentions and decisions of these committees). To succeed, committees with the responsibility of reforming hiring and orienting need the same kinds of self-confidence and self-esteem that help make up *self-management* for individuals.

Finally, distribute guidelines for recruiting and orienting and take immediate action to assess the extent of their implementation. And as a measure to ensure the broad-based participation of departments and recruitment and orientation committees, enlist higher administrators to lead evaluation teams. When recruitment and orientation efforts take on an air of *social networking*, the enthusiasm can be contagious.

TEN

Retention and Tenure

The trial period in the careers of new faculty, from the time of settling in until the tenure decision, may be more vital than we generally suppose. It is here, as we have seen, that new hires usually lock into habits as teachers, writers, and colleagues. And it is here that many faculty members may bond or fail to bond with their campuses. At the study campuses already described, tenure reviews may have been executed badly. For one thing, the mysterious, rumor-laden prospects of tenuring decisions elicited defensive styles of adjusting to campus, especially in teaching. For another thing, the tendency of evaluators to give faint praise but ready disapproval humiliated many new faculty members at a time when they were desperate for reassurances.

This period was one when the new faculty members who left did so because they saw the demands for tenuring as unpleasant and perhaps unachievable (Boice, 1991e). Many who won tenure were left with a debilitating bitterness. This comment from an inexperienced new faculty member illustrates a typical reaction:

> I will never, ever forget this [the tenuring process]. I'm left feeling that they didn't really want me, that they begrudged me the tenure and pro-

motion. I can't believe that for as hard as I worked at setting up the new program in [my field], it didn't seem to count at all. Instead, they harped on their reservations about my teaching, which, as far as I can tell from the student rating numbers, is near the department mean. And I was pained, that's the word, by their reticence in accepting my articles and presentations as worthy of this great department. After all, my record easily outstrips the achievements of some of the people on the [department tenuring] committee. [In response to my query about what effects this experience would have] Lots. I'm going to look for other jobs. I want to go to a place where I will be appreciated. [In response to my probe about whether her colleagues knew how she felt] I doubt it. They certainly haven't asked. And I don't think either of us cares.

One of academe's curious failings in administration of critical life events such as tenure is that we rarely inquire about what it was like for the person being evaluated or how the process could be improved. We may also be remiss, some of us, in attending to what the literature has to say about retention and tenuring. Many of the findings and practices are well worth considering.

Retention

Handled properly, retention and tenuring become interdependent. If we work effectively at retention from the initial contacts with new hires, tenuring decisions will be foregone conclusions. Done properly, retention programs should ensure that no new faculty members are surprised at the decision about their tenure and should maximize the opportunities for gaining tenure, humanely and effectively. One way to appreciate what we must do to enhance the retention of new faculty is a study of what causes them to leave.

Why New Faculty Leave

Some new faculty members set themselves up for failure. And to some extent, the atmosphere of isolation and self-determination surrounding new faculty members helps make them even more vulnerable. Because they are so afraid of being evaluated, they often establish narrow, short-term goals, confuse their colleagues' judgments with their own self-worth, and resent the pressures that they feel (Boice, 1991a; Braskamp et al., 1984). And as we have seen in earlier chapters, new faculty resist asking for help.

New faculty members forced out of their jobs in the retention and tenure process are often perceived as incompetent, quarrelsome, and socially inept (Caplow & McGee, 1958). Evidently, the publish-or-perish rule is overestimated as a cause for dismissal; well-liked new faculty who teach adequately and who act as good departmental citizens (for example, share committee assignments and advising) are often promoted with few or no publications at campuses that claim to require publishing (Boice, 1990b).

New faculty members who leave campus voluntarily to take better offers do so for mostly intangible reasons (Matier, 1990). Of the seven reasons cited by such emigrants in Matier's study, only one concerned tangibles, and that one—money—was not one of the highest-ranking reasons. The other six reasons point out the importance of collegial relations and other nurturing supports in holding faculty: (1) congeniality of colleagues, (2) rapport with department leadership, (3) research opportunities, (4) reputation of the department, (5) reputation of the campus, and (6) reputation of associates. New faculty members who leave for other jobs because they expect to fail in the tenure process where they already are point out a related reason: they can see no prospects of getting the help from colleagues that they would need to master demands for things such as writing productivity (Boice, 1991e).

One more dimension of retention helps complete this preliminary picture. New faculty who look to leave, get offers, and are coaxed to stay receive salary increases far in excess of what their less restless colleagues receive (of some 30–40 percent with matching offers from the home campus, compared to the 7–8 percent increases for other faculty; Matier, 1990). Thus, attrition, or even the prospect of it, is expensive for campuses. It is also costly for those rejected. New faculty members who fail and are forced out are usually devastated. My own surveys of individuals denied tenure suggest that their long-term career outcomes are worse than those of counterparts who do not finish their Ph.D. degrees, and include personal experiences of extended grief (Boice, 1991e). Campuses that dismiss a new hire face the expense of recruiting a replacement and, more importantly, of having hosted the failed colleague for several years of discomfort and inefficiency.

Faculty members who survive the tenuring process but become estranged by it may be the most expensive of all. These are individuals who often lose their currency as scholars, their enthusiasm as teachers, and their congeniality as colleagues. Moreover, they may maintain these stances as difficult, undermining colleagues for three and even four decades (Boice, 1986b). The greatest cost, however, to campuses and to students may accrue when underrepresented new faculty, such as blacks and members of other minorities, do not make it as full-fledged members of the professoriate. According to my own surveys of unsuccessful new faculty members, they are especially in peril.

What Can Encourage New Faculty to Stay

So far, we know surprisingly little about ways of enhancing the retention of our new hires. One of the few relevant studies about faculty deals with their commitments to campus.

Equal Rewards and Friendly Colleagues. There is, as Neuman and Finaly-Neuman (1990) note, a rapidly growing literature on organizational commitment in nonacademic settings. Commitment means that workers accept organizational values and goals, exert themselves on behalf of the organization, and express a desire to maintain their membership in the organization. Its benefits include heightened job performance and organizational effectiveness. Neuman and Finaly-Neuman's study of forty research university departments indicates that commitment is higher among applied than among pure science faculty. And in the sciences, at least, the most productive faculty are also the most committed to campus. Neuman and Finaly-Neuman also use their analyses to suggest what campuses can do to build commitment: provide clear equity criteria for faculty rewards and provide support by a friendly group of colleagues and/or chairperson. Both, in theory, should be easy to arrange.

Involvement. There may be another, related means of facilitating retention, the key to which is involvement. That, at least, is the message from a thoroughgoing approach to the study of retention with college students. Astin (1985) makes the point this way: Effective education and effective retention depend on student involvement. Student involvement in campus activities such as student organizations and interactions with faculty is more predictive of student change and retention than are entering characteristics or institutional characteristics. Conversely, the passivity that presages lack of change and dropping out is often characteristic of minority and disadvantaged students. So it is, Astin concludes, that addressing student involvement is a matter of educational equity.

Astin's notions about the costs of passivity become all the more riveting when we take a look at the facts about normal activity patterns of undergraduates. Only a minority of them engage in the kinds of activities that signal involvement and maximized educational performance (Baird, 1990, p. 277): "First, the most predominant character of that experience involves class work, studying, and interactions with friends. A great many of the experiences involve solo academic activities. . . . Even such activities as looking up basic references seem to represent a fairly low level of involvement. Many activities in student organizations, sports, art, music, theater, and science, even at the level of being an observer, were also uncommon. . . . The college experience of many students, then, may be a rather prosaic, uninvolved affair.''

Does this general lack of involvement generalize to new faculty? My own surveys at three campuses indicate two similarities. One is that the majority of new faculty members are involved in little beyond their classes, their labs, and occasional chats with a few friends. The second similarity is that the new faculty members most likely to succeed and to stay on campus are those most involved in campus activities other than committees (participation in choral groups, attendance at theater and other fine arts presentations, exercising with colleagues). Recall from the description of quick starters (Chapters Six and Seven) that exemplary new faculty members are relatively atypical in practices such as spending substantial amounts of time at social networking about their research and teaching. Quick starters are also atypical in recruiting undergraduates to work in their laboratories. Put simply, quick starters excel at involvement—their own and others'.

Why would involvement foster success and retention? Part of the answer may lie in IRSS theory. Motivation comes in the wake of, not in advance of, regular practice and hard work. (That is, it comes most readily when the seeker is solving the right problem—starting with involvement.) Thus, new faculty who establish regular involvement in writing, regardless of busy schedules, find ideas, momentum, enthusiasm, and productivity as writers (Chapter Six). In contrast, new faculty members who become commuters and spend the minimum of time on campus are necessarily isolated from (and probably misunderstood by) their colleagues. Similarly, Astin (1985) is among the researchers who find that students who live in residence halls have the most contacts with peers and professors, express the most satisfaction with campus, and exhibit the highest retention rates.

How to Encourage Involvement

Involvement may not be as easily arranged as it sounds. Most of us may have excelled as students and as professionals while

remaining unaware of how uninvolved our peers generally
were. This routine comment of a new faculty member adjusting to teaching helps illustrate the point:

> You know, I hadn't realized how different most
> students are from me—that is, from the kind of
> student I was. I guess that I failed to notice how
> generally uninterested most of the students
> around me were. No doubt, now that I think on
> it, most of my fellow students were like that when
> I was an undergraduate. Now that I'm teaching,
> I'm having to learn to tolerate normal students.

Why is noninvolvement the norm among students and
even new faculty, those formerly excellent students? It may be
that the root of passivity is largely a matter of task representation. Most new faculty may not know how to arrange the
tasks facing them in ways that permit them to engage in a
wide and rewarding range of activities.

How, then can we encourage it? One means, obvious as
it sounds, may be to simply point out the importance of
involvement to new faculty. I know of only a few orientations
or workshops for new faculty that make this point explicitly.
This tradition is, as Sternberg and his colleagues might point
out, an example of keeping vital knowledge tacit (Sternberg
et al., 1990). Another strategy comes from studies of writing
productivity where involvement is facilitated with contracts.
When new faculty contract to work regularly at writing during busy daily schedules, they in effect arrange for a new task
representation: they agree to transfer writing from its peripheral status (as something to be done only when everything
else is under control) to a status of everyday awareness and
involvement. Accordingly, they set out to manage writing in
brief daily sessions instead of waiting for binges. The effectiveness of such contracts relies on social pressures (say, meeting with a colleague for regular writing times) and on the
regimen of contingency management (for instance, making a
more desirable activity, such as newspaper reading, contingent

on first completing a set amount of writing). Once under way, contracts usually work with documentable success (Chapter Seven).

Again, this transformation may not be as easy as it sounds. Even when they are shown evidence of the success that this regularized involvement in writing brings to colleagues, new faculty members are rarely eager to abandon their familiar misrepresentation of the task. Unproductive (that is, uninvolved) new faculty members suppose that good writing demands a number of preestablished conditions, including motivation, a clever idea and clear plan, and a big block of undisrupted time. They fail to recognize, in my experience with them, the importance of seeing that writing depends on learning from experience, on the momentum of already being involved, and on social responsiveness to "ideas in the air." And all too often, they mistakenly believe that involvement in academic careers may exclude them from involvement in the sense of social attachments.

What, in the final analysis, keeps new faculty from taking this leap? The usual hindrance is the same one that keeps support programs in general from succeeding—noninvolvement and failure to master the subsequent IRSS factors. One effective way of ensuring that new faculty get involved and receive regular coaching on skills such as self-management and social networking is to initiate another familiar activity, cataloguing.

Cataloguing

We have seen some of the rationales for cataloguing in the chapters on mentoring (Chapter Five) and self-help (Chapter Eight). Briefly, it consists of having new faculty summarize what they have done as teachers, colleagues, and researchers and writers, what they are doing, and what they plan for the next several years. Nowhere, in my experience, is cataloguing more likely to be considered than when dealing with new faculty and tenure.

Links to Growth Contracting. Cataloguing has roots in growth contracting. The idea of growth contracts is immediately attractive: faculty are coached to plan individualized contracts (Gaff & Wilson, 1971) that include a profile of strengths and weaknesses, a scheme for addressing weaknesses, and a means of assessing progress, including an advisory committee. One such example (Carlberg, 1981) was based around competitive grants to faculty who met prepared reports to meet these guidelines:

1. *Self-assessment:* Carlberg directed his colleagues to assess their strengths and current interests as well as their weaknesses and dislikes. Specifically, he asked them to indicate shortcomings directly related to current institutional responsibilities (for example, an inability to teach discussion-based classes).
2. *Statement of current roles:* Next, faculty contracting for growth listed institutional responsibilities, such as specific teaching duties, and other responsibilities, such as family time commitments.
3. *Long-range projections:* Applicants wrote a statement projecting the roles and responsibilities that they hoped to fill for the next two to five years.
4. *Synthesis:* Next, contractors assessed the compatibility of their self-judged strengths and weaknesses in regard to current responsibilities and outlined their plans for change.
5. *Profile:* Then, with the self-evaluations in hand, applicants asked their deans for feedback, advice about redefining their plans, and support for their developmental efforts.
6. *First draft of the annual development plan:* Applicants were directed to write out specific goals for strengths and weaknesses, plans for meeting the goals, and the evidence that would document attainment of goals.
7. *Sharing the plan with an advisory committee:* The seventh step in this classic format for growth contracting deals with evaluation. Carlberg had advisory committees approve the plans and later assess faculty members' progress

in their growth contracts. I quote his caution: "The advisory committee is likewise encouraged to proceed on the assumption that an honest and thorough assessment is in the best interest of the participant's development" (p. 71).

In spite of the persistence of reports of campus efforts at growth contracting, few such programs have survived. One reason for the poor survival record of contracting programs may be that they relied entirely on ready volunteers. The actual numbers of faculty members who sustained participation may not have been enough to lend credibility to contracting programs. A second reason is that most contracting schemes called for faculty to assess their own weaknesses and then for advisory committees to grade progress. Because nothing substantial (such as tenure decisions made by the advisory committee) was at stake, nothing much may have happened. And because they are often unaware of their most basic problems in working effectively, new faculty members may not have suggested the most helpful plans for change in the first place. Bennett (1983), a pioneer in the study of effective department chairing, lists some of the steps necessary to make contracting effective. The key, in Bennett's view, lies in seeing evaluation as a constant part of academic work, one that is best made explicit and planned for when expectations and assessments of progress are regularly communicated to faculty members. One is that, given the advantage of specific directives and feedback, the faculty members perform better. Another advantage is that evaluations can be conducted with a minimum of discord, for both the evaluator and the person evaluated (Bennett & Chafer, 1984).

Roots of Cataloguing. Bennett's guidelines for continuous evaluations form the first root of cataloguing. Done well, cataloguing includes constant planning, revision, and feedback. Done frequently and supportively, cataloguing loses most of the usual unpleasantness associated with evaluations. One reason for the diminution of evaluation anxiety is the habituation that repeated exposure bring. Another is the sharing of responsibility for setting and evaluating goals; with consensus about what is expected and what will indicate change, neither evaluator nor the person being evaluated is surprised. The final reason for the lessening of anxiety harkens back to something we considered in earlier chapters, procrastination. Procrastination thrives on lack of planning and on infrequent performance checks; even while the procrastinator puts off goal-directed activities, he or she builds anxiety and resentment that may be directed to the evaluation that eventually points out failures to act in timely fashion.

The second root of effective cataloguing is the extension of planfulness to a broad-based set of plans with guidance that amounts to coaching. When new faculty prepare their first catalogues (often beginning with scholarly writing), two initial considerations are critical. First, new faculty need to see models of an ideal catalogue (we will see some examples of catalogues in Chapter Eleven); without this, they tend to wordy and obtuse products. Second, they need preliminary feedback from a relatively nonjudgmental colleague on the first draft of the catalogue. New faculty often prove to be surprisingly unaware of cultural subtleties of their departments and campuses. They may not, for example, know what kinds of writing count toward tenure, which outlets for writing are acceptable (often certain scholarly journals only), or the direction in emphasis that the department would prefer them to take.

But effective coaching goes beyond advice about cultural norms. It also proves essential in getting new faculty past their usual passivity (at least in the public arena) in responding to collegial evaluations (Braskamp et al., 1984). While new faculty initially disagree with the collegial feedback that they get about the quantity, quality, and direction of catalogued accomplishments and plans, they complain only until they are involved in solving the right problems. Sometimes, incidentally, the "right" problems are agreed on after the cataloguer and his or her committee agree to a compromise; the goal of cataloguing is not unthinking compliance. The stage for compromise is set when problems such as misunderstandings arise. For example, evaluators may misread the message of a planned paper and assume that it is disconnected from the stated plan of research and scholarship, or an evaluator may suppose that a coauthored manuscript will not count toward tenure while the graduate training of the person being evaluated emphasized collaborative projects with two or three coauthors.

To help ensure the effectiveness of these communications and compromises, campus practitioners of faculty development must be involved, at least as coaches for the evaluators of catalogues. My experience indicates that coaches' roles should be to encourage catalogue evaluators to help compose a temperate written response to be communicated to the new faculty member; to remind committees about scheduling a follow-up conference; and to give evaluating committees feedback about how their communications and adjustments compare to those of other cataloguing groups.

The third root of cataloguing is also new to general practice in faculty development, career counseling, and planning. In their landmark call for improving the lot of faculty, Bowen and Schuster (1986) recommend faculty career counseling as a central step in retaining the best and brightest hires. Wheeler (1990), a long-time practitioner of career counseling for colleagues, provides schemes for doing it. Because career counseling works on a one-to-one basis, it addresses vital issues such as help with socialization to a profession and campus, with establishing collegial relationships, with coping with work overloads, and, of course, with formulating realistic plans.

The extension of career planning to cataloguing comes naturally. Once faculty are involved in making long-term plans, they address things usually left ambiguous. Cataloguing turns out to be an occasion for doing much more than finding out how much is enough for tenure; it is also an occasion for considering timely changes and clarifications.

Evaluations of Cataloguing. Cataloguing has proved effective in helping faculty achieve a variety of specific goals, including increases in productivity, reengagement in the collegial management of a department, and establishment of rapport and acceptance with students (Boice, 1986b, 1987a). The biggest improvements for cataloguers, compared to peers who did not catalogue, came in ratings of comfort, trust, and campus identification. This typical comment from a cataloguer reinforces the point:

> At first, I didn't like it. I valued my privacy. I wanted the freedom to change my plans (although it turned out that I didn't sacrifice that), and I wanted to make it entirely on my own, without any help. My dream was to work in relative obscurity for a few years and then to suddenly submit a package containing all my marvelous accomplishments. Of course, by the time I got into cataloguing, I was getting nowhere with that dream. Once I got involved, the relief in the pressures I felt, in the uncertainties of what I should be doing, and in how I would actually be judged was enormous. When I knew what I should do, when I had improved my plans to make them more realistic and compatible, and when I knew pretty much exactly what I needed for tenure, I was able to start doing a much better job at almost everything, including teaching. I am a great fan of cataloguing; I am going to recommend it to other new faculty.

Resistance to Contracting and Cataloguing. If cataloguing works, what would prevent its widespread adoption? We can, for starters, revive the reasons generated earlier in the book for other new approaches: inertia, lack of time, encroachment on academic freedom, and so on. But, in fact, none of these reasons has proved significant in practice. The time demands are really not excessive; cataloguing takes much less time than, say, traditional mentoring of the sort described in Chapter Five. And while participation has been kept voluntary, even reluctant new faculty members are quick to see the advantages of ongoing evaluations that provide no surprises in formal decisions.

The real obstacle to cataloguing is posed by the evaluators themselves and is remarkably powerful. Consider this comment from a new faculty members who had just realized, without prompting, why his department would remain ambivalent about cataloguing as an ongoing evaluation leading to renewal and tenure decisions:

> Oh, I see the problem. If everything is out in the open, if everyone has agreed to precisely what I have to do, there is no freedom of choice left. You see, if I do what I am supposed to do, if I meet my plans for coteaching the course with cooperative learning, for example, and if I stick to the schedule for getting things written and published, then the decision about tenure is preset. That means that the chairman and the R/P/T committee will have almost no power when the decision, the formal decision, is made. It's fascinating, don't you see; if they decide they don't like me, or whatever, they will have little or no power to put subjective components into the equation. My chairman won't go for that.

A related and more justifiable reservation is routinely posed by the evaluators. They worry about contracting becoming too concrete. In the first kind of problem usually anticipated, a new faculty member might plan, say, three articles in a particular journal, but the result could be less than intended by the evaluators—the three articles that get published could be brief coauthored reports to which the contract signer has contributed little. When they elaborate on the ways by which cataloguers can cheat departments by means of technicalities, senior faculty and chairs also suppose that having set a weak precedent, they will have to let other new faculty get by with similar transgressions.

But there is a simple answer, one built into the regular communications of cataloguing. Initial and ongoing specifications can be revised and detailed to clarify expectations, including the type of article (or the kind of student performance) that will be satisfactory. And to ensure that new faculty do not get to the tenure decision before learning that their articles are too brief or their teaching innovations are ineffective, cataloguing committees can give cataloguers timely feedback about the acceptability of activities.

The second premonition of trouble is less easily resolved. An example of this hindrance that stands out in my own notes of coaching cataloguing groups is typified here in the concerns of a chairperson heading an evaluation team:

> All right, suppose that after being clearly on track, after doing all the things we agreed he would do, he comes up on a charge of sexual harassment—a student comes in to me the week before the tenure vote with strong evidence that gets corroborated. Then what happens? With cataloguing we could be stuck.

Part of the answer, of course, could lie in specifying the conditions under which tenure will not be granted; there is no harm in using the contract to remind new faculty that moral turpitude and related misbehaviors are generally conditions for terminating employment. And part of the answer can be found in the coverage of contracting in the chapter on self-help (Chapter Eight). Cataloguing is intended to promote communication about expectations, about needed changes in expectations and in plans, and about progress that meets expectations unambiguously. It does not work, in my experience, if the communication takes on legalistic tones, with written documents exchanged and filed as binding. Instead, the comments from the evaluators work best if they are generally unwritten. Verbal comments directed to the new faculty member indicate a general sense of progress without making ironclad guarantees. The point of cataloguing, after all, is to provide improved communications, not to provide promises.

In the end, of course, evaluators could easily break the spirit of the cataloguing plan. But in my experience with more than forty cases, no complaints of this sort have been lodged. When cataloguing is carried out over several years, the ongoing contacts between evaluators and new faculty create an atmosphere of trust and even support. As a rule, while they maintain their stance of enforcers of the agreements that emerge from cataloguing, evaluators become advocates of the people they are evaluating and hope to see them meet their goals. The bottom line is this: new faculty have to enter into cataloguing with a modicum of trust in their colleagues. Cataloguing depends, in part, on the same results-first approach advocated throughout this book. It also depends on precedent; as new faculty and their evaluators learn of already successful cataloguing exercises, they may feel more confident about trying it. Finally, when it comes down to a willingness to improve the processes of retention and tenure, administrators may have to admit that things will work more smoothly without the subjective judgments and the surprise decisions. Who said that to get control, we must first give it up?

Cataloguing, then, with its tendency to arouse concerns about evaluation, presages what usually does not happen until later in the experience of new faculty—the actual tenuring decision. Because it makes the tenure review a more gradual, more reflective process, cataloguing renders the whole evaluation of new faculty easier.

Tenure

In considering the tenuring process, we have access to a lot more information than is available on retention. The literature on faculty evaluation is extensive; and, after all, the matter of tenure review is a matter of evaluation. There are, for example, continuously updated reviews of how liberal arts colleges evaluate faculty (for example, Seldin, 1984).

Such polls suggest that faculty evaluation is being done ever more widely and systematically. With experience, we are growing better informed about how best to conduct faculty evaluations.

Model Programs

One of the pioneering efforts at modeling a successful evaluation program for faculty was Grasha's (1977) list of essential principles and details. He offered rules including reminders that there is no perfect evaluation system, evaluations should be broadly based on several indices, evaluations must be linked to the reward structure of the organization, assessments must allow for individual differences and personal qualities, and evaluations should emphasize a developmental focus while avoiding quantification.

While Grasha's rules still constitute sound advice about evaluating faculty, a variety of other valuable points have been made by other practitioners. Braskamp's (1980) inventory of necessary considerations is one of the best:

1. Begin by recognizing the inherent paradox in evaluating faculty; that is, while faculty cannot stand to feel that they are constantly under scrutiny, they need some feedback about their goals and progress made toward them in order to achieve excellence.
2. Evaluations should serve both formative (developmental) and summative (administrative and judgmental) purposes.
3. Evaluations must be fair (reliable, valid, and bias-free) if they are to be taken seriously.
4. Evaluations must be useful to intended audiences (recall the instance from Chapter Two of a campus whose committees had carefully redesigned a student evaluation of teaching only to fail to notice that few faculty members got the results).
5. If their performance is to improve, faculty must become better self-evaluators, analysts of what works and what

doesn't, and problem solvers (as in what Cross & Angelo, 1988, later called classroom research).

Inherent Problems in Evaluating Faculty. Practitioners involved in evaluating faculty recognize a host of difficulties, but they are not alone. Rice (1985) concludes that evaluations are done badly almost everywhere. He starts with the small solace that fewer than 10 percent of American organizations have good evaluation systems. Personnel experts are understandably dissatisfied with the usual procedures of performance review, evaluation, appraisal, and ratings.

Why are evaluations as a rule done badly, in and out of academe? Rice supposes that one source of the problem is a lack of agreement about the purpose of evaluations (for example, should they be just formative or summative?). Another problem owes to widespread perceptions of evaluations as subject to personalities, to the vagueness of qualities being rated, and to irrelevant criteria. When faculty or others under evaluation see evaluations as unfair, they react to them defensively. Rice's solutions, based on an extensive inquiry into the best evaluation programs, are refreshingly simple. He advises keeping the number of items for evaluation to five to nine categories and placing the most importance on ratings of performance at the extremes (that is, exceptionally good or poor); ratings in the middle of distributions contain little information value. His final bit of advice may be the most important. To guard against "false memories" at evaluation times, evaluators should refer to the thorough documentation already collected. The temptation, even where such data exist, is to base evaluations on what comes to mind immediately.

One of the most interesting articles about the pitfalls of assessing faculty deals with the legal implications of evaluations that may eventually find their way into court. Sacken (1990) concludes, first of all, that most of faculty's activities are inherently difficult to assess. Teaching, in particular, is a diffuse enterprise, often with unspecified outcomes or with results (say, critical thinking) that are hard to measure. There is, at least for legal purposes, no validated hierarchy of teaching skills, no history of equating teaching to learning, and, in Sacken's view of how the legal system sees us, no credible reason to believe that instruction will improve. The result, when campuses dismiss faculty for reasons of inadequate teaching, is that faculty are at a loss to counter the vague arguments of their campuses that casual evaluations (usually restricted to student ratings) suffice to prove their incompetence. So it is that Sacken makes the following argument: if better informed, faculty themselves could be the agents of improving their evaluations (and the chances of more objective treatment). Among the things needed to make evaluations fairer are more multiple and global measures of faculty performance and clearer links between performance and rewards and consequences.

Dimensions of Evaluating. The greatest consensus about improving evaluations of faculty is for the necessity of multiple measures. But if we venture beyond the familiar grounds of student evaluations, where do we go next? An exemplar for making sense of the dimensions that ideally make up a checklist is Menges and Brinko's (1990) model for planning and assessing faculty progress. One dimension is organizational (for example, including considerations about the department, college, community, and profession); the second is temporal (that is, stage of career, such as probationary); and the third depicts faculty roles (instructional, scholarly-creative, service, personal). In all these dimensions and categories, development can be planned and progress can be assessed. Ideally, the two efforts of planning and of assessment work in concert.

In Menges and Brinko's scheme, the resulting checklist is overseen by a committee that would match institutional and faculty activities within each role, make sure that support exists for the roles considered important, and ascertain whether any subgroups of faculty (including minorities) have special needs that are not being met by the program for planning and assessment. What this design adds to approaches such as cataloguing is an attractive and useful visualization of the whole scope of areas that demand evaluation and assessment.

A Final Caution About Evaluations. For all this accumula-
tion of wisdom about how to improve faculty evaluations,
one void remains. Perhaps because experts have not queried
new faculty at length about their reactions to evaluations,
they may not recognize the problem caused by the usual lack
of reassurance and praise in the renewal and tenuring process.
Hints about how to counter this problem come from outside
the literature on evaluation.

Social psychologists offer an interesting reminder about
the difference between constructive and destructive criticism
(see Baron, 1988). Destructive criticism is neither precise nor
considerate; it tends to attribute failures to causes lying within
the person being criticized. This pattern resembles the perception of feedback received by new faculty in studies
reviewed earlier. The parallel extends to what social psychologists find comes in the wake of destructive criticism: an
increase in anger, tension, resistance, avoidance, and conflict.
Curiously, destructive criticism works to elicit these negative
responses more powerfully than even jurisdictional disputes
or competition.

Thus, whatever else, evaluations of new faculty must
be based in constructive criticism. An impressive plan for
combining the role of evaluator and coach comes from a composition teacher struggling with the conflicts between teaching and grading (Elbow, 1983). It is, Elbow supposes, this
conflict in roles for teachers—being an ally as they teach and
an adversary as they grade—that forces many of our colleagues into maladaptive stances. Some end up as "hard"
teachers whose loyalty to knowledge wins out. Some become
"soft" by directing their loyalty to students alone. And some
develop into "middling" teachers who tolerate the tension or
detachment of being "sort of" loyal both to standards and to
pleasing students. Elbow (1983, pp. 335-336) advocates an
alternative to the three usual positions, one that embraces
both the hard and soft stances alternately:

> My present oppositional theory tells me I should
> exaggerate . . . my gatekeeper functions rather

than run away from them. The more I try to soft-
pedal assessment, the more mysterious it will
seem to students and the more likely they will be
preoccupied and superstitious about it. The more
I can make it clear to myself and to my students
that I do have a commitment to knowledge and
institutions, and the more I can make it specifically clear how I am going to fulfill that commitment, the easier it is for me to turn around
and make a dialectical change of role into being
an extreme ally to students. . . . That is, I feel
better about being really tough if I know I am
going to turn and be on the student's side more
than usual. And, contrarily, I do not have to hold
back from being an ally of students when I know
I have set really high standards.

Elbow's insight is not, of course, limited to the students
with whom we must play the dual roles of developer and
evaluator. What he says about students applies to new faculty
as well. Where we separate our roles, we can begin with and
persist in high standards and expectations in one role; as we
set clear expectations and establish ongoing feedback, we can
communicate our other role, that of an ally who will help
coach new faculty to their best performance. As coaches, to
use another of Elbow's ideas, we can move to a stance where
we can point out what is being done well and where *we* must
work harder to achieve success. So, in the end, what may
matter most in evaluating faculty is not so much the mechanics as the stance; we may accomplish more by simply
separating, strengthening, and alternating the two roles that
ordinarily conflict.

One other thing fascinates me about Elbow's oppositional theory: it is tacit knowledge. It is information that
operates at a more fundamental level than the mechanics usually emphasized in the literature on evaluating faculty. Indeed,
the most important thing that Elbow's method accomplishes
is comfort in handling the two usually contrary roles. Where

do Elbow's points about balance and the other rules about making evaluation a fair, broad-based, and useful practice leave us? In my view, the method that best addresses the cautions we have reviewed is cataloguing. We return to cataloguing for one last time in this section on tenuring with a final look at its advantages and possible problems.

Cataloguing Revisited

As we reconsider some of the advantages of centering tenure decisions around a process such as cataloguing—one that begins early, sets clear and high standards, and evaluates frequently and supportively—we are reminded of four related things. First, by clarifying what it is that we want faculty to know and do, we can figure out what it is that we must provide in the way of support programs to help them meet those goals. Second, by separating our roles of developer and evaluator (and by inducing new faculty to take on some of this role by learning to be effective self-evaluators), we make the process of tenuring less aversive and more constructive. Third, by setting high standards at the outset, we can make teaching an activity to be taken more seriously (Boice, 1990b). Fourth, as we practice the simple and direct methods of cataloguing, we might even manage to coach and evaluate new faculty in that most difficult of dimensions, ascriptive (subjective and personal) traits. That is, hiring and tenuring are indeed affected by qualities such as style and manner, whether we like to admit it or not (Exum, 1983; Daniels, 1979; Lewis, 1975; Smelser & Content, 1980).

Cataloguing offers an opportunity to address what Elbow calls the slippery factors of evaluation. We could recognize the inappropriateness of counting ascriptive factors toward tenure at all. Or we could decide that personal qualities are essential to collegiality, to effective teaching, and to scholarly success and that we are going to specify the relevant expectations and support. We might, at the least, encourage the establishment of mentoring relationships with mentors who can model and teach the usually tacit knowledge called social skills.

As we bring more openness and support to the tenuring process, some other desirable results should follow. One is the perception of tenuring as a system of evaluations and support that properly begins during recruitment and continues through orientation and retention. The second is that we will see more specific needs for supporting new faculty; faculty development based on little more than instructional improvement may become a thing of the past. The third is that the prospect of surviving in academe may seem less mysterious and more manageable. New hires from underrepresented groups should be the particular beneficiaries of improved evaluations (see Chapter Eleven); at present, they see academe as an exclusionary culture that works to discourage them with unwritten and subjective rules (Boice, 1991e).

What, finally, will work against improving faculty evaluations? We have already seen some of the reasons why faculty and administrators resist thoroughgoing evaluations: the possible violation of academic freedom, the difficulty of specifying adequate performance, the interpersonal strains of being both colleagues and evaluators or those evaluated, and the time demanded. But where evaluations can be conducted more gradually so as to foster clear communication, to include support such as coaching, to involve faculty in ongoing involvement as planners and self-assessors, and to identify the essential components of effective faculty performance, usual reservations may be supplanted. Instead of seeing tenuring as typically competitive and rejecting, we may realize its potential for supportive and collegial interaction.

 ELEVEN

Tailoring Programs
to Special Needs

The problems of recruiting and retaining new hires who thrive in academe, discussed in preceding chapters, are magnified and clarified by the most difficult cases. This chapter focuses on the needs of special populations of new faculty. It depicts the special problems faced by minorities, women, and other marginal groups, including adjunct faculty and librarians new to campus.

The literature on minorities and women in academe reminds us of the magnitude of their special problems, of a tragedy in the making. Consider some preliminary examples. The representation of Afro-Americans as students and as faculty is actually dropping on our campuses; blacks make up less than 4 percent of our faculty (National Center for Education Statistics, 1989). Minority and women faculty members characterize their experiences with words such as *hardship* and *victimization* (Exum, 1983; Simeone, 1986) and express disbelief when confronted with the claims of higher administrators that campuses are doing everything they can to locate and nurture minorities and women (Bowen & Schuster, 1986) and that discrimination is a thing of the past (Payne, 1989).

My own firsthand looks at the experiences of underrepresented and marginal new faculty have been just as sobering. This example of a new Ph.D. with joint appointments expands on the usual finding of isolation among white males as new hires:

> It isn't that I'm lonely. That could be a result of my own making. Sometimes scholars like to be alone. It's more a matter of disinterest and disapproval from my colleagues. I'm surrounded by snobs. They rarely talk to me without mentioning that they are from Harvard or wherever. They routinely complain about the blue-collar, unsophisticated students they have to teach here. I find myself thinking, "What about me? You could just as well be describing me." I wonder if, as they demean the students, they are intentionally putting me down. What hurts the most, though, are hints that I am here only by the grace of affirmative action. Or maybe what hurts as much are the subtle rejections. Slights. They turn and walk away, in mid-sentence, as I'm being introduced or as I'm making a point. I don't feel that I am taken seriously by [my] department.

Another example, from a woman faculty member new to a humanities department, enlarges the point about feelings of exclusion and nonsupport:

> The chairman and his cronies are the ultimate old-boy club. They meet and play poker and smoke cigars and make decisions about how the department is run. When I am with them at departmental functions like parties, they rarely miss a chance to make sexist remarks around me. They joke about where my husband is and the probabilities that he is being unfaithful to me. They make sly comments about how attractive I am. But when they discuss research and professional things, they exclude me. They make me feel like a child. And yet they had no reserva-

tions about sticking me with a large introductory class. I am unappreciated, overworked, and out of place.

The third example comes from a new hire in the library, a member of a group of faculty usually neglected in support efforts:

Do I feel welcome on campus? That's a laugh. The faculty treat me as an inferior; they even expect me to call them doctor as they address me by my first name. They expect me to drop everything to make a presentation to their classes. The fact that I have so-called faculty status is a joke.

To some extent, the accounts of special groups of new faculty sound like those in Chapters Two through Four. Feelings of isolation dominate the experience of new faculty. But most new faculty do not report having suffered the condescension of racist, sexist, and careerist remarks. They do not have to face the added problem of colleagues who doubt their credentials and their worth. When these pressures are appended to an already difficult load of adjusting to campus, the result can be intolerable.

Special Populations of New Faculty

What lies ahead for those of us who take the problem of special populations to heart and to action? The famous Kerner Commission provides a reminder: as education and opportunities increase, so will unrest, protest, and progress (Kerner, 1968). Even if we accept the prospects of disruption and of extra expense, what will be likely to keep us from effecting real change? One obstacle may be our academic values; we may need to suspend our usual and cherished dispassion as scholars to make decisions guided by emotion (Gordon & Meroe, 1991). Another may be that we have not tried hard enough to assume the perspective of the new faculty who comes from an underrepresented and underappreciated background. Those of us who have prospered as academics may need to begin by resolving to listen to complaints about a revered old institution.

Afro-American Faculty

We have already seen indications of isolation and rejection. When we ask the victims to reflect on that experience, they may refer to earlier events, often graduate school. Feelings of anger about academic careers often begin before the doctorate. The discriminations are subtle and painful; over time, they make their recipients feel crazy (Winkler, 1988). While still in graduate school, as in their later professorial experiences, Afro-Americans often feel pressured to give up their racial and ethnic identities. There, as later, they are discouraged from studying their own cultures and problems as colleagues express doubts about whether such research is "real." And there, blacks often miss the role models and social support that seem readily available for white males.

Moreover, blacks come to a new campus disadvantaged in other ways. They may not have had substantial mentoring as graduate students (Blackwell, 1989). They are likely to have been trained in the least prestigious universities (Finkelstein, 1984). Once on campus in a professorial role, though, blacks often discover that discrimination intensifies in both overt (Moore, 1988) and covert (McKay, 1983) ways. In addition to carrying at least a normal load of expectations for productive scholarship, often with minimal collegial support, they are expected to welcome a host of extra roles—as consolers, advisers, and advocates for students and as participants in radical groups (Banks, 1984; Suinn & Witt, 1982).

Further, as new professors, blacks are reminded again and again of the dominant culture in academe to which they are expected to become socialized. Beckham (1988, p. 77) described it as "an ingrained Eurocentric haughtiness that describes the curricula of American Higher Education." Traditionally, the professoriate has been anything but diverse;

professors come from the upper strata of society, socialize mostly with colleagues, and consume high culture with a flair. However, as many as three out of five black faculty members come from below-average economic backgrounds, where intellectual and cultural values may have not prepared them for academic careers (Finkelstein, 1984). Once in professorial roles, black faculty may be counseled to stop complaining and to bury themselves in their work (Banks, 1984). When they demur, they are reminded about the value of being liked, of getting along by going along (Exum, Menges, Watkins, & Berglund, 1984).

For all those discouragements, the most undermining kinds of discrimination entail concerns about one's credentials and competence, especially when hired in an affirmative action program: "Once the powerful white male establishment had linked affirmative action to a lowering of standards, any and all women and minorities entering academia faced a dilemma. No matter how exemplary the training and credentials of individual women and minority faculty members, they were always vulnerable to insinuations that merit was not always the main factor in their appointment" (Banks, 1984, p. 333). Not everyone has the sense of worth and social support, Banks notes, to enable them to react as Painter (1981, p. 22) did to the accusation of an unemployed white male Ph.D. that she got her job only because she was black and a woman:

> I never questioned the justice of my position. I should have a job, and a good one. I had worked hard as a graduate student and had written a decent dissertation. I knew foreign languages, had traveled widely, and had taught and published. I thought I had been hired because I was a promising young historian. Unlike the man beside me, I didn't think my teaching at a first-rate university required an extraordinary explanation.

Reasons for Exclusion. The scholarly inquiries into causes of the persistent underrepresentation and mistreatment of blacks are useful and far-reaching. We can use them as a foundation for understanding the problems of other marginal groups of new faculty. Exum (1983) is exemplary in explaining the plight of blacks in academe. Instead of resorting to emotional, moralistic, or legalistic reasoning, he opts for economic explanations as the only ones that matter. His assumption is that the problem is one of supply and demand—that both are low and, apparently, bound to remain that way for some time.

The supply of blacks for professorial slots is diminishing (see also Bowen & Schuster, 1986); the few doctorates taken by blacks are mostly in education and the social sciences. Blacks who want and who are selected for professorial positions occupy the lowest ranks and receive the lowest salaries, usually at the least prestigious campuses. The demand, despite the claims by campuses of extraordinary efforts to recruit, is constrained by actual practices. Recruits report subtle discouragements during interviews; once hired, they report a dearth of support, including role models. By simply not trying hard, campuses can undermine the recruiting and retention of minority faculty.

Exum uses an organizational theory to offer a compelling reason why campuses may maintain this stance. Etzioni (1976) distinguishes campuses on the basis of their nearly unique goal; unlike other organizations, colleges and universities aim for cultural, not economic, ends. Because we typically rely on agreement instead of financial gain, we try to use normative consensus, not coercion, to achieve cooperation. And so it is that campuses are slow to change, inclined instead to rely on tradition. Exum uses Etzioni's ideas to explain why affirmative action offends most campuses. First, because they rely on normative consensus, campuses see themselves as deliberate and fair; affirmative action questions that assumption. Second, because of their goals of cultural improvement, campuses act as gatekeepers of quality, status, and privilege. As such, they resist interference from outside agencies that do not share their interest in limiting access to professorial life. Thus, the traditional ideologies of merit and autonomy provide a legitimate, seemingly nonracist reason for resisting affirmative action programs.

Exum then uses examples from the most thoroughgoing affirmative action programs to corroborate his point. Even after setting up elaborate procedures for identifying and recruiting minority faculty, campuses still make hires in the conventional way, on the basis of contacts with applicants' sponsors. Exum's closing points follow from the quandary just seen, where minorities are hired in the same old ways, with or without affirmative action. In the final analysis, sponsors count. And so do ascriptive traits, the personal qualities of style and manner, of conforming behavior, that affect perceptions of the likability and desirability of candidates as colleagues (Daniels, 1979; Lewis, 1975; Smelser & Content, 1980). Because these mechanisms of sponsorship and personality are kept subjective and behind the scenes, practices of hiring minorities and other nontraditional groups remain capricious.

Exum and his colleagues extended this analysis with an interview-based examination of the academic labor market as a specific obstacle to equal opportunity hiring (Exum et al., 1984). The logic of their analysis goes like this: The major currency of the academic marketplace is prestige. This, combined with perpetual pressures to save that lesser kind of currency, money, leads to four problematic practices. The first is the preference for internal hiring. Hiring someone already on campus saves money, time, and risk of mistakes. The internal hire is already known and proven; expenses of searching and training are reduced. Affirmative action, in contrast, demands expanded searches, more elaborate grievance procedures (especially for minority and women applicants who are denied jobs or retention and promotion), and greater investments of time and energy by faculty and administrators.

The second problem of traditional academic markets is its ambiguity in describing and advertising professorial openings. Job advertisements in academe are masterpieces of unclarity; as a rule, they emphasize competencies desired but say little about the actual behaviors necessary. And position openings are poorly communicated. Most academics are ignorant of formal job advertisements and usually obtain jobs by way of sponsors and informal networks.

The third difficulty follows from the second. Expectations about positions remain ambiguous even after hiring. Once on campus, new faculty receive only vague cues about what they should be doing. Some make frantic efforts to mimic the actions of visible colleagues. Some, especially minorities and women, discover what they should have been doing after the fact, during the performance reviews and tenure evaluations that come too late for remedy. Moreover, the least tangible factors, of being liked, of being seen as a team player, may be least apparent to minorities and women operating on the periphery.

The fourth problem with the academic market is that it encourages ineffective evaluations. Exum and his colleagues recount the kinds of information most typically used by minorities for self-assessments of their progress as professors. They rely, for one thing, on personal standards. These are attractive in a culture that values autonomy, but they are dangerous because of their privacy and subjectiveness. Another vital source of information for minorities is the institutional assessment that is included in informal reviews. Because formal evaluations are infrequent and delayed, new faculty supplement them with informal comments from students and colleagues (often misleading). The final kind of information source is the most interesting and problematic. Because they are not well known on campus and because their research and scholarship focus may be on nontraditional subjects, minority faculty rely heavily on outside evaluations. This extraordinary reliance signals shortcomings:

> The fact that our informants placed such great emphasis on external sources of evaluation suggests another dimension of the ignorance problem noted earlier: These faculty not only have a hard time learning and knowing what to do,

> but even after hiring they may not be known
> very well by the university. This emphasis also
> suggests that the university has to some degree
> abdicated oversight of employee performance to
> what one respondent described as the "invisible
> college" of the profession. Again, reliance on
> influence networks helps solve an ignorance
> problem, though in ways that may or may not
> benefit women and minorities [Exum et al.,
> 1984, p. 315].

Other scholars add useful insights about what keeps
affirmative action from working more efficiently. Epps (1989)
makes the point of many writers most simply: success at educating, recruiting, and promoting minority faculty is not
valued on campuses; this sort of achievement carries no status
in academic cultures that deal in prestige. Collett (1990)
makes a related point, to which we will return in considering
solutions: we may need to change our normative expectations
about minority students. If we are serious about increasing
student (or faculty) diversity, we may have to learn not to
judge people as students and as colleagues quickly and severe-
ly, on the basis of verbal skills, emotional nonreactivity, and
individual competitiveness.

Consider another insight from the rich literature on
student development: Astin (1985) makes an interesting observation about what might discourage disadvantaged students
from liking school or from planning careers as teachers. College teachers come from the most educated families. They
value displays of brilliance (that is, verbal fluency and productivity in research and scholarship) in students and in colleagues. So it is, Astin concludes, that professors value the
demonstration of intellect over the *development* of intellect:
we favor students and colleagues who arrive with the proper
intrinsic motivation, manifest brilliance, and social tone (see
also Tobias, 1990). Stated another way, academe is ideally
suited to perpetuate the social Darwinism discussed in earlier
chapters.

Solutions. The same observers who chronicle the dilemmas in attracting the best new faculty also offer solutions for recruiting and retaining black and other minority faculty. Wheeler and Schuster (1990) propose some common but important solutions, such as reducing the pressures for "relevant" committee work and facilitating peer support groups. Bowen and Schuster (1986) propose a more detailed program: identifying promising minorities as sophomores, awarding them portable fellowships and encouragement to pursue academic careers, and then hoping for the best. Certainly, in the scope of federally funded projects for academe, their scheme is a modest and needed program.

Proposed solutions from minority professors themselves suggest that notions such as Bowen and Schuster's could fail because they do not begin by addressing more basic problems than identifying and supporting prospective professors (Green, 1988). Some solutions we have already seen, such as Exum's (1983) insistence that we must increase the demand as well as the supply. Some, such as Gilkes's (1982), recommend abandoning attempts at fitting into the academic culture; blacks may simply do better to rebelliously identify with community achievements and the approval of kindred colleagues. And some (Epps, 1989; Moore & Johnson, 1989) return to economic arguments: affirmative action may never work until universities reward successes of individuals who recruit and support minority faculty.

When everyone has had their say, it may be that student development practitioners will have the most practical suggestions for faculty development. Collett (1990), again, suggests beginning by reexamining our normative ideas about teaching (and takes a perspective that may strike some readers as given to stereotypes):

1. We may overvalue conformity, discipline, and quick learning; we need to find ways to cope with students who seem unmotivated and disorderly.
2. We may profit in appreciating cultural differences in verbal and nonverbal styles of expression; for example, a

student's manner of speaking may be an invitation for participation by other students, an event that would put him or her more at ease.

3. We may need to reexamine our assumptions that students will base their esteem more on competitive success than on group success and standing within the group.

4. While we value the importance of interaction of students with faculty, we often neglect those interactions, especially with minority students.

I suspect that we can benefit by translating Collett's prescriptions for teaching minority students into supports for new faculty. That is, we may need to caution ourselves against overemphasizing traditional expectations of how new hires must show motivation, nonverbal expression, competition, and collegiality. To do so, we could mimic Collett's method of beginning by observing and then inquiring about the function of the styles that minority and other special groups bring to academe. Just as we expect new hires to demonstrate involvement, we could model the process by getting involved in the cultural experience of nontraditional faculty on our campuses.

I believe that we can also glean useful insights from another group of professionals learning to communicate effectively with minorities: counseling psychologists. Sue (1981) summarizes the actions of a culturally skilled counselor, a list that might just as well apply to practitioners and colleagues supporting new minority faculty:

1. Be aware of your own cultural baggage and values (for example, the values placed on coming from a home with cultured, educated parents).

2. Understand how the dominant culture treats minorities, in overt and in subtle ways.

3. Find comfort with and acceptance of cultural differences (for instance, relative emotional impassivity or expressiveness).

4. Make sure that the client has access to culturally similar support and role models (that is, for all your sensitivity

and good intentions, you may not be able to provide enough).

Cataloguing: A Useful Solution? In my own efforts at arranging supports for Afro-American faculty, I have found the kinds of suggestions listed above helpful. My patient interviews conducted over semesters and years have provided the best opportunities for understanding and help. Still, I have yet to see admonitions for better administrative commitment or more generous financial commitments have lasting effect. While guidelines for recruiting and retaining women and minority faculty may have improved (Green, 1988; Lessow-Hurley, 1989), notably to the point of getting underrepresented candidates to campus and even into tenure-track slots, equal opportunity programs pretty much stop with the opportunity to gain access and to prove one's mettle.

I see the entrenched elitism of campuses as the chief obstacle to treating women and members of minorities as equals who merit the collegial supports traditionally accorded to white males. Campuses take their role as gatekeepers of privilege very seriously; so it is that they value demonstrations of brilliance over development of brilliance. It is elitism, the most insidious kind of social Darwinism, that keeps faculty development programs on the periphery, along with minority faculty.

What works in the face of these daunting barriers? The hint comes from Exum and his colleagues. They see the ambiguity of job descriptions and of job evaluations as the chief means of restraining minorities and women. Each step of the process, of specifying the ideal persons for the position and of identifying acceptable performance of professors, leaves room for subjective and discriminatory practice. Each stage of the traditional mechanism involves ignorance, reliance on influence networks to recruit and to make judgments of performance, and vulnerability for faculty with nontraditional backgrounds.

Help for women and minorities awaits the kind of specification of expectations, feedback mechanisms about progress, compromise about the expectations over time, and support for developing the brilliance and style necessary to success that we have already seen in cataloguing strategies. No groups can benefit more from participation in cataloguing, in my experience, than faculty at risk. Members of minorities and other marginal groups can use it to form an objective, negotiable set of expectations that specify what has to be done and improved. Cataloguing, as we have seen it in preceding chapters, clarifies adaptive actions, ensures collegial feedback and support, and helps identify timely corrections. The faculty who need cataloguing most are those with the least information about what professors should do, with the fewest ready models of success, and with the strongest suspicions about the fairness with which they are being treated.

In this case, though, two things can be added as a matter of course to the cataloguing procedures outlined in previous chapters. First, to help recruit minority and women faculty and to ensure that they understand expectations from the outset, cataloguing (or at least the clear prospect of it) can begin as soon as they are candidates. The prospect of cataloguing can help assuage the fears of minority and women faculty about the demands and support they will receive at a new campus. It can help demonstrate the commitment of a campus to helping its faculty develop and flourish. And it can help ensure that expectations are mutual. Many are the new faculty members who have told me that they would never have come to campus if they had known what was really expected of them. Second, cataloguing must identify the expectations, also in negotiable form, of off-campus reviewers who will evaluate the potential and progress of new faculty from the outset. Panels of evaluators should, then, be arranged in advance and not formed just before tenure reviews, as is traditional practice.

Models and Guidelines for Cataloguing. With any new faculty members, minority or not, we can facilitate cataloguing with examples of exemplary catalogues. And with any group of evaluators, we will fare best by offering examples of feedback, negotiation, and coaching interactions that clearly help new faculty thrive. With experience, these models of excellence come from ongoing instances of the cataloguing process on one's own campus. Until then, I find that campuses can benefit from the brief set of examples and guidelines that follow (to guard the identity of the small numbers of black faculty on my study campuses, I have combined and disguised their comments and written materials).

1. First approximations to catalogues are almost invariably uninformative. Consider this representative attempt to describe plans for future teaching:

> I plan to teach the same courses I am now teaching, probably introductory psychology and the other courses that I have already listed under current teaching. I might, someday soon, like to teach a graduate seminar on my specialty. As for plans to improve my teaching over the long run, I anticipate doing two things: getting a grant to reduce my teaching load and using the extra time to prepare a better set of notes.

Note that, despite instructions to the contrary, little has been said that is specific to growth: setting an overall theme for teaching; finding links between teaching and other academic activities, such as research and collegiality. In my experience with some forty cases of cataloguing carried out for at least a year, something else surprising happens in this first approximation: cataloguing committees typically do not see problems with so brief and uninformative a plan. Academicians are simply not used to making plans explicit and useful, especially plans about teaching and collegiality.

2. Minority faculty initially display special difficulty in specifying plans for building collegial networks. Their first efforts at catalogue descriptions of anticipated interactions are commonly as impoverished as this:

> The plan for collegial networking over the next two years is to stay in touch with my dissertation

adviser. He and I have plans to do several papers together.

Here again, black new faculty and newcomers in general evidence trouble in translating instructions (for example: "Consider specifying colleagues whom you would benefit in knowing, for professional and personal reasons"; "Speak to possibilities of finding a mentor"; "Speculate about contacts you can make, on and off campus, with colleagues pursuing kindred interests in research and teaching"). When I asked new faculty why they provided such terse plans, their responses indicated frustration and uncertainty:

> I'm still not sure what exactly you want. I just can't see into the future. I'll have to wait to see how things develop. For the time being, I don't think I have the time to be visiting and calling a lot of people. What's more, I'm not sure they have time for me.

3. Cataloguing committees need to take quick action in coaching and modeling useful catalogue entries. As a rule, what works best is to briefly and supportively share expectations of progress in teaching, in collegiality, and in research, writing, and creativity at the time when decisions will be made about retention and tenure. Ideally, committees can illustrate their expectations with examples of junior faculty who have recently fared well in evaluations. At a minimum, committees can coax from new faculty members verbal descriptions of plans that will be translated into writing. In the case of plans for teaching, the result of a fifteen-minute interaction typically looks like this:

> I hope to teach introductory psychology only every other year. Doing it every semester may burn me out on big classes. When I do it, I would like to work at restructuring the whole class so that I have a better repertoire of demonstrations,

small-group problem solving, and practice tests. And I want to develop a new class, sometimes offered as a graduate seminar and sometimes as a senior undergraduate class, on my specialty, where I would focus the semester on having the students do research projects and learn the literature. Given my rather disappointing student ratings, especially in introductory psychology, I plan to try to find out what I am doing wrong. Specifically, I have arranged to have Bob Boice visit my class and examine my teaching evaluations as a source of ideas.

In the case of the plan seen above for building collegiality, coaching from a cataloguing committee (often with behind-the-scenes advice from me) would likely help produce this kind of plan:

I have two specific plans. First, I have already agreed to consider my cataloguing group as mentors. I have agreed to have meetings with all three of them for fifteen to twenty minutes every other week for purposes of getting advice and encouragement. Second, I plan to follow up on my committee's contact with a leader in my field who has agreed to talk with me on the phone monthly about manuscripts in progress that I will mail to him.

4. Committees and new faculty members work best in a spirit of understanding, explanation, and compromise. A key to success in cataloguing is the kind of ongoing communication about plans and expectations that produces limited resentment about misunderstandings and no surprises. Consider how a typically brief and annoying comment from a cataloguing committee can evolve in something more useful:

Our first reaction is that you are not devoting enough time to writing and devoting too much

time to talking with every minority student who
comes to your office.

New faculty members' responses to such feedback are usually
made most directly to me, in my temporary role as an
intermediary:

> That doesn't do much for me. They haven't even
> taken the trouble to understand my situation. Do
> they know that I am doing some writing? Do
> they know that the black students are desperate
> for someone to talk to? Where do they expect me
> to find the extra time?

When I coach committees to ask new faculty members
for candid reactions to their feedback, they commonly get similar information. Then, with a bit of coaching to committees
about becoming more informed, encouraging, and specific,
the feedback is easily transformed into a statement like this:

> First of all, we have enjoyed getting to know you.
> We have learned a lot more about you from visit-
> ing your classes and perusing your lecture notes.
> And a look at your manuscripts in progress
> proved reassuring that you are getting under way
> here. Overall, we are pleased with your progress.
> For the moment, though, we would like you to
> consider two changes in your daily routines that
> could help make your beginnings here more pro-
> ductive and enjoyable. One is trying to find brief
> times for writing each day (Bob Boice has volun-
> teered to help coach you on this). The other is
> finding a model who can guide you in ways of
> meeting the needs of minority students without
> undermining your own career. We have got a
> black professor on campus who has experienced
> a similar dilemma to agree to sit in on your office
> hours as an observer and commentor if you want.

Of course, these four basic steps of managing cataloguing, as I see them, can be guided by IRSS theory. In essence, making cataloguing effective is a matter of involvement (for example, immersing oneself in the experience of new faculty), of regimen (meeting regularly, even when too busy or not in the mood), of self-management (solving the right problem, such as helping coach balance between teaching and writing), and social networking (the act of cataloguing itself).

While the strategy for cataloguing for black new faculty operates on basics that should be generalizable to all newcomers, we might wonder how useful the consideration of black faculty will be for other special groups.

Generalizability. The experience of Afro-Americans as new faculty is specific in some ways, particularly in regard to the debilitating effects of racism. But much of the account of black experience in professorial roles, including the causes of exclusion and mistreatment, applies as well to other marginal groups of new faculty. In the brief account of supporting special populations of new hires that follows, the cases of other peripheral groups will be used to expand on the pattern already established.

Other Minority Group Members as New Faculty

What happens to other members of minorities as new faculty that does not happen to blacks? In my own observations, members of other minorities provide the same kinds of distressing reports—of colleagues parading their credentials, their cultured mannerisms, and their disdain for affirmative action. The exception seems to be Asians as new faculty. They are the fastest-growing minority in academe. They no longer qualify for affirmative action on most campuses. But they are nonetheless often made to feel unwelcome, and they add at least two complaints to those we have already seen. One is that when a minority group does achieve success, campuses may move to make certain that they are not overrepresented. Asians have reason to suspect that some campuses exercise biases in admissions policies, much as once happened with Jewish applicants. The second is that Asians get lumped together in naive ways; Hsia (1988) notes that Asians comprise some twenty nations and sixty ethnic groups, with commensurate differences in cultures and needs.

Again, an essential lesson in examining the plight of new faculty with atypical backgrounds is that campuses are notoriously slow to change their conservative and exclusionary policies. We might even expect this phenomenon to extend to campuses where members of minorities are the majority. Smith and Borgstedt (1985), for example, describe the experience of white faculty at predominantly black colleges as follows: (1) Negative stereotyping was a real problem, more so from black colleagues than from black students. The general experience was one of "familiar distance," of colleagues who seemed superficially friendly but who never got close in terms of friendship. (2) White faculty perceived inequality of treatment from administrators.

Women

In some regards, women face seemingly insurmountable odds in the struggle for equality. They continue, as students and as faculty, to suffer discouragements in the verbal and nonverbal behaviors of their male counterparts (Wright, 1985). They are made to feel incompetent, invisible, and unwelcome (Daley, 1991; Simeone, 1986). They are, much like minorities, concentrated in lower ranks, with the lowest salaries. And academe has managed an impressively powerful kind of discrimination by keeping most of its women in sex-typed locations and fields (for example, the arts and humanities). Membership in these marginal groups typically carries disadvantages such as second-class citizenship (Fox, 1985).

Problems of Women Faculty. According to emerging research, women generally evidence more anxiety, stress, loneliness, and recurrent physical illness than do their male colleagues (Thoreson, Kardash, Leuthold, & Morrow, 1990). The optimistic con-

clusion that men and women in the professoriate are getting to
know and respect each other (Bowen & Schuster, 1986) may say
too little about the need for improvement. Overall, the evidence
weighs against the "feminization" of academe (Lomperis, 1990);
more than ever, women are likely to be untenured, off track, and
part-time. And to complete this discouraging picture, women
are perhaps three times as likely as men to get caught in the
academic revolving door (Rausch, Ortiz, Douhitt, & Reed, 1989;
Rothblum, 1988). Their special difficulties in adjusting to campuses include a stronger need for affiliation, approval, and competent colleagues. They are also less likely than men to have been
assigned an official mentor, to have received written guidelines
for tenure, or to have found adequate resources for child care.

What happens when women enter positions traditionally closed to them? One result is expected: they enter as
"solos," as the only women in their departments, and they
adjust with much more difficulty than do their male counterparts. They are, as Laws (1975) puts it, tokens. Tokenism
carries expectations of the token remaining alone and deviant.
The second result is just as troubling. Women who infiltrate
male-dominated departments tend to lower ratings of group
satisfaction, at least in the short run (Crocker & McGraw,
1984). And, as a rule, women who initiate first entries are
more unhappy than are their colleagues, especially at the most
prestigious universities (Finkelstein, 1984). What is it that
women do to discomfit their male colleagues and themselves?
In addition to challenging traditional beliefs about running
departments fairly and objectively, women may bring unset-
tling styles of behaving to staid academe. One fascinating
example is crying in formal situations (Hoover-Dempsey,
Plas, & Wallston, 1986). Males see it as weakness. Women,
who as a rule are not asked for their perception of its function, may see it as a desperate sign of wanting to be heard. A
potential lesson is this: male colleagues may learn that as
women bring their relational and affective emphases to campuses, crying will prove a healthy form of release and communication in an institution traditionally steeped in tension
and politics.

Solutions. Part of the answer to problems of inequality may lie in numbers. Women now account for most of the small growth in hiring of full-time faculty members; they constitute an even larger part of the graduate student population (Bowen & Schuster, 1986). With this slow growth, prospects of mutual social support may improve. Another part of the solution may be seen in the exemplary leads that women have taken in publicizing the traditionally tacit knowledge about succeeding in professorial careers. In Chapter Seven, we saw examples such as Scarr's (1982) landmark manuscript on the secrets of getting published. In areas such as psychology, women (especially those new to academe) are faring as well as their male colleagues in publishing (Boice et al., 1985). Still, women may need some places of their own, even campuses, to thrive (As, 1985).

Part of the solution may already exist. White women, more readily than minorities of either gender, can evidence the cultural and educational backgrounds most valued in academe. They are at least as likely as males to have highly educated parents, to have attended prestigious schools, and to have acquired stylistic qualities such as social tone. But even these seeming advantages do not compensate for the sexism and stigmatization that women continue to experience. They are as likely as blacks to conclude that they are victimized by unclear expectations and subjective evaluations (Finkelstein, 1984). A critical step for ensuring more equitable and encouraging treatment for both groups may, again, lie in processes such as cataloguing and planned mentoring. Along with more objective treatment, another factor may help. Women in academe are taking the lead in educating colleagues to share their perceptions of "chilly climates" in workshops that let whole groups see how racism and sexism affect individuals (Rosser, 1989).

Traditionally Female-Dominated Disciplines

Both female and male faculty in areas of campus traditionally dominated by women face types of discrimination similar to those already reviewed. Despite their traditional obscurity on campus, they too have something to teach us. My own decade of collecting systematic reports from new faculty has produced interesting insights into ghettos of women faculty in departments such as home economics, social work, and nursing. The reaction of these faculty to being excluded from the mainstream of interaction and respect on campus is mixed. To a certain point, they are content to be left alone to do their work. And to some degree, they feel like second-class citizens whose accomplishments go unrecognized. Only rarely do they feel that they belong to the greater enterprise of the campus or that they have been assisted to achieve their potential as professors.

New faculty in particular suffer from this exclusion and its resulting ambivalence. They are, in my experience, far less likely to get the resources available to other new faculty, including small grants and release time. At one campus where I consulted, I investigated reasons why faculty in the humanities (a highly sex-typed area on campus) received by far the fewest in-house grants. A glance at the application folders suggested at least one probable cause. Letters of advocacy and support from department chairs and deans were brief and unenthusiastic. Letters in the sciences, where applicants fared best, were polar opposites: chairs and deans evidenced intimate knowledge of their applicants' qualifications and project plans and of what awards committees wanted. When I discussed this discrepancy with awards committees, they were surprised at my alarm; they had, they assured me, never expected humanities faculty to be serious contenders for grants requiring systematic projects. Humanities administrators, similarly, remarked that they did not expect fair treatment in university-wide allocations. They stuck to this stance of hopelessness and victimization, at least for a while, despite the fact that they had increasingly hired new humanities faculty who had records of systematic research and who faced the same pressures for publications as their counterparts in the sciences.

My favorite group for study in sex-typed locations is one even more neglected than the departments and areas already mentioned. The most documentably mistreated of faculty are those who work in libraries. Consider, for starters, that their colleagues on the rest of campus may not know that librarians are increasingly being given faculty status (Batt, 1985; Boice, Scepanski, & Wilson, 1987). In the quotations that opened this chapter, we saw one of the manifestations of the second-class status afforded to library faculty. More traditional faculty treat them as clear inferiors, often expecting librarians to call them by title. Many campuses, intentionally or unintentionally, exclude library faculty from orientations for new faculty, from campus grants and sabbatical programs, even from faculty clubs. My own long-range study of library faculty, in collaboration with two librarians (Boice et al., 1987), revealed other obstacles to full membership in the academic community. While some faculty from the rest of campus knew how steeped in scholarship their colleagues in the library can be, few were willing to list them as coauthors of manuscripts, even when their inputs clearly merited it. Nor, despite the eagerness of some library faculty to teach courses in their specialty areas, usually gratis, did most other faculty want them as colleagues in teaching. And to complete the picture, librarians may have handicapped themselves with their extraordinary emphasis on teamwork. They viewed taking time out for scholarly writing as letting down colleagues who might have to give inadequate service to library patrons.

Library faculty, more than any group of new faculty I have seen, also suffered from unclear expectations. While they were expected to publish, much like more traditional faculty, they were unsure where to find the time, whether to publish on pure or applied topics, or whether collaborations with nonlibrary faculty or with each other were legitimate. It was not until some of their peers came up for tenure review that they got information, albeit vague, about what counted and what did not. Here, too, cataloguing would have helped. What definitely did help, at least for a small group of library faculty who tried it, was a kind of involvement. Where library faculty set aside time for scholarly writing, especially in collaborative efforts, they produced a slow but steady stream of manuscripts for publication (often starting with moderately difficult levels of refereed acceptance criteria in outlets such as ERIC documents). Concomitantly, they felt more a part of the campus and its scholarly mission. Self-rated increases in self-esteem and job satisfaction also came with teaching in academic departments, especially when classroom presentations were shared with faculty from those departments. The results of this study, then, run counter to usual assumptions that librarians need little more than a good work climate and sensitive supervisors (Goodman, 1980).

Adjunct Faculty

Faculty hired in non-tenure-track positions, full- and part-time, are becoming more and more a part of academe. By the 1980s, some campus systems had employed adjuncts to carry as much as one-third of the teaching load (Pollack, 1986). Pessimists suppose that by the turn of the millennium, adjuncts will carry the bulk of teaching, often without much accountability.

The temptations for campuses to utilize adjuncts are obvious in a setting where budgets are shrinking. Adjuncts cost less per classroom hour in terms of salaries, benefits, and office facilities, and resources such as laboratories and secretaries. Moreover, adjuncts are unlikely to effectively question administrative decisions, including the one to increasingly rely on non-tenure-track faculty.

Experiences of Adjunct Faculty Members. We know little of a systematic sort about adjunct faculty; by definition, they are marginal, nearly invisible. My own interviews with new faculty include a sizable sample of lecturers. Some were part-time and some were full-time. But none of these new faculty felt engaged in anything more than a fast-moving mirage, often one that took them from campus to campus:

> This is just one of three campuses I teach at.
> Have you heard of freeway fliers? I sometimes

have to stop to remind myself where I am and
what course I am getting ready for. So I do not
feel settled, that I belong anywhere. That's a
disappointment. I had hoped that this lecturing
would last only a year or two, but it's in its fifth
year for me.

And, as a rule, adjuncts expressed some cynicism about their
teaching:

Nobody here except the chairman knows me, and
I met him only once. He seemed interested in
whether I could cover the material in [my
courses], not in how I would teach or how well I
would. The students will know, but they probably won't count. It's ironic in a way, because it is
people like me (and I don't even know who most
of the other poor bastards are) who carry a large
part of the teaching responsibility here. I wonder
that the regular faculty don't keep an eye on me.
[In response to my question about how much a
part of the campus he felt] Not at all. I'm just an
employee doing a job that the faculty don't want
to do. [In response to my inquiry about his plans
for improving his teaching] None, frankly. I'm
trying to find a tenure-track position. Publishing, not teaching, will count.

The saddest adjuncts were those beginning to realize
that their status of isolation from colleagues and scholarly
research was inexorably taking them away from their plans:

You know, all I do is teach. I'm a traveling teaching machine. The irony is that I really don't like
to teach, at least not like this. I have no one to
talk to except students. They rush off after class,
and so do I. I have to realize, especially when I
have these talks with you, that I am no longer

much of a scholar. I'm not keeping up with the journals; it's all I can do to keep up with the teaching. It is a dead end, really.

Overall, adjunct faculty, like other new faculty on the margin of academe, experienced the same problems as their mainstream, tenure-track counterparts, only in exacerbated fashion. Loneliness, which for white male faculty members eligible for tenure seemed unbearable, was reportedly even worse for adjuncts. They had no opportunities for collegiality and no prospects for improvement. They worked even longer hours and reported even more stress. But the doubt was always about how long adjuncts could maintain the pace, continue to neglect their families and/or social lives, and sustain the dream of a professorial career.

Help for Adjunct Faculty. Concern for adjuncts is growing, especially at community colleges, the site of strongest support for faculty development. Leslie and Gappa (1991) are compiling the first book on adjunct faculty that includes an accounting of support programs for this growing group of new faculty. A single instance of current programs shows how far we have come and how far we have to go: Two community college campuses in New Jersey, Burlington County College and Raritan Valley Community College, are considered exemplary for offering a little more than orientations, collegial dinners, and a modicum of mentoring. The former offers a handbook for adjunct faculty that could serve as a model for other campuses (McCadden, 1989). In addition to a welcome and a history of the campus, it lists instructor responsibilities, grading policies, faculty evaluation procedures, and departmental resources.

Another sign of promise is the pamphlet *A Survival Handbook for Part-Time and Temporary Faculty* (National Education Association, 1989). It includes a brief history of the growth of adjuncts in academe (up at least 22 percent since 1970), information that needs to be obtained during the hiring process (including fringe and retirement benefits, rights to reappointment, responsibilities, and evaluation procedures), and the goals of the National Education Association (NEA) for improved treatment:

1. Equitable compensation, including benefits
2. Academic due process, including grievance procedures and objective, fair evaluations by peers
3. Participation in campus governance
4. Humane working conditions, including reasonable hours, office space, and administrative services

Perhaps the NEA, in its advocacy for adjuncts, would agree that cataloguing should be extended to part-time and temporary faculty. My own attempts to institute such a program at two campuses have met with obstinate resistance; there is, I have been told, already too much paperwork, too much evaluating, to think of extending it to temporary faculty, many of whom stay only a semester or two. If it ever becomes commonplace, cataloguing may come last to adjuncts.

For the time being, I have had success helping adjuncts via more indirect means. I have found the clue to what might help in my surveys of what kept them from advancing beyond adjunct status. One reason stood far above others: these are often individuals who have procrastinated about dissertations and other scholarly writing. Campus-based programs for adjuncts as writers with formats such as those described in Chapter Seven proved dramatically helpful in several ways: (1) Adjuncts were able, despite their busy schedules, to manage regular productivity that led to satisfaction and to publishable manuscripts at rates comparable to those of other new faculty. (2) Adjuncts saw benefits of productivity extending to classroom teaching; as they felt more confident about scholarship, adjuncts reported teaching with more ease and patience. (3) And as adjuncts became productive, especially in finishing dissertations, they began to socialize more with colleagues, including their tenure-track counterparts on campus. Part of this expansiveness was invariably a search for a better job. Just as adjuncts seem to experience the dilemmas of new faculty in exaggerated form, they evidently respond to support in similarly strong and appreciative fashion.

Teaching Assistants

Are graduate teaching assistants (GTAs) new faculty? In a sense, they are, as apprentices learning to teach and to master the other skills essential to professorial life. The chief differences from tenure-track faculty may lie in the nature of teaching assignments (GTAs are more likely to head discussion sections), in the consequences of teaching (GTAs who elicit poor student ratings do not imperil their chances for tenure— or, perhaps, for much of anything), and in the likelihood of being trained as teachers (GTAs are far more likely). The clearest difference is one of status. Campuses reluctant to offer programs on teaching improvement for new faculty because of concerns about academic freedom give little thought to requiring graduate students to participate in TA training.

Why is teaching training so much more common for graduate students than for new faculty? My guess is that as the prestige of a campus grows more important, so does the likelihood that development (as opposed to demonstration) of competence is deferred more to graduate students. Faculty, no matter how new, presumably come to campus properly armed with skills and motivations—ready to demonstrate, not acquire, their brilliance. Indeed, the faculty development programs at most prestigious universities consist almost exclusively of TA training. Some of the premier talent among faculty development practitioners has been devoted to graduate students as teachers (J.D.W. Andrews, 1985; Mentor, 1987; Nyquist et al., 1991), especially to nontraditional GTAs who do not speak English fluently.

Why Most TA Training Fails. When we talk about efforts to train TAs, we are more open and fluent about our (or their) failings than we are when we consider programs for faculty. The TA literature, more than any other in faculty development, is literate, practical, and honest. It offers, first of all, a refreshingly candid accounting of its failings. Here again, the lessons from a peripheral group can be applied to new faculty.

Staton-Spicer and Darling (1989) specify a limitation in training GTAs that surely generalizes to new faculty. Because they are evaluated by faculty in general ways beyond teaching, GTAs go to faculty with only the most superficial questions about teaching. Inquiries that could imply a lack of competence (contrasted to a need to learn simple, technical information) are deferred in the hope of self-identified solutions.

Chism (1988) addresses other shortcomings of GTA training that take place largely in orientations: there is no continuity into seminars when GTAs need help most; orientations lull administrators into supposing that needs for instructional development are being met; the faculty or paraprofessionals assigned to TA training often have too little credibility to influence changes; and few campuses hold departments accountable for the teaching of their GTAs. In these regards, GTAs are treated as peripheral; they and not new faculty get the bulk of training, but that training is not effective or consequential.

Lessons from TA Training. Still, there is hope to be gleaned from TA training. Demands persist for this form of faculty development, in part because of demands for new faculty and for faculty who can better teach students ways of handling an information overload (Nyquist, Abbott, & Wulff, 1989). And with these demands comes more useful information about what makes a difference for fledgling teachers, such as opportunities for students to learn from and have fun with each other (Wulff, Nyquist, & Abbott, 1987). Some of the most useful lessons about helping novice teachers emerge from the literature on international teaching assistants (ITAs), usually considered the toughest cases for development.

Taken together, several studies (for example, Bailey, 1983) on ITAs reinforce a point about the basics of teaching, a point that we reviewed in earlier chapters; ITAs whose teaching results in good student evaluations and effective student learning are those who establish rapport, informality, and approachability with their students. ITAs who fare less well in ratings apparently believe that their lack of fluency in English makes teaching difficult; evidently, as they retreat into formality, students become less likely to make the effort to get involved and learn.

The irony in the growing practice of TA training is that it builds on the assumption that graduate students are more in need of training and more compliant about training than are new faculty. On my own campus, a rationale among administrators for TA training is the expectation that most of our graduate students will end up at lesser schools, places where teaching is taken more seriously. Still, TA training is like any other affirmative action effort; we must hope that slender beginnings will grow into something more substantial and habitual. Because of the people conducting it, TA training has the promise of reforming support for new faculty. The critical step awaits the realization that new faculty also need development; the transition between GTA and new faculty is less abrupt and complete than we may remember it. I end this chapter with a recounting of these and other lessons that we can learn from the difficult exercise of looking more closely at our outlying new faculty.

IRSS Theory and Lessons Learned

First, the needs of outlying new faculty are the most urgent; they are more vulnerable than any other new faculty to deficits in collegial support and clear expectations. And they may seem even less desirous of accepting our support than the usually stubborn autonomous new faculty depicted in earlier chapters. To use IRSS terminology, they suffer from problems, external and internal, of getting involved.

The second lesson is pivotal. No matter how sensitive and enlightened we become, our efforts to help new faculty may be doomed without careful attention to clarifying their positions and their evaluations. Cataloguing or something like it may make the biggest difference in supporting special populations of new faculty. In IRSS theory terms, the second challenge for nurturing marginal new faculty is ensuring regimen through regular observations and thoroughgoing programs.

The third lesson is a variation on involvement. What may block us from helping minority and other marginal faculty are cultural values of which we are unaware. The traditional valuing of educated families and attendance at the most exclusive of schools, for instance, may be far more off-putting to new colleagues with different backgrounds than we might have imagined. We can learn much that is valuable by studying cultural diversity (Flannery & Vanderpool, 1990). Stated another way, the problem with many of our efforts to support minority and other marginal new faculty may have been a matter of task misrepresentation, of supposing that solutions lie largely in affirmative action.

The fourth lesson, though it may seem redundant, is worth mentioning again. Much of our resistance to affirmative action and to support programs that would make full partners of outliers, including library faculty and adjuncts, has roots in our traditional goals of preserving standards. We worry about lowering standards and thus fostering a less worthy enterprise. We may not be ready to make such people full partners, members of our social networks, until they have proved themselves.

A solution to this thorny dilemma of preserving standards while acting as allies to special populations can be found in Elbow's (1983) paper on embracing contraries. He speaks from his own experience: by specifying exactly what he expects as a teacher, he can move on to indicate his willingness to coach students in ways of meeting those goals. And, in so doing, he takes pressure off himself. His students, in turn, know what they have to do and that they can get help. In this way, he accomplishes both the goals of most teachers, goals usually kept in imbalance: maintaining standards and acting as an effective ally of students.

A final thought takes us back to the first point. The key first step is involvement, for ourselves and our new faculty. It takes repeated, patient contact to get to know new faculty on the margin. Involvement is also a key for minority and other marginal new faculty. More than anything else, it provides collegial support, modeling, and other information about mastering professorial skills. We cannot realistically expect minorities and other disadvantaged new faculty to generate the requisite skills or motivation before they are involved, before they have come in from the periphery. And, once more, we cannot expect them to come in until we reach out in open, accepting ways.

TWELVE

Enlisting Chairs
and Other Administrators

What about the traditional ideal of faculty development—faculty being solely responsible for their own development? It is an attractive notion, one consistent with the reason most of us took up academic careers: autonomy. Faculty ownership also has a practical side. Ultimately, all of us have to take responsibility for our own development. Yet, in its customary form, the ideal of autonomy has failed. Chapters Two through Four remind us of the usually poor outcomes of relying on what new faculty themselves request as faculty development (usually release time from teaching). As the intervening chapters have shown, a more directive approach of providing programmatic support and incentives for new faculty helps make their survival process more egalitarian and cost-effective.

One lesson from those active support programs has not yet been mentioned: effective faculty development programs grow from more than a grass-roots movement of faculty ownership alone. Ownership of the support process properly extends to campus administrators. This chapter, then, broadens the franchise for faculty development in a way that, until recently, would have been exceptional. It begins with a look at one of the sources of change in considering the importance of involving administrators.

The Bush Foundation Project Evaluations

As in other areas of faculty development, closer observation of what works and what doesn't has forced us to reexamine our traditional beliefs. A turning point may have come in the landmark studies of Eble and McKeachie (1985). As we saw in earlier chapters, they scrutinized the Bush Foundation Faculty Development Project at some thirty midwestern campuses; among their conclusions were confirmations of the expected: the most successful campus programs demonstrated careful planning, substantial enrollments of faculty participants, skills training (versus mere exhortations for improvement), and sensitivity to already heavy faculty work loads. But Eble and McKeachie also unearthed a surprise. They had started with the hypothesis that faculty ownership of programs would be of paramount importance to their success. Instead, they found a variation on that presumption, the importance of balance: "Relating these measures to our various outcome measures, we found that those institutions in which there was balanced faculty-administrative planning were significantly more successful than those where administration dominated or where faculty dominated" (p. 203). More specifically, "The colleges and universities characterized by the highest level of faculty satisfaction were those where faculty rated administrative support most highly $(r = .55)$" (p. 169).

In analyzing the optimal role of administrators in faculty development programs, Eble and McKeachie drew a parallel to the conclusions of Deci and Ryan (1985): the best way to motivate faculty is via an administrative orientation toward autonomy and toward support that informs rather than controls.

More Localized Studies of
Administrators' Effects on Programs

In the wake of the Bush Foundation evaluations came other, more localized studies of programs that added to the evidence for the crucial role of administrators. One example draws on the studies we overviewed in the early chapters of this book; new faculty with supportive chairpeople were far more likely to report successes and satisfaction than were counterparts with unsupportive chairs (Turner & Boice, 1987). Indeed, on the Bush campuses, chairpeople seemed to be more vital to the welfare of new faculty than were any other groups.

My own observations indicate that chairs are in a position to do much more than simply give a program their blessing and funding. New faculty are more likely to become involved and to benefit when chairpeople encourage their faculty to participate and reward that participation than when they are uninterested. This theme of the importance of enlisting higher administrators to authorize support programs and of involving chairs as recruiters, models, and even practitioners in faculty development dominates the rest of this chapter.

Other Indications of Importance

While attitudes about the importance of administrators are changing, the active involvement of these campus leaders and providers in support programs continues to be the exception. In some ways, administrators can seem like natural adversaries of faculty development.

Negative Indications

Do chairs and other campus administrators harbor suspicions about professional development programs? Moore (1983) joins several writers in drawing such a conclusion: administrators that he surveyed, including deans, almost never participated in professional development programs on topics such as management training. Only slightly more than half of them had mentors, and only half of those valued the mentoring that they received. On the whole, deans seemed to be exemplars of academics who make it on their own. In a separate study, deans reported that they valued faculty who showed responsibility, discipline, maturity, and self-initiation (Morris, 1981).

And to complete the point, even when deans claimed strong support for teaching, they typically did not communicate this commitment to their faculty in any visible way (Bowker, 1982).

How well do administrators foster their own professional development? To date, the most systematic data come from chairs. In one large survey of psychology chairs, stresses were reported as enormous, relief as rare, and costs to productivity and careers as unacceptably high (Boice & Myers, 1986). Stress for chairpeople came most obviously from colleagues who misbehaved, cajoled, and resented evaluations; chairs recognized that faculty, far more than time or work pressures, made the job difficult. Relief came all too often from escape strategies such as alcohol use. On the whole, then, we have no evidence that administrators take good care of themselves.

Nor, in the main, can we conclude that they are ready supporters of faculty development programs. In the study of chairs just mentioned, few of them saw development programs, for themselves or their colleagues, as solutions. Their primary goals as chairs were to gain appreciation from colleagues for their behind-the-scenes work and, sooner or later, to stop chairing. As for their faculty, chairs claimed that they wanted little more than autonomy for them; ideal faculty were seen as those who find productivity and self-sufficiency on their own. For the most part, chairs wanted to be left alone, especially by a few troublesome faculty; they almost never supposed that difficult colleagues could be helped (or deserved help).

Eble and McKeachie (1985) also saw a general disinclination for faculty development among chairs. At most of their study campuses, even those provided with an impressive set of strategies and resources, chairs gave faculty development "unfocused support." To them, faculty development was little more than another time-consuming administrative responsibility.

Positive Indications

Still, the Bush Foundation evaluations provide hope. Some chairs got involved, and some showed special effectiveness when they brought faculty together for more than conducting business. These chairs, whose faculty shared skills and built common purposes, made an obvious difference in the success of faculty development programs. Moreover, as we have already seen, campuses where higher administrators expressed strong support for Bush Foundation projects evidenced the most positive effects. A small but growing literature based on other settings confirms the point. At one campus, the simple advent of a dean who became a visible supporter of a faculty development project made a difference in its success (Arends, Reinhard, & Sivage, 1981). When the faculty involved in that project were asked what about the dean's behavior was most important to them, they listed his accessibility, his participation in meetings, and his other gestures of closeness to them.

Arguments for involving administrators, especially chairs, become more compelling when they specify the roles that these campus leaders can play in faculty development. Some of the studies reviewed below reveal the types of obstacles that are likely to emerge as support roles are resisted and how such obstacles can be surmounted.

Roles for Administrators

My experience indicates that most administrators who move beyond mere endorsement begin by playing the part of the open-minded skeptic; they doubt that faculty development will work, but they wouldn't mind being contradicted. When faculty developers face the predicament of administrators waiting for proof, they will do well to ask for a period of grace of, say, at least three years so that the program can win over skeptics. During this period, some administrators can be convinced to assume an accustomed role: they can act as advocates, often by encouraging chairs and faculty to give the program a chance to prove itself. This stage is so crucial to programs for new faculty that I consider it as the first of specific roles for administrators in support programs.

Administrators as Advocates and Arrangers

Anyone who has started a faculty development program knows the challenge of asking chairs and deans for their support. My own initial contacts were so dramatic and educational that I decided to collect systematic information that might help other faculty developers.

A Study of Deans and Chairs. I undertook the initial study over a decade ago, just as I began to realize that basing faculty development on faculty ownership alone is not sufficient. I had noted that successful developmental programs in industry (Miles, 1983) and in employment assistance programs (Thoreson, Roberts, & Pascoe, 1979) had not prospered by distancing themselves, as I thought mine had done, from their administrations. And with the encouragement of a few forthcoming chairs, I had also begun to spend more time asking middle-level managers for suggestions about ways to improve my programs for faculty. Chairs and deans offered useful insights on the needs of their faculty, and I began to agree with them that faculty, especially those immersed in specialized studies, were not always in a position to give complete direction to support programs.

I also noticed the potential of chairs and deans as advocates. A simple endorsement at chairs' councils or faculty meetings sufficed to impel faculty to seek out my programs. This excerpt from my notes from conversations with a recruit new to a program for new faculty illustrates faculty's typically ambivalent but action-oriented attitude toward administrative endorsement:

> When Dean [name] recommended this, I decided you must be doing something worthwhile. But I do want to know two things. Are you working for him or for me? Is he going to know about my coming here?

An Aside About Confidentiality. There is, of course, a potential cost in accepting favors from chairs and deans. I quickly learned that they wanted me to hear out their complaints; no one else, they invariably explained, was available as a safe and patient listener. I didn't mind that function, because it taught me a lot about the administrative domain of academic functioning.

Their second demand was more of a problem. Even as deans and chairs gave me advice and encouragement, they often tried to break two cardinal rules of faculty development: that faculty participation should be voluntary and that it should be confidential. For one thing, they commonly wanted to force a difficult faculty member to work with me; such assignments were typically conveyed to the faculty member as a condition of avoiding punishment. In another common scenario, administrators would ask whether a particular faculty member was already working with me (and, if so, what I was accomplishing).

Because I came to these encounters with a background in clinical psychology, where patient confidentiality is a moral, practical, and legal necessity, I was practiced in responding to these requests. But deans and chairs, I discovered, are remarkably effective in catching me off guard and in making compelling arguments for exceptions to the rules. So in the interest of my own survival, I formulated two firm rules for handling their pressures: (1) The response to inquiries about who is working with me and how much they are accomplishing must always be the same. I remind the inquirer, with a friendly smile, that faculty will stop working with me if I break confidentiality. The exception comes only when faculty directly request that I share information about their participation and progress with specific individuals. (2) My response to involuntary assignments of faculty to work with my program is always the same. I remind administrators that my program will suffer if it is associated with remediation and punishment, that involuntary participation will probably produce less than optimal results, and that I usually disapprove of forcing faculty to make adjustments. (Where, in contrast, faculty evidence problems such as substance abuse or sexual harassment, I help chairs and deans find referrals for faculty to other agencies.)

Then I recommend that the chair or dean simply suggest that the faculty member talk to me privately about participation. The administrator must, I explain, make it clear that he or she will not know whether the visit took place.

While these safeguards work, they can lead to another quandary. In my experience, when faculty in trouble *do* come for voluntary help, they are unlikely to praise my efforts later. These faculty, more than any other, keep the credit for what they have managed to themselves, perhaps justifiably. Faculty development, like teaching and scholarly writing, is best done for implicit satisfactions and not for public recognition.

Interview Results. As I concentrated on the deans and chairs that I had come to know, something else occurred to me. I realized that I had probably begun with an atypical sample; every administrator whom I had asked for advocacy was already primed to offer it. These were the few deans and chairs who took the initiative to seek me out before I was established on campus. To learn something more useful, I decided, I needed to sample a more representative group of chairs and deans. As in my contacts with new faculty, I used a standardized format for interviewing and following up (Boice, 1986a).

I started by having the campus dean who already championed me ask the other campus deans to agree to an appointment with me. When I had interviewed the deans, I asked them, in turn, to petition their chairs to agree to a similar interview. All but one of the six chairs who refused to see me later, some after having made appointments, worked under the only dean to openly express reservations about my program after the initial interview.

Summaries of my interview notes produced the following differences between deans and chairs faced with requests for advocacy of my faculty development program:

1. Deans, unlike chairs, usually kept me waiting and then put me on the defensive with an initial comment such as "I'm not sure that this is going to be a good use of our

time." Chairs were immediately friendly and encouraged
me to talk while they listened patiently.

2. Deans talked in unhurried fashion, but they did most of
the talking early on, often explaining the recent history
of their college or school; some listed their reservations
about faculty development (for example, "I think it's a
boondoggle"). Chairs continued to listen for a while.

3. Deans asked assertive, direct questions about my qualifications and accomplishments in areas such as faculty
development; chairs, once they had listened to me, moved
energetically to lists of complaints and questions about
one or two difficult faculty members (for example, "What
should I do about someone who wrote me obsessive
memos almost daily and then followed them up with
late-night calls to my home?")

4. Deans began to react positively once they had listened to
the program descriptions. They were surprisingly creative
in conceptualizing applications of my programs to their
colleges or schools (for instance, suggesting that I become
part of the interviewing sequence for minority faculty
applicants, explaining the support available to new faculty). Chairs, at about the same juncture, reacted in the
opposite way. They worried aloud about the likelihood
that their support of faculty development would offend
colleagues. Then they became defensive, supposing that
few, if any, of their faculty actually needed help.

5. Once they became enthusiastic, deans took action to help
me. They made calls and dictated memos to arrange for
my contacts with their chairs. They helped me arrange
faculty development workshops for collegewide faculty.
They asked new faculty, not all of them in trouble, to
attend the workshops. And, as a rule, they promised to
follow up with supportive comments to chairs and higher
administrators. By the end of their interviews, chairs had
shifted back to admitting that they had one or a few problem faculty members but insisted that I could not help
their "deadwood." One chair labeled this position the
"moral weakness hypothesis":

These are faculty who are just weak, morally weak. They just don't care. They just don't try. And they can't change. I'm sure of it. You wouldn't be doing anyone, including them, a favor by trying.

Unless prodded by their deans, few chairs volunteered to have me present workshops or talks to their faculty.

Administrators as Instructional Developers

When administrators decide to move beyond advocacy, I observe two patterns to hold true. First, it is usually chairs who become more than advocates as they take an active role in helping new hires improve their everyday functioning, probably because of their already greater involvement with faculty. Second, their involvement usually focuses on teaching improvement (see Lucas, 1989).

Sharing Chairs' Own Solutions. Wilhite (1990, p. 113–114) collected problem-solving strategies from chairs that they were willing to share with their peers. One case that she describes concerns a new faculty member as a troubled teacher: "One 'freshly minted Ph.D.' with an extremely good academic background was described by his chairman as 'a little arrogant,' and this was impeding the faculty member's effectiveness with students and colleagues. . . . We just sat down and chatted about it. It turns out there were on-campus and off-campus training programs. One of them dealt with teacher effectiveness; the other dealt more with interpersonal relationships." The new faculty member followed his chair's advice and participated in the training programs, with good results. During the next couple of years, the problem, along with his poor student ratings, disappeared.

Practical Advice About Teaching for New Faculty. Another strategy for chairs as instructional developers also offers simplicity (Boice, 1991d). In a first step, I determined the conditions under which new faculty ask their chairs about teaching. New faculty's inquiries typically come in the wake of student evaluations. Left alone with only casual impressions of how their classes succeeded, most new faculty might not have sought advice on teaching. But even with this prod to new faculty, chairs did less than an optimal job as instructional developers. Consider the usual outcome of conferences between chairs and new faculty about teaching evaluations:

Generally, the chair and the new faculty member focused on a single, global rating item (for example, "rate the instructor") and ignored items that gave more feedback on what could be more easily changed (such as "rate the instructor's accessibility"). And, as a rule, they kept an eye on departmental means. If the score for a global item was at or above the mean, the conclusion was usually that the new hire was "on track." Even where global ratings were below the norm, chairs rarely gave advice about learning from specific rating items or about changing specific teaching behaviors. Instead, they exhorted their new hires to improve with generalities such as the importance of being better prepared and of learning from experience.

When I followed up with new faculty on their meetings with chairs about the need to improve teaching evaluations, a few troubling facts emerged. The new faculty, especially those most clearly in trouble, still saw no substantial problems in how they taught. They generally blamed their disappointing ratings on the evaluation instrument and on the students (most commonly, they supposed that students were punishing them for pressing high standards in classes). The obvious solution, in the minds of new faculty, was to lower standards by easing up on assignments and grading more liberally. When they checked with their chairs about this plan, it commonly met with quiet approval.

As a rule, then, the process of a new hire going to his or her chair for advice about teaching improvement may not be very productive. What clearly works better is coaching chairs to do better jobs of counseling their colleagues on what ratings mean and on what kinds of alternative teaching tactics are most likely to help new faculty with poor ratings. I find that limiting my advice to a few points helps get chairs to adopt them (because they are already overscheduled and want something that works easily). First, chairs should be given a sense of the usual shortcomings of new faculty (for example, preparing too much material for lecturing at a comfortable, interactive pace). Second, they should be encouraged to recruit senior colleagues who excel in one or more aspects of teaching to invite new faculty to observe their classrooms. As a rule, new faculty reciprocate with an invitation to a senior colleague who seems supportive and discreet. With some preliminary coaching, the senior colleague can be encouraged to attend to specific factors crucial to new faculty, such as pace of lecturing, rapport with students, and classroom comfort. Third, chairs should be urged to model the practice of administering early, informal evaluations (Chapter Six) in their own classes, pointing to its advantages in correcting problems before classes have ended and in establishing rapport with students. And they should be given an incentive to carry out this suggestion, in the form of a respite from formal administrative evaluations for a year while the formative evaluations are being used. Finally, once they are comfortable and successful with this strategy, chairs should be counseled to share it with other chairs.

An Excellence-Based Approach. Perhaps the most impressive compilation of information about what chairs can do to facilitate colleagues' teaching comes from a study of 200 chairs nominated as excellent by their colleagues (Creswell, Wheeler, Seagren, Egly, & Beyer, 1990). This analysis of excellence in chairing offers, first of all, a sense of what chairs can do to help themselves (self-development, including time management) and their colleagues in general (setting goals collaboratively). And it includes specific pointers about what excellent chairs do to support new faculty: for example, helping them to improve the use of their time, clarify their needs (especially unrecognized needs) and expectations, find and reward successes, and establish collaborations. Finally, Creswell and his colleagues use the exemplars to suggest a stepwise scheme for facilitating teaching, including what Lewis (1988) calls a preobservation interview (to clarify goals and objectives), direct observation of the new faculty member's teaching, encouragement of alternatives in teaching, modeling and mentoring of alternatives, and advocacy, once improvements occur, for the colleague's being supported as a recipient of rewards and recognition.

Administrators as Facilitators of Scholarly Productivity

We have already seen schemes for helping new faculty find more productive habits and attitudes as writers, usually by means of campuswide programs and self-help regimens (Chapters Seven and Eight). Chairs, it turns out, can supplement these programs with some surprisingly elementary but effective actions. In my experience, four strategies work well for a variety of chairs, regardless of their own productivity as writers (Boice, 1988a).

Discussion Groups. This is a favorite with chairs who want to establish a culture of interest and support for writing in their departments. Discussion groups are easy to set up, create a valuable sense of collegiality, and promote scholarly writing. Yet they are not widely used. When I sampled one hundred social science departments at a variety of campuses by phone, I found fewer than 25 percent of doctoral programs and fewer than 8 percent of master's-level departments where such groups met at least once a semester. With only a few exceptions, though, faculty at inactive departments volunteered the opinion that discussions are worthwhile activities. When I followed up on my inquiries with the departments carrying on discussion groups about manuscript writing, I found dramatic differences between them. Where faculty participants rated their groups highly, they generated a common list of the qualities of successful groups (rank ordered here from most to least common):

1. The group generates and shares ideas for writing.
2. The group meets at least once a month.
3. The group shares practical knowledge about getting writing finished and published.
4. The group builds cultural acceptance for scholarly writing.

But this list, based on faculty's self-reports of what they liked most about their groups, may be misleading. Contrast that list to a list of the qualities of groups that were associated with the greatest actual changes in manuscript pages written by members:

1. The group pressures members to bring and share recent writing.
2. The group discusses maladaptive beliefs and habits of writing.
3. The group regularly includes the chair.
4. The group helps arrange collaborative writing.

Except for some superficial features, there is no overlap between what faculty say they like about discussion groups and what corresponds with facilitating productivity. It also turns out that chairs play a critical role in the latter but not the former set of circumstances.

Enlisting Faculty Models. Another simple but effective strategy for chairs is asking successful authors in the department to share their expertise. At one campus, four faculty members who had mastered the brief daily regimen of writing (Chapter Seven) volunteered to publicize their writing habits and productivity to select groups of department colleagues through the intervention of their chairpeople. The long-term result for the faculty members who attended sessions with the models was that nine of the twelve attempted similar regimens, with reliable increases in their writing outputs.

Making Brief, Casual Visits to Faculty Offices. Chairs can prod colleagues gently but effectively by stopping in the offices of colleagues who volunteer for reminders and encouragements as writers. In a study where twenty-four such faculty members were visited by their five chairs, the results were dramatic, even after a year. These faculty members averaged some 7.0 pages per week, compared to 1.5 pages for a matched group of faculty members who intended to write more but had no visits about writing from their chairs. The chairs in this study were not only surprised by the effectiveness of their ministrations; they marveled at how little they had to do to effect the changes. The expectation that colleagues would have some writing to share each week was effective in itself. But these chairs thought they also helped by reassuring colleagues when writing was going slowly or had been rejected, by discussing solutions to problems in writing, and by offering occasional bits of praise for what had been written. My sampling of faculty's perceptions of the support process virtually duplicated their chairs' list.

Heading a Workshop Series. Some chairs decided to focus on workshops run jointly with their faculty. The formats for successful workshops are varied (Boice 1988b, 1990d) and readily adapted to most faculty groups. In a typical format, workshops involve members in free-writing exercises, in time-management practices, in collaborative support, and in strategies for coping with criticism (see Chapter Seven). Most such workshops can be led by chairs and faculty with no special expertise; exercises such as free writing tend to run themselves. But they benefit by integration of the knowledge of colleagues experienced in editing, publishing texts, and producing grants. Again, where chairs take a leading role in organizing and leading workshops, faculty attendance and benefits are greater.

Administrators as Models and Faculty Developers

Once chairs become active in supporting the productivity of their new faculty, they typically become more productive themselves. For a variety of reasons, the act of supporting the writing of colleagues by promoting ways of generating ideas, momentum, and cooperation leads to practicing what is being taught. Several studies show that these gains for chairs are substantial and lasting (Boice, 1987a). In turn, not surprisingly, the chairs who make this transition apparently stimulate even more productivity in their faculty (Boice, 1986a).

What would keep chairs from participating in programs that bring such uniform evidence of success for their junior faculty and themselves? In fact, the topic of writing, especially for those of us who feel remiss about getting it done, elicits a powerful array of objections. The list that follows rank orders the reasons expressed by a sample of fifty chairs approached for participation in programs like those just depicted:

1. Busyness (that is, claiming an overload of work)
2. Concerns about offending faculty with implications that they are doing too little; concerns about violating the academic freedom of colleagues
3. Negativism expressed about writing for publication (typically, "too much poor quality writing is being published already")
4. Claims that facilitating writing lies beyond the responsibilities of chairs
5. Doubts about being qualified to teach colleagues much about writing

What worked best to get chairs past these hesitancies was a combination of information (descriptions and data from already successful projects with chairs in the role of faculty developers), modeling (seeing other chairs on campus demonstrate success in getting past such reservations), and simple leaps of faith (by reminding chairs that the alternative of letting new faculty master productivity on their own is not working; by encouraging them to give the programs a brief trial). What rewards chairs most, in my experience, is seeing colleagues profit from the programs, receiving appreciation from colleagues for assuming the role of faculty developer, and managing more scholarly productivity for themselves.

Wilhite (1990) offers an insight into what helps get this method under way. In her view, the exemplary chairs do at least three things: they work to identify problems early, they assume that most of faculty's problems do not solve themselves, and they use innovative ideas to help support faculty (such as coaching them to say no to requests for committee participation).

Administrators as Promoters of Collegiality

Much of what we have suggested for the roles of chairs in promoting the survival and happiness of their new hires presumes cooperation and support among faculty. Teaching and writing both suffer in ordinary practice for the isolated, collegially unsupported ways in which they are done. This subsection adds a specific suggestion about helping chairs arrange collegiality that goes beyond mentoring and other strategies that we have covered in prior chapters. Here, we consider the key role of chairs in coaching new faculty to break out of difficult, oppositional patterns. As a rule, when we think of difficult, disillusioned colleagues, we picture senior colleagues who have long assumed the stance of outlier and underminer. In my own studies of what I called middle-aged, disillusioned faculty (Boice, 1986b), I discovered several interesting characteristics of these colleagues who exist on the periphery of departments, often with chronic anger and suspiciousness. For one thing, they join their administrators in concluding that they are beyond help, that they cannot change. For another, they admit to long-standing feelings of not fitting in, of not trusting colleagues, and of not having fair access to rewards, feelings that date to their first few years on campus. As a rule, outliers assume their stance soon after they come to campus.

Characteristics of Outliers. When chairpeople identify faculty members as outliers, they typically attribute a number of negative characteristics to them (Boice, 1986b). They feel that such faculty members are (1) inactive as scholars (71 percent), (2) prone to shirk responsibilities re committees and student advising (49 percent), (3) socially isolated from colleagues (34 percent), (4) oppositional and undermining in department meetings and affairs (32 percent), (5) openly unfriendly toward the chair (24 percent), (6) explosive toward students and/or colleagues (22 percent), (7) a frequent source of student complaints (22 percent), and (8) paranoid (12 percent). The list in itself confirms what we already know about disillusioned colleagues; they are unhelpful, unliked, unhappy, and unproductive. In collaboration with several long-term chairs, I have developed a tentative list of characteristics that may identify outliers early in their careers: (1) social isolation (especially combined with bitterness and suspiciousness), (2) busyness displays combined with a lack of scholarly productivity and elitism, (3) lack of balance between maintaining high standards and student approval, and (4) obsessiveness and explosiveness.

Interventions for Outliers. Coaching colleagues out of their isolation and contrariness is much more difficult than spotting it. Here, I abstract the strategies that I have developed and outlined in articles for chairs elsewhere (Boice, 1987a). In essence, the strategies resemble those for managing difficult students (Sorcinelli, 1990), especially the preventive notion of reducing misbehavior by reducing the anonymity of misbehaviors.

Step one is casual visits to all faculty members' offices. This simple gesture not only offers advantages for chairs (for example, it puts the bulk of interactions with faculty in their offices, where meeting length is far more under the control of the chair); it also makes faculty members feel that they are cared about. Moreover, it helps some colleagues get past the feeling that meetings with chairs occur only when problems arise. But it is especially valuable as a means of contacting faculty members who ordinarily do not visit the chair's office. Attempts to establish rapport and request behavior changes with outliers will be made more comfortably in the faculty members' offices than in the chair's. As a rule, these visits should be no more than five to ten minutes long so that chairs have time to visit all their faculty at least biweekly. Some of the visits should be devoted to small talk (despite its foreignness to many of us). At the same time, I encourage chairs to avoid the temptation to engage in guilt induction (for instance, noting the absence of the faculty member at recent faculty meetings). Instead, chairs fare better by saying that they value their colleagues' involvement and inviting them to attend.

Another thing that helps is resisting the temptation to respond in kind to angry or guilt-inducing statements. If a colleague becomes angry in questioning why the chair should want him or her to attend a faculty meeting, the chair can respond by finding something in that statement with which to agree ("Yes, I can understand why you or any colleague would object to feeling pressured to attend faculty meetings"). Doing this defuses the tension that would otherwise build and helps put the discussion back on course. Once the chair acknowledges the colleague's complaint, he or she can offer an unemotional, truthful response ("It isn't that I deny your right to refuse to say hello to me in the halls. It's more that your participation in the department is important to me. I worry when anyone is left out, and so I'd like your help in putting me more at ease in this job"). While faculty see the transparent motives in these requests, they also see the truth in them. In my experience, difficult faculty members almost always comply with these requests. So-called difficult faculty rarely enjoy their reputation and inertia. They need, as they later admit, a face-saving way of getting back into circulation.

When I coach chairs in carrying out these suggestions, I find that two things are especially helpful. One is rehearsal; trying to adopt new, unpracticed styles once emotions arise is an invitation to failure. The second is reminiscent of the results-first approach that we have seen in earlier chapters. Once the strategies are rehearsed, the next thing is to plunge in and give them a try. They work, both for the chair and for the problem faculty.

Step two, conveyed briefly here, in practice is at least as lengthy and demanding as the first. It consists of coaching new faculty into more productive patterns of working and socializing. As we saw in Chapters Four through Seven, this is largely a matter of facilitating involvement and first-factor components.

Step three, the final step for reengaging outliers, is decisive but is often overlooked. In fact, what keeps most programs for outliers from working is a lack of meaningful incentives. Because they have not been rewarded and see themselves as cut off from usual reinforcements, outliers are reluctant to get involved in reengagement programs. They imagine that even with the agreed-upon improvements, the rewards (say, merit raises) will be denied to them. How can a chair with limited resources promise the prospect of rewards to more faculty members than there are, say, merit raises available? Some departments use a lottery system to give all those who deserve rewards a chance to win material prizes. Others use the inexpensive expedient of public praise.

Administrators as Those Evaluated

As this chapter ends, we examine administrators and evaluation in a new light: in the role of those being evaluated. Here there are three related messages: Administrators can benefit from evaluation and its concomitant development. Administrators who engage in evaluation and self-development are apparently more likely to support similar efforts for their faculty. And administrators themselves are often new to campus (or to their roles) and so merit some of the same considerations that we have been giving to new faculty in nonadministrative positions.

Self-Study. A curious quality of those who assume administrative positions in academe is that few of them read the literature about their roles. In my workshops with new chairs and deans, for instance, fewer than 10 percent of them had thought of reading the literature about their jobs. But to their

credit, they are interested once exposed to this growing literature. New chairs, for instance, show a ready curiosity about
research and lore on what makes them effective, what stresses
them, and what can help make their positions more effective.
I put together annotated bibliographies that summarize points
such as these:

- Fiction about chairpersons can be illuminating; Brace's
  (1968) novel *The Department* speaks to the quandaries of
  chairing: "A chairman . . . is treated respectfully by the
  administration and the public. But his colleagues take
  other attitudes. They are grateful to him for doing the
  dirty work. They resent it that he has certain powers of
  decision" (p. 34).
- Workshops on chairing offered by the American Council
  on Education typically use Bennett's (1983) book and
  emphasize his conclusions about the transitions that
  make chairing difficult: (1) from specialist to generalist,
  (2) from individualist to collectivist (for example, sharing
  credit), and (3) from loyalty to one's discipline to loyalty
  to one's campus.
- Research on chairing suggests that the most effective
  chairpersons are rated high on both task and people
  dimensions (Knight & Holen, 1985).
- Surveys of chairs indicate that they resign for reasons
  such as work load, feeling unappreciated by deans and
  higher administrators, finding faculty unresponsive, and
  having to settle petty arguments (Miles, 1983).
- Forecasts of chairing indicate increasing roles as fund
  raisers, recruiters, and managers (McMillen, 1985).

One result of exposing new chairs to knowledge about what
they do is an increased inclination toward self-evaluation,
especially when the sharing is done in groups.

Self-Evaluation. Once chairs reflect on what stresses and what
rewards them, on what contributes to efficiency and what to
failure, they are ready for the next step. Just as feedback is

essential to rapport, comfort, and improvement in teaching, it provides similar opportunities for administrators to learn from the people under them. In fact, though, such evaluations are far less common than are student evaluations.

Perhaps the clearest aspects of this neglect of evaluation are the reasons why administrators resist evaluations. While a number of writers have produced lists of objections (for instance, management is an art that cannot be measured by an evaluation device), Seldin (1988), a leader in academic assessment, states the matter in terms of how to get past resistances (for example, devise flexible devices that take diverse roles into account). Seldin is also clear about what factors ensure successful evaluations for administrators: ratings from multiple sources and accounting of subtleties and nuances of management. But Seldin's key contribution may lie in linking evaluations to development programs. He lists ten qualities of good administrative development programs (including the importance of nonthreatening, supportive programs, clearly defined goals, and modest expectations). I use these guidelines in establishing workshops and support programs for new administrators; the premise, much as with new faculty, is that ongoing evaluations provide the most important information for functioning comfortably and effectively. The major difficulty in basing administrative development on evaluations is the same as that with faculty's teaching evaluations: most administrators dislike criticism. They would rather, much as would classroom teachers, continue to rely on casual comments and impressions to judge how well they are doing.

I have found two strategies to help administrators get past this obstacle: I ask exemplary senior chairs and deans to act as mentors for newcomers, and I encourage participants, new and experienced, to begin with the Painless Evaluation Instrument for Chairpeople, or PEIC (Boice & Creamer, 1989), shown in Exhibit 12.1. In practice, the list of continua is longer than shown in the exhibit; the chairs and other administrators being evaluated help devise the items to fit their interests and styles. The important thing is to design continua

Exhibit 12.1. The Painless Evaluation Instrument for Chairpeople.

Indicate the changes you would like to see your chair make by drawing an arrowhead in the desired direction for the continua below. To indicate no change, draw the arrow pointing upward:

more autocratic _____ more democratic

prompter action _____ deferred action

objective, detached _____ emphatic, involved

stable policy _____ flexible, evolving policy

less communication _____ more communication

emphasis on administration _____ emphasis on interpersonal

so that neither label is necessarily good or bad. When items are designed properly, they give those evaluated a sense of how they may need to change direction without feeling criticized.

The real purpose of the PEIC (as with the early, informal evaluations of teaching that we saw in Chapter Six) is to generate supportive and instructive communication between the evaluators and the person being evaluated. My experience indicates that the most important colleagues to involve in these evaluations are new faculty. In the midst of facing a variety of new evaluations themselves, they are comforted by seeing that their leaders are open to similar scrutiny.

Once chairs and other administrators discover the values of evaluations, two other things tend to happen. First, they become open to more direct, riskier evaluations from faculty, such as the Departmental Evaluation of Chairperson Activities for Development (DECAD) (Hoyt, 1977). Second, they begin to translate suggestions for change into alternative ways of carrying out their roles. In the main, they discover that faculty and administrators who work under them want more communication, clearer expectations, and more reinforcements. As they effect these changes, they become administrative and faculty developers.

Closing Reflections

This chapter makes two main points: that support programs for new faculty profit by engaging administrators as part owners and operators and that new administrators, like new faculty in novel surroundings and roles, can benefit from development programs that parallel those discussed in earlier chapters. Ultimately, both new administrators and new faculty benefit by being helped to establish the IRSS components of involvement, comfort, rapport, balance, collegial networks, and improvement goals based in ongoing evaluations. On reflection, it makes little sense to separate administrators from the design and execution of support programs for new faculty.

 THIRTEEN

Strategies for Getting Programs Under Way

This final chapter is about endings and beginnings. It provides a finish in the form of a brief review of information conveyed earlier in this book, especially lessons that seem most likely to be generalizable to a diversity of campuses. It adds to lessons about support for new faculty by drawing parallels to information generated outside faculty development, some of it from better-established fields, such as organization development. And in considering this broader base for generalization, it specifies strategies for beginnings, for starting and building support programs.

Beginnings: Advice About Starting Programs

I begin this last chapter with what practitioners have told me they most want considered: a succinct review of how to start support programs. In this section, I overview a classic example of advice about starting programs for faculty in general, first summarizing the counsel of the first prescriptive book on support programs for new faculty and then showing what the present book adds to those prescriptions.

General Sources on Faculty Development

One of the best guides for establishing programs was one of the first. Gaff (1975) not only details many of the mechanics of establishing faculty development on campuses but prefaces this information with useful cautions about taking care of other things, such as politics and demand. For example, he speaks to the ambivalence that faculty development elicits on most campuses: as one staff member observes, "We have a condition of high need but low demand for our services" (p. 120). Gaff's book deserves a look just for its useful advice about coping with reticent administrators. For instance, he suggests pointing out that funding for faculty development deserves to be as least as munificent as that set aside to cover the depreciation of campus buildings (see Jarvis, 1991, for a similarly powerful argument about the underfunding of faculty development). Gaff adds a second point worth reemphasizing: faculty development programs also need nonmaterial rewards, including praise, direction, and time.

Gaff's specific counsel about making programs viable includes no surprises, but his brief lists function as valuable checklists of what to do in advance (for example, determine program costs), how to determine what programs on other campuses are already doing, and what sorts of colleagues make good program directors (probably generalists rather than specialists).

The best general source is Lewis and Povlacs (1988). Its chapters by established practitioners include one on consulting programs (Fink, 1988), one on linking consultation to workshops (Mann, 1988), and one that offers an observational system for diagnosing teaching problems (Lewis, 1988). Still, when I consult with campuses about programs for new faculty, they want advice tailored specifically for new hires. The first such book, by Jarvis (1991), not only is exclusive to new faculty but has a basis in data about the new faculty experience.

Jarvis's Junior Faculty Development: A Handbook

Jarvis (1991) builds his advice for establishing programs and practices on interviews with "over one-hundred faculty members at eight universities and colleges in the United States. We asked these professors what they felt was important for success in their own careers and what they felt would help new faculty members develop as scholars, teachers, and citizens of their university" (p. v). His application of these data is usable and readable (in part because he presents fictional and wryly humorous scenarios to make his points about what will work). He also anticipates the problem of campus diversity by offering scenarios for programs with maximal and minimal support. For campuses with ample resources, Jarvis recommends a specific list of possible beginning components, summarized here as follows:

1. A faculty development committee (which will be subject to predictable inertia that can be overcome with actions such as those listed next)
2. A weekly noon seminar for new faculty, with sessions including an orientation to campus, the basics of college teaching, and research strategies
3. A mentoring program for junior faculty with mentors drawn from senior faculty, especially those just retiring
4. An annual weekend retreat for new faculty, whose attendance is encouraged by invitations from their deans to discuss their experiences during the first year on campus
5. A faculty handbook amended to balance materials related to teaching and research
6. A summer research program that provides funding for one-third of new faculty
7. Services from the campus research office, including editing of manuscripts
8. Monthly symposia ("potluck seminars") held at faculty members' homes that include junior and senior faculty as equals
9. Travel monies specifically for junior faculty, set aside from travel funds for all faculty
10. Personal computers and network connections (for example, BITNET) for all junior faculty
11. A plan to perpetuate the program by hiring a full-time director of faculty development for the campus

After listing all these ideal resources, some of them impractical for many campuses, Jarvis completes his advice with a reminder of what really matters: "A great deal can be done in the area of junior faculty development for a very modest capital outlay: The main requisite is the vision. We agree with the Lilly Endowment Program report on its junior faculty program: ". . . lack of imagination, initiative, and drive—not lack of money—accounts for the failure of institutions to concern themselves with the development of their junior scholars into senior professors" (Bornholt, 1980, p. 9.12).

What This Book Adds to Predecessors

This book adds several points to the sound advice of Gaff and other practitioners. A review of those additions provides an opportunity to revisit some of the practices covered in earlier chapters.

Beginning by Getting to Know New Faculty. The first addition is a basis in data from new faculty themselves, even if provided only in casual observations, interviews, or surveys of new faculty. Several practitioners, including Fink (1991), Gainen (1991), Sorcinelli (1988), and van der Bogert (1991), have helped set the current mood for this approach. In this book, a beginning with immersion in the new faculty experience is considered irreplaceable for several reasons. New faculty often reveal problems and needs that their senior colleagues and administrators have either forgotten or bypassed. Moreover, new faculty themselves may not apprehend their real problems until they are given extended chances for reflection and self-monitoring. A final reason for getting to know newcomers completes what could be a longer list. Contacts with new faculty, especially in their offices and classrooms, help recruit them to participation in support programs. Faculty developers who wait for faculty to come to them may end up serving those colleagues least in need of help.

Beginning with a Democratic Orientation. The second addition to traditional emphases is more notable. Few development programs have aimed to involve all faculty; most have focused on "winners." Earlier in this book, we saw a variety of arguments against variations on social Darwinism. I think that two specific arguments have special merits. One harkens back to Astin's (1985) profound insight about why campuses rarely manage to improve their teaching: it is because academe, with its emphasis on intelligence and prestige, values demonstrations of brilliance, not its acquisition. As a result, many professors may be content to teach in incomplete ways that allow only the most brilliant of students to demonstrate their prowess. The problem with this emphasis on "winners," for both students and new faculty, is that it means that we may fail to attract and retain people with unrealized potential (Tobias, 1990). In fact, as we have seen, the basics of brilliance can be taught and mastered (see Sternberg et al., 1990). The second argument against social Darwinism in academe is that it can lead to the exclusion of traditionally disenfranchised individuals from optimal careers as professors. Without specific attention to a democratic base for support programs, these individuals may be most likely to miss out (Exum, 1983).

Given inevitable shortages of time and other resources, how can faculty developers manage to be accessible to all new faculty? Again, part of the answer is getting to know new faculty via systematic inquiries to document their problems, their coping strategies, and their successes. The simple act of contacting new faculty to learn about their experiences also provides an opportunity to invite them to participate in further support. When senior faculty are asked why they have not participated in faculty development programs, their answer is nearly uniform: it is because, in their view, no one has asked them in a meaningful way.

Including Exemplars. While I reject the notion of focusing programs on the new faculty members most obviously likely to benefit, I do advocate a related idea. As we saw in earlier discussions of quick starters among new faculty, there is much to learn from exemplary individuals; with some coaching, other new faculty members can master equivalent success at balancing daily activities, building more positive attitudes, and establishing a greater readiness to accept help from colleagues and students. What makes the use of exemplars vitally different from less democratic approaches is this: once efficient patterns are established, they are shared with all new faculty who can be enticed to practice them.

Emphasizing Ongoing Evaluations. While most of us, including me, reflexively avoid evaluations, we cannot deny the importance of providing ongoing feedback to new faculty. The format prescribed here, cataloguing, provides a clear sense of what colleagues expect of new faculty, including a negotiable set of goals, ongoing feedback about progress toward those goals, and ready opportunities for evaluators to offer help. Ongoing evaluations may be the single most important element of survival and success for new faculty, once they are engaged in support programs. Ongoing evaluations may also be the most crucial component of ensuring the success and survival of support programs themselves.

Emphasizing Holistic Development. The narrowness of traditional faculty development is obvious to new faculty struggling to survive: it falls short in neglecting both collegial supports and scholarly productivity as elements of its program. As we have seen, teaching does not occur in isolation. Moreover, mastery of collegiality and productivity carries valuable lessons for the mastery of teaching. For example, as new faculty generate time and momentum for networking and writing, they typically learn to prepare for classes in more efficient ways, including going to classes ready to involve students as more active learners. Whatever else, I hope that the data presented in earlier chapters show that the establishment of productivity in new faculty does not necessarily undermine excellence in teaching.

Reliance on a Theoretical Orientation. In their overview of the literature on faculty development, Menges and Mathis (1988) emphasize a single deterrent to progress in the field: a lack of theories to organize and direct research and practice. By now, even the most casual of readers will have noticed the persistence of IRSS theory as an organizer in this book. Each of its four components, as we have seen throughout, helps suggest specific actions for support programs.

Involvement, as we have noted, is essentially Astin's (1985) notion of the necessity of immersion for progress and persistence to occur. It suggests, among other things, the value of getting to know new faculty, of extending the support process to interviews and other preliminary contacts with potential new hires, and of making administrators co-owners and collaborators. And it reminds us that the majority of new faculty members who remain uninvolved in faculty development programs are being underserved, possibly even undermined. Immersion, in my experience, also helps faculty developers surmount a particularly troublesome barrier. They often imagine that new faculty would see them and their requests for interviews as intrusions. Once they visit new faculty, however, this apprehension is soon forgotten. Recall from the descriptive studies in chapters Two through Four that new faculty almost invariably come to cherish these opportunities to complain, to elicit comparative information about their progress, and to soak up support and advice.

Specifically, then, IRSS theory posits that the first step in building or rebuilding programs is involvement. Involvement in such activities as establishing productive and successful writing optimally precedes much of the planning process for support programs. Once practitioners are immersed in the problems and successes of new faculty, planning will occur as needed, especially if programs include ongoing evaluations. In our study of mentoring, as we saw in Chapter Seven, campus support for a major program came more easily when my collaborator and I had first established momentum, credibility, and a viable sense of direction in patiently conducted pilot research.

In the area of *regimen,* in what amounts to task management, the lesson is that balance and moderation result in increased accomplishments in teaching, collegiality, and scholarly productivity. For example, new faculty wrote more and wrote more successfully when they abandoned their customary preference for bingeing in favor of brief daily sessions. New faculty who mastered this component of working at tasks such as lecture preparation in moderation described the result as "getting more from less."

Self-management is also an idea borrowed from outside traditional faculty development. It is Flower's (1990) idea of constantly checking to see whether the right problem is being solved. This essential step can help support programs to determine, preferably by means of ongoing evaluations, whether interventions are addressing the real problems of new faculty. An example from Chapter Eight helps make the point: when new faculty are asked (without much chance for reflection) what would help them, most suppose that they need release time from teaching. But as we saw, time is not the real problem. The problem that needs solving is how workdays can be used in more efficient and balanced fashion.

With *social networking,* a compelling confirmation of IRSS theory was seen in the habits and attitudes of the exemplary new faculty labeled as quick starters. They began with emphases on the kinds of actions usually left untaught, such as comfort and balance, and thus short-cut the usual socialization process. And from the outset, they built involvement and other basic skills as a result of their inclination to solicit and welcome social contacts; they sought advice, modeling, and encouragement from colleagues much more than did other new faculty.

This study of quick starters is not, however, the only instance of investigators specifying similar qualities of exemplary faculty. Cole (1986), for instance, studied the careers of his own students who went on to excel as teachers. Among their unique qualities were the positiveness and eagerness to learn more that characterized quick starters here. A better-known study of exemplary faculty labels them as "vital faculty" (Clark & Lewis, 1985), professors who show the most concrete goals, carry out the most complex careers, rely the most on external resources, and take the most risks (see also Finkelstein, 1984; Kanter, 1981).

The kinds of strategies suggested by IRSS theory can also be used by faculty developers who are starting programs. My own observations of a variety of support programs for new faculty show that involvement, regimen, self-management, and social networking all underlie thriving. One way to uncover the tacit skills required to be an effective practitioner is the tactic of shadowing an already experienced faculty developer in his or her daily rounds. Sometimes, consultants to new programs are best followed around on their home campuses. These shadowing experiences tend to accomplish three things. First, they demonstrate the simplicity of faculty development; in the main, it requires no special skills beyond putting new faculty at ease, listening with patience and empathy, and sharing what has been learned from other new faculty. Second, shadowing helps prove that new faculty are generally receptive and open to contacts, especially after they discover that the visits are worthwhile. Third, experienced practitioners can reveal the usually unspoken and unwritten competencies involved in carrying out faculty development.

When I asked four practitioners who spent a day or more shadowing me to specify examples of tacit knowledge with special value for their own practices that they had learned, these responses were the most common:

1. The importance of positiveness, especially in assuming that new faculty would welcome inquiries and advice
2. The value of patient listening, especially of pausing after questions
3. The value of enthusiastic interest in the experiences of new faculty and sharing of information about the commonality of experiences with them
4. The value of suggesting collegial contacts to new faculty

Each of these kinds of tacit knowledge is, of course, a matter of nuances; it may be easier and more effective to learn them through observation than through reading. But why not simply plan to learn tacit knowledge on our own, through trial and error? Because then we would take the risk of duplicating the inefficient and painful procedure that most new faculty members undergo in learning the professorial ropes. If we can learn from each other and short-cut the process, so much the better for support programs.

Done properly, networking with other practitioners extends well beyond campus. It includes a growing variety of resources for the relatively new field of faculty development. Organizations that hold conferences, conduct workshops and seminars, and issue publications for practitioners include the Professorial and Organizational Development Network in Higher Education (POD) (Hilsen, 1990; Lewis, 1988); the National Council for Staff, Program, and Organization Development (NCSPOD) (Svinicki, Kurfiss, & Stone, 1986); and the American Association for Higher Education (AAHE) and the American Educational Research Association (AERA) (Mentkowski & Chickering, 1987). Centers that act as clearinghouses and as orchestrators of research about faculty development include the National Center for Research in Postsecondary Teaching, Learning, and Assessment, a consortium of institutions based at Pennsylvania State University; and the New Jersey Institute for Collegiate Teaching and Learning, Seton Hall University. Agencies that provide funding for faculty projects include federal programs (for example, FIPSE, the National Science Foundation, and Health Resources & Services Administration) and a variety of private funds (such as the Ford Foundation). Finkelstein's (1990) review of recent progress in faculty development includes a useful list of funding opportunities.

One of the essential steps of involvement and networking is reading. Journals of higher education, such as the *Journal of Higher Education* and *Research in Higher Education.* The *Chronicle of Higher Education* commonly includes articles about faculty development and notices about workshops in that area. I have found that authors and workshop presenters are usually willing to send materials and spend time on the phone. These conversations are an important contributor to a feeling of membership in faculty development.

What, on the other hand, will keep many of us from feeling that involvement and kinship? More specifically, what would discourage the kind of stepwise investment in support programs just outlined? In my experience, part of the problem is simply inertia; part of it is concern that we will be imposing on new faculty or will not have enough time and resources to conduct a substantial program; and part of it is reservations derived from concerns about generalizability—should we suppose that the kinds of results and advice presented in this book will apply to other kinds of campuses and settings? The next section of this final chapter addresses generalizability and ways of enhancing it.

Generalizations: Ways of Making Information Applicable

The main limitation of information about supporting new faculty is the narrowness of its base; as yet, too few of us are collecting information and sharing strategies (see Fink, 1991, for an annotated bibliography of the surprisingly few articles and books on new faculty). In this sense, we have made the barest of beginnings. Until more of us investigate for ourselves and communicate what hinders and helps our new faculty, generality will remain limited.

The assumption here, though, is that enough information exists to make useful beginnings. In what follows, I suggest the most generalizable of the findings presented in this book. The attendant assumption, to be developed after the generalizations, is that we can broaden the knowledge that we have by relying on its better-developed counterparts in fields such as organization development.

Where to Find Generality

Recall a general principle stated throughout this book: balance is likely to hold as a principle for new faculty at all campuses. If support programs did little more than getting new faculty to spend moderate amounts of time on activities such as teaching preparation, they could count themselves successes. Other prospects for generality are listed below. In each case, I cite brief examples of research on development from outside the narrow confines of information about new faculty so as to enhance its generality.

Involvement. Collecting data about the experiences of new faculty shows the value of involvement, which cannot help but apply to any campus. While this strategy has some support in the research mentioned above (Fink, 1991), the case for collecting developmental data has been more strongly made in better-established fields. The most productive example is student development, the focus of Astin's (1985) theory and research on involvement. Baird's (1990) study of what typical students do shows that only a small minority of them do the things that we suppose they should: using the libraries much, getting to know professors, joining clubs, going to cultural events. As Astin would note, the result of this uninvolvement, especially for disadvantaged undergraduates, is a lessened likelihood of succeeding or remaining in college. The data presented in this book about new faculty, most of whom are similarly uninvolved and inefficient, suggest that the same general principles apply to them.

Regimen. What we know about support programs so far suggests that the next step to be taken once new faculty are involved is helping them establish a regimen of balance and moderation. In my experiences as a consultant at more than twenty campuses, some groups of new faculty have needed relatively more help with collegiality (especially at commuter campuses), with scholarly productivity (particularly at campuses where pressures for publication were new and where the culture for research and writing was not especially strong), or with teaching (notably at campuses where excellence was rewarded with reductions in teaching loads). Nonetheless, some generalities do apply. One, again, is balance. While faculty on almost all campuses seem to suppose that they need reduced teaching loads (even when the existing responsibility is for one course per semester!), in reality they benefit more from balanced distributions of time and energy (Chapters Five through Eight). The powerful generality of this principle can be seen in research on student procrastination (Rothblum, 1990). Put simply, failures at academic tasks have little to do with the availability of time. Instead, unproductiveness owes to fears of failure, to poor work habits, to seeing the tasks as aversive, and to low self-esteem.

Self-Management. The third general rule also follows the structure of IRSS theory. New faculty at any campus will need to acquire practical knowledge about finding comfort, confidence, and efficiency. In this case, the best evidence for generality comes from studies, some of them massive (Howard & Bray, 1988), about the qualities essential to success among corporate managers. The three most reliable of these qualities, resilience, insight, and identification, are eminently coachable (London, 1985). Moreover, these same three qualities apply to managers in a wide variety of settings and were also typical of new faculty who coped best in the studies described here (Chapters Two through Eight). However, each of them is usually untaught; it seems, certainly, that this same tacit knowledge needs to be taught at any campus making serious efforts to support its new faculty.

Social Supports. The fourth general rule restates the notion of helping our new faculty find social support: it says that new faculty everywhere should profit by learning to let others do some of the work. One source of evidence for the generality of this notion comes from research on writing. Where faculty have access to collegial networking and collaboration, their productivity is enhanced (Creswell, 1985). Evidence for the power of sharing work also comes from the literature on organization development. Consider examples from a growing literature about assessing and developing career motivation (London & Bray, 1985), predicting labor-force changes (Rousseau, 1991), gain sharing (Doherty, Nord, & McAdams, 1989), and team building (Neuman, Edwards, & Raju, 1989).

Taken together, these illustrations help confirm the general importance of building social support as part of professional development. But here, more than with the other parallels, doubts arise. Are not faculty different from corporate workers on dimensions such as autonomy and, presumably, needs for collegiality? A reply can be found in the data from Chapter Two showing that new faculty's most salient complaint, at least at one large comprehensive university, is social isolation and intellectual understimulation.

Conclusion

A final instance of general rules helps provide specificity. It is the notion, presented most often as the scheme for cataloguing, that all support programs must revolve around ongoing evaluations. Cataloguing can help establish a democratic community where the evaluators and those they are evaluating agree on what will be evaluated, what needs changing, and how changes should occur, thereby minimizing unnecessary ambiguity. Even so, as we saw at the outset of this chapter, we profit in seeing specific instances where we can expect successes in our practices beforehand. In the next section of this closing chapter, I link the ideas just mentioned to other programs in faculty development. Thus, in this final look at generality, I list five already successful approaches as specific models for planning ahead.

Futures: Building on Parallel Beginnings

We have already seen examples of the emergence of national and local programs for coordinating and supporting faculty development across campuses. These centers and consortia provide attractive and adaptive ways for campuses to begin or strengthen support programs.

Programs Organized Across Campuses

The Lilly Foundation provides a structured format for installing a mentoring program, funds to encourage the involvement of mentors and protégés, and conferences where participants interact with colleagues from other campuses. The Lilly projects have been evaluated as effective at several universities (Austin, 1990). Perhaps an even better example is the kind of center that is open to participation by programs at any campus, rather than the handful of campuses funded at any one time by programs such as the Lilly Foundation's. The New Jersey Institute for Collegiate Teaching and Learning (NJICTL) stands out as an exemplary program, one that is being emulated by systems such as the California State University. In the few years of its existence, the NJICTL has broadened its network to campuses in and out of state. It offers small grants (with campus matching funds) for new projects on topics such as support for adjunct faculty; it recruits fellows-in-residence (including leading experts on practices such as motivating minority students to interact with faculty in the system); it trains campus directors of support programs through workshops and networking; it promotes conferences where its own practitioners and those from around the nation interact; and it provides a scheme for making faculty development programs somewhat uniform across campuses—the Katz approach to a master faculty program.

Two points about the NJICTL suggest future trends. First, more states and regions are planning to organize similar ventures. Second, those of us in areas without such networks might do well to begin by helping organize them. The main reason that more practitioners are not part of a regional center may be that no one has asked them.

Master Faculty as Mentors and Colearners

The master faculty approach is well known; its basics are covered in *Turning Professors into Teachers* (Katz & Henry, 1988). An excerpt gives a sense of the scheme: "The observing colleague takes careful note about the process of the class . . . [and] notes the content the teacher presents and its organization, the how of presentation, the teacher's interactions and rapport with the students, and the pace, mood, posture, and other nonverbal behavior. . . . These observations furnish data for analysis at the meetings with the professor, and they are considerably enriched by further information obtained from interviews with students" (p. 12). That is, master faculty (mentors) function as observers and advisers; their analyses are combined with feedback from a student who provides similar observations as a basis for new faculty members to consider alternative ways of teaching. In Chapter Six, we saw that one of the first changes to occur in this format is a lessening of pace in presenting lectures. The telling aspects of the Katz paradigm are these: First, it provides a tested, credible format for beginning programs on a modest level; once effective, it can be expanded. Second, it models the essence of IRSS theory. The program director or others can act in the roles of master faculty member and coordinator who collects data and facilitates discussion groups of pairs. As a result, several fundamentals are ensured: involvement in the experience of new faculty as teachers; coordination of a surefire program of support and thus solving the right problem (because the inductively based format necessarily points out problems that need solutions); transmission of tacit knowledge about what helps with teaching and with mentoring, and other support; and establishment of social networking that includes colleagues, new faculty, and students all looking at the same teaching.

Program Research

With program research, the precedent is only partially established. It is based on Cross and Angelo's (1988) approach to classroom research. Recall from Chapter Six and elsewhere in this book that classroom research is largely a matter of making students into ongoing evaluators and collaborators in improving teaching and learning. What makes classroom research somewhat unique is also what makes it overdue: it emphasizes student learning.

Program research would develop along similar lines. It would involve new faculty as ongoing evaluators of their support programs and of what they had learned. By constantly querying new faculty about what they were doing differently and how the supports affected their successes and satisfactions, faculty development could take on a more democratic and credible style. For one thing, it would help ensure program effectiveness. For another, it might help model the kind of evaluations that we want new faculty themselves to carry out with those they evaluate. That is, program research should help generate classroom research, and vice versa.

Quality Improvement Programs

We have just seen three examples of emerging approaches to faculty development with special promise. But a look at related areas in organization development suggests many other possibilities, chief among them the emphasis on quality improvement programs (QIPs). In the corporate world, QIPs emphasize the IRSS values of balance, moderation, teaching of essential skills, and, above all, cooperation and communication. Two examples of QIPs help introduce this seemingly foreign concept; we will see below that it is not unknown in academe.

AT&T and Quality Improvement. The first example is a system developed at AT&T (Blount, 1987). Its perspective seems immediately different from faculty development, not only in its quality councils and quality improvement teams but especially in its two criteria for success: customer satisfaction and employee satisfaction. Those of us in academe do not, at least in overt ways, worry about student and faculty satisfaction on most of our campuses. But we could. AT&T works to effect those related goals by means of quality councils, quality improvement teams, and individual efforts.

 Quality councils, much like faculty development committees, demonstrate the need for development, create the environment for change, and direct the quality improvement programs; specifically, these leaders obtain resources, recognize and communicate the progress of teams that they supervise, coordinate the efforts of different teams, assist in solution implementation, and bring in outside consultants for ongoing evaluations of program progress. *Quality improvement teams,* much like departmental groups of senior colleagues and new faculty carrying out a cataloguing project, work toward specific goals of improving their customers' and their own satisfaction in a specific area of endeavor; in particular, these teams work to improve the quality of specific products and services, to train members in target skills and abilities, and to promote communication and teamwork as the primary means of achieving these changes. Finally, employees make *individual efforts* to include quality improvement as an integral part of their work.

The key to making this interlinked approach work, according to Blount, is data collection. Team members constantly gather data to identify quality improvement opportunities, to analyze the root causes of problems, to test the effectiveness of solutions, and to track success in improving quality (primarily in terms of customer and employee satisfaction). Quality consultants play a role similar to that of evaluators, but they also do something more: they act as advocates with higher management for soliciting resources and supports for councils and teams.

Not surprisingly, AT&T's QIP is comprehensive enough to include the details of what teams can do to promote success, such as ways of prioritizing the most needed quality improvements (solving the right problem), establishing clear criteria of success (specifying the difference between what is and what should be), and communicating results so as to elicit support from higher management. Would AT&T's approach be compatible with a faculty development program such as cataloguing? Imagine the power of structuring the mentoring teams as quality councils and organizing appropriate groups of new faculty as quality improvement teams, some of whose goals for improvement would be team-based. Imagine the impact of aims for change that include customer and employee satisfaction. And envision the usefulness of an outsider who acts as an evaluator and advocate.

Organizational Dynamics and TQIS. A second well-known approach to quality improvement teams adds even more useful ideas to an already intriguing picture. Labovitz (1987) summarizes the workshops that the consulting firm Organizational Dynamics Inc. uses to train for what he calls total quality improvement systems (TQIS). The five modules of the presentation are summarized as follows:

1. Identifying the benefits of quality for your organization. The result will be customer-oriented, not product-oriented; it will stress prevention; it will be part of employees' daily work; and it will focus on the long run.
2. Identifying the costs of quality. This analysis includes breaking costs down into avoidable and necessary costs; it aims at demonstrating cost-effectiveness.
3. Identifying new ways of seeing work; for example, recognizing that everyone in your organization is both a customer and a supplier; asking questions about what co-workers and customers need from you, what they do with what you give them, and what gaps exist between the two.
4. Identifying means for continuous improvement through the use of charts that plan and track actions to improve your work.
5. Identifying ways to make quality happen, mainly by picking a leader who is effective as a champion, model, and mentor.

We can easily extend the insights about teamwork and planfulness just listed. In academe, more than anywhere else, we need to build support programs that ensure that quality is a real part of professorial experience. QIPs could, for instance, help bring balance between productivity and quality in scholarly productivity in at least two ways. One would be the result of teams and councils simply paying more attention to quality in ongoing fashion (for example, in reviews of early reports of research and its written manuscripts). The other would be making improvement a more cooperative, moderated effort by having teams of new faculty act in concerted fashion. Team members could monitor the quality of each other's work with the goal of improving quality for the group. And they could be helped by the lessening of demands for competitiveness issued by councils. Emerging plans by campuses to limit the number of publications acceptable for review in tenure and promotion committees (Cooper, 1991) should help enhance the quality of what is written and, possibly, of the teaching that is done when there is less overall pressure on new hires.

Just Communities

This final exemplar of an existing approach that lends itself to adoption by support programs for new faculty involves everyone in the responsibility for development, even students. The best-known and most revered purveyor of this approach to development is Kohlberg (Power, Higgins, & Kohlberg, 1991). His notions of "just communities" advocate a return to educational democracy by way of a plan of regular community meetings of students and teachers. Just communities decide what should be learned, how everyone can help effect that learning, and how fair decisions can be made about everyone's progress. And they do more: they serve as a moral agent, focusing on teaching moral values consistent with their aims (say, protecting the rights of individuals by limiting group pressures for conformity). To accomplish all this, the teachers must, of course, take positions of leadership at times, particularly by advocating their own positions and by being invested in what and why students decide.

What is the application of the just communities program as tested and proved effective for students and their moral culture? Just communities should transfer with ease to the same cataloguing situations discussed under quality improvements. The difference is a matter of making an addition—of democratically involving another layer—mentors and evaluators for new faculty—in the planning and evaluation of development. Everything else could remain pretty much the same, including attention to moral considerations such as justice. This addition of a just communities component to cataloguing projects could help new faculty carry out cataloguing and related strategies, such as mentoring, in more cooperative, communicative, and trusting fashion. Still, the temptation may be to formalize too much of our programs. The usual failing of democracy, if not monitored for quality, is bureaucracy (Morone, 1990).

The Last Word: Comments from Participants and Observers

In looking for an ending, I thought back to how this book began. Our first views of new faculty highlighted their misery as isolated and overwhelmed newcomers to campuses. Our closing vista should reflect the success story that this book tries to tell, again by sampling the comments of program participants. Note that, this time, the excerpts come from more people than just new faculty; the successes and satisfactions of support programs accrue to almost everyone on campus.

A great many remarks have come in written notes, often from new faculty who began as pronounced skeptics, as did this person:

> I wanted to send a note of appreciation. I'm doing much better, and I owe it to FISO [the Faculty Instructional Support Office]. Things worked out just as you said they would. How much easier this was than waiting until the end of my probation period and then trying to make changes. My teaching is going much better. My students and I understand each other much better. Students told me they wanted me to stay longer after class instead of being the first one out of the door (I hadn't realized I was doing it). You were right about another thing. I have been able to find time for writing. With a little practice, I was able to make use of short periods of

time. I hope your ideas spread [new assistant professor, year 3 on campus].

I have also come to value the briefer comments that new faculty make when we meet on campus, including this one:

I appreciate your interest and the fact that your
programs work. Frankly, I wasn't sure that a
black person would get that kind of help here.
But I am.

But I am also relieved to see that more senior colleagues are
seeing benefits in the support programs:

You know, FISO has been a breath of fresh air. I
was dubious at first. Making things easier for the
assistant professors makes it easier for us, too. I
feel relieved that we have made our expectations
clearer about what is going to be necessary for
tenure. But what I also like is that I am being
asked for advice by junior faculty. I didn't like
being ignored.

And I know that when higher administrators join the chorus
of complimenters, a support program is starting to work:

I wanted you to know that I have been bragging
about our faculty development program to academic vice presidents from other campuses. I told
them about the luncheons that the president and
I had with small groups of new faculty and how
the newcomers gave the same enthusiastic response to our questions about what was going
well. Without fail, they volunteered praise about
your programs.

Ultimately, though, the evaluation that counts most is
the practitioner's. My own experience of conducting support

programs for new faculty has been the highlight of my career. In the end, as new hires have become my friends, my collaborators, and my teachers, I may have benefited the most.

 RESOURCE

Questionnaire Used to Interview New Faculty

1. Describe prior academic and teaching experience:

2. Rate (1–10 scale) extent to which this campus meets career expectations and add comments) _____

3. Estimate, in years, how long you plan to stay (and add comments) _____

4. Rate (1–10 scale) the quality of collegial support you've gotten of late _____; of intellectual stimulation _____

5. Rate own need (1–10 scale) for collegiality _____; rate self (1–10 scale) re friendliness toward colleagues _____; re giving collegial support _____

6. Specify the number of campus colleagues with whom you have at least weekly interactions that are more than small talk _____; with whom you pursue off-campus friendships _____; with whom you are collaborating in projects

that will lead to publications or grant proposals _____
and/or in classroom teaching _____

7. Rate the recent supportiveness (1-10 scale) of your chairperson _____; of other administrators with whom you are
familiar _____ (specify the individual:)

8. Describe experiences on campus as protégé or mentor:

9. Rate desire (1-10 scale) for mentoring _____

10. Rate your identification _____ with this campus
_____ What keeps you from giving a higher rating?

11. Estimate typical workweeks this semester in average
number of hours per week re:
    A. Classroom teaching _____
    B. Lecture preparation _____
    C. Grading and handouts _____
    D. Student contact outside class (separate for under-
        grads and grads _____; _____
    E. Scholarly reading (not for lecture preparation)
    _____
    F. Research and analysis exclusive of reading
    _____
    G. Grant writing _____
    H. Writing manuscripts for publication _____
    I. Committees _____
    J. Administration _____
    K. Other (   ) _____

12. Rate yourself (1-10 scale) in terms of recent busyness (where 10 would be the busiest you have ever been) _____; in terms of stress _____

13. Rate yourself (1-10 scale) in terms of your resilience in coping with pressures and disappointments this semester _____

14. Plans for productivity this semester (compare counts for year prior):
    A.   Conference presentations _____ (_____)
    B.   Manuscripts completed and submitted to refereed outlets _____ (_____)
    C.   Manuscripts published _____ (_____)
    D.   Grant proposals submitted _____ (_____)

15. Specify the ideal number of refereed publications for you per year once you are settled on campus _____ (current total for career _____)

16. Specify social network on campus (and off) for research/scholarship:

17. Rate your own productivity compared to your peers' (1-10 scale where 5 = average) _____; your own expectations _____

18. Describe writing re these dimensions:
    A.   Writing pattern

    B.   Writing location

    C.   Writing medium (word processor?)

D. Writing blocks (and strategies for getting unstuck)?

E. Strengths as a writer

F. Weaknesses as a writer

G. Motivation to write for publication

19. Rate your perception (1–10 scale) of external pressures on campus to publish _____; to get grants _____; internal pressures to publish _____; get grants _____

20. Describe own style as a classroom teacher (preferably in a current undergrad class):

21. How students would describe you as a teacher to friends:

22. Strengths as a teacher:

23. Weaknesses as a teacher:

24. Recent ratings from students of your teaching (numerical and descriptive) and how they compare to peers':

Rate (1-10 scale) the usefulness of the ratings _____

25.   Plans to improve teaching:

26.   Indicate interest (or current practice) re the following
strategies as teacher:
   A.   Routinely knowing students by name

   B.   Arriving early and chatting informally with
        students

   C.   Giving early samples of test questions and scoring

   D.   Administering early, informal evaluations

   E.   Discussing formal, end-of-semester evaluations
        with a colleague

   F.   Previewing and/or outlining lectures

   G.   Involving students by waiting patiently after ask-
        ing question

   H.   Specifying clear learning goals for class

   I.   Talking about own research/scholarship in class

   J.   Teaching critical thinking

27. What changes, if any, do you plan for your teaching?

28. Rate (1-10 scale) the quality of undergrads in your classes _____; of grads _____

29. Describe social network for discussing teaching in your department and elsewhere on campus:

30. Are your interests primarily in teaching _____, research _____, equal _____.
Which should count more toward tenure and promotion:

31. Indicate the kinds of assistance for teaching you have received of late on campus:

32. Estimate the probability (0 to 1.0) that you will receive tenure in a timely fashion _____
Rate the probability that you will win some kind of teaching award on campus, sooner or later _____

33. Estimate the probability that you will participate in campus faculty development programs within the next year (please be candid) _____

34. Can you think of any questions that I should have asked you (or do you have any questions for me)?

References

Alleman, E., Cochran, J., Doverspike, J., & Newman, I. (1984). Enriching mentoring relationships. *Personnel and Guidance Journal, 62,* 329-332.

Andrews, H. A. (1985). *Evaluating for excellence.* Stillwater, OK: New Forums Press.

Andrews, J.D.W. (1985). Editor's notes. In J.D.W. Andrews (Ed.), *Strengthening the teaching assistant faculty,* (New Directions for Teaching and Learning No. 22, pp. 1-5). San Francisco: Jossey-Bass.

Angelo, T. A. (1990). Classroom assessment: Improving learning where it matters most. In M. D. Svinicki (Ed.), *The changing face of college teaching* (New Directions for Teaching and Learning No. 42, pp. 71-82).

Arends, R. I., Reinhard, D. L., & Sivage, C. A. (1981). The educational dean: An examination of behaviors associated with special projects. *Journal of Teacher Education, 32,* 14-20.

As, B. (1985). A feminist university. *Women's Studies International Forum, 8,* 391-394.

Association of American Colleges. (1985). *Integrity in the college curriculum: A report to the academic community.* Washington, DC: Association of American Colleges.

Astin, A. W. (1985). *Achieving academic excellence: A critical assessment of priorities and practices in higher education.* San Francisco: Jossey-Bass.

Astin, H. S., & Bayer, A. E. (1979). Pervasive sex differences in the academic reward system: Scholarship, marriage, and what else? In D. R. Lewis & W. E. Becker (Eds.), *Academic rewards in higher education* (pp. 211–229). New York: Ballinger.

Austin, A. E. (1987). Comparison of faculty perceptions of the workplace at low and high morale colleges. In A. P. Splete, A. A. Austin, & E. E. Rice (Eds.), *Community commitment and congruence: A different kind of excellence* (pp. 6–10). Washington, DC: Council of Independent Colleges.

Austin, A. E. (1990). *To leave an indelible mark: Encouraging good teaching in research universities through faculty development.* Nashville, TN: Vanderbilt University.

Austin, A. E., & Gamson, Z. F. (1983). *Academic workplace: New demands, heightened tensions.* Washington, DC: Association for the Study of Higher Education.

Axelrod, J. (1973). *The university teacher as artist: Toward an aesthetics of teaching with emphasis on the humanities.* San Francisco: Jossey-Bass.

Bailey, D. (1983). Foreign teaching assistants at U.S. universities: Problems in interaction and communication. *TESOL Quarterly, 17,* 308–310.

Baird, L. L. (1990). The undergraduate experience: Commonalities and differences among colleges. *Research in Higher Education, 31,* 271–278.

Bakker, G. R., & Lacey, P. A. (1980). The teaching consultant. In W. C. Nelson & M. E. Siegel (Eds.), *Effective approaches to faculty development* (pp. 32–37). Washington, DC: Association of American Colleges.

Bandura, A. (1990). Conclusion: Reflections on nonability determinants of competence. In R. J. Sternberg & J. Kolligan (Eds.), *Competence considered* (pp. 315–362). New Haven, CT: Yale University Press.

Banks, W. M. (1984). Afro-American scholars in the university: Roles and conflicts. *American Behavioral Scientist, 27,* 325–338.

Baron, R. A. (1983). *Behavior in organizations*. Needham Heights, MA: Allyn & Bacon.

Baron, R. A. (1987). Research grants: A practical guide. In M. P. Zanna & J. M. Darley (Eds.), *The compleat academic* (pp. 151-169). New York: Random House.

Baron, R. A. (1988). Negative effects of destructive criticism. *Journal of Applied Psychology, 73*, 199-207.

Batt, F. (1985) Faculty status for academic librarians: Justified or just a farce? In P. Spyers-Durand & T. W. Mann (Eds.), *Issues in academic librarianship*. Westport, CT: Greenwood Press.

Beckham, B. (1988, Winter). Strangers in a strange land: The experience of blacks on white campuses. *Educational Record*, pp. 75-78.

Bem, D. J. (1987). Writing the empirical article. In M. P. Anna & J. M. Darley (Eds.), *The compleat academic* (pp. 171-201). New York: Random House.

Bennett, J. B. (1983). *Managing the academic department*. New York: Macmillan.

Bennett, J. B. (1985). Faculty evaluation: The roles of the department chair. *Department Advisor, 1*, 1-6.

Bennett, J. B., & Chafer, S. S. (1984, Spring). Evaluating the performance of tenured faculty members. *Educational Record*, pp. 38-41.

Beynon, J. (1985). Institutional change and career histories in a comprehensive school. In S. J. Ball & I. F. Goodson (Eds.), *Teachers' lives and careers* (pp. 158-179). Lewes, Sussex: Falmer.

Blackburn, R. T. (1981). Cloning in academe. *Research in Higher Education, 15*, 316-327.

Blackwell, J. E. (1989). Mentoring: An action strategy for increasing minority faculty. *Academe, 75*, 8-14.

Bledsoe, G. B. (1988). *Entering the profession: Advice for the untenured*. Washington, DC: National Education Association.

Blount, M. F. (1987). *Quality improvement process guidebook*. Basking Ridge, NJ: AT&T.

Blum, D. E. (1990, September 26). Younger scientists feel big pressure in battle for grants. *Chronicle of Higher Education*, pp. A1, A16.

Boice, R. (1982). Increasing the writing productivity of blocked academicians. *Behaviour Research and Therapy, 20,* 605–611.

Boice, R. (1983a). Contingency management in writing and the appearance of creative ideas. *Behaviour Research and Therapy, 21,* 537–543.

Boice, R. (1983b). Experimental and clinical treatments of writing blocks. *Journal of Consulting and Clinical Psychology, 51,* 183–191.

Boice, R. (1984). Reexamination of traditional emphases in traditional faculty development. *Research in Higher Education, 21,* 195–209.

Boice, R. (1985a). Cognitive components of blocking. *Written Communication, 2,* 91–104.

Boice, R. (1985b). The neglected third factor in writing: Productivity. *College Composition & Communication, 36,* 472–480.

Boice, R. (1985c). Psychotherapy for writing blocks. In M. Rose (Ed.), *When a writer can't write.* New York: Guilford Press.

Boice, R. (1986a). Differences in arranging faculty development through deans and chairs. *Research in Higher Education, 23,* 245–255.

Boice, R. (1986b). Faculty development via field programs for middle-aged, disillusioned faculty. *Research in Higher Education, 25,* 115–135.

Boice, R. (1986c). A program for facilitating scholarly writing. *Higher Education Research & Development, 6*(1), 9–20.

Boice, R. (1987a). Coping with difficult colleagues. *Department Advisor, 2*(4), 5–8.

Boice, R. (1987b). Is released-time an effective device for faculty development? *Research in Higher Education, 26,* 311–326.

Boice, R. (1988a). Chairs as facilitators of scholarly writing. *Department Advisor, 3*(4), 1–5.

Boice, R. (1988b). Helping faculty meet new pressures for scholarly writing. *To Improve the Academy, 7,* 135–148.

Boice, R. (1989a). Procrastination, busyness, and bingeing. *Behaviour Research and Therapy, 27,* 605–611.

Boice, R. (1989b). Psychologists as faculty developers. *Professional Psychology: Research and Practice, 20,* 97–104.

Boice, R. (1990a). Countering common misbeliefs about student evaluations of teaching. *Teaching Excellence, 2*(2), 1–2.

Boice, R. (1990b). The hard-easy rule and faculty development. *To Improve the Academy, 9,* 3–12.

Boice, R. (1990c). Mentoring new faculty: A program for implementation. *Journal of Staff, Program, and Organizational Development, 8,* 143–160.

Boice, R. (1990d). *Professors as writers.* Stillwater, OK: New Forums Press.

Boice, R. (1991a). New faculty as colleagues. *International Journal of Qualitative Studies in Education, 4,* 29–44.

Boice, R. (1991b). *New faculty as scholarly writers.* Manuscript submitted for publication.

Boice, R. (1991c). New faculty as teachers. *Journal of Higher Education, 62,* 150–173.

Boice, R. (1991d). Practical information about teaching for new faculty. *Department Advisor, 6,* 7–8.

Boice, R. (1991e). *Survey of recent Ph.D.s who avoided or fled academe.* Manuscript in preparation.

Boice, R. (1991f). *Why typical orientations for new faculty are ineffective.* Manuscript in preparation.

Boice, R. (1991g). *Writing blocks.* Manuscript submitted for publication.

Boice, R. (forthcoming). Lessons learned about mentoring. In M. D. Sorcinelli and A. E. Austin (Eds.), *Developing new and junior faculty* (New Directions for Teaching and Learning No. 50). San Francisco: Jossey-Bass.

Boice, R. (1992). Quick starters. In M. Theall (Ed.), *Effective practices for improving teaching* (New Directions for Teaching and Learning No. 48, pp. 111–121). San Francisco: Jossey-Bass.

Boice, R., & Creamer, L. (1989). Painless evidence for academic chair evaluation. *The Department Advisor, 4*(4), 6–8.

Boice, R., & Johnson, K. (1984). Perception and practice of writing by faculty at a doctoral degree granting university. *Research in Higher Education, 21,* 33-34.

Boice, R., & Jones, F. (1984). Why academicians don't write. *Journal of Higher Education, 55,* 567-582.

Boice, R., & Kelly, K. A. (1987). Writing viewed by disenfranchised groups. *Written Communication, 4,* 299-309.

Boice, R., & Kurfiss, J. (1990). Current and desired faculty development practices among POD members. *To Improve the Academy, 9,* 73-82.

Boice, R., & Myers, P. E. (1986). Stresses and satisfactions of chairing in psychology. *Professional Psychology, 17,* 200-204.

Boice, R., & Myers, P. E. (1987). Which setting is healthier and happier, academe or private practice? *Professional Psychology: Research and Practice, 18,* 526-529.

Boice R., Scepanski, J. M., & Wilson, W. (1987). Librarians and faculty members: Coping with pressures to publish. *College & Research Libraries, 48,* 494-503.

Boice, R., Shaughnessy, P., & Pecker, G. (1985). Women and publishing in psychology. *American Psychologist, 40,* 577-578.

Boice, R., & Thomas, C. T. (1989). Diagnosing academic cultures. *Journal of Staff, Program, and Organizational Development, 7,* 165-171.

Boice, R., & Turner, J. L. (1989). The FIPSE-CSULB mentoring project for new faculty. *To Improve the Academy, 8,* 117-139.

Bornholt, L. (1980). Foreword. In A. L. Beeman (Ed.), *Toward better teaching: A report on the post-doctoral teaching awards program of the Lilly Endowment, Inc.* (pp. i-iii). Indianapolis: Lilly Endowment.

Bowen, J. R., & Schuster, J. H. (1986). *American professors: A national resource imperiled.* New York: Oxford University Press.

Bowers, P. (1979). Hypnosis and creativity: The search for the missing link. *Journal of Abnormal Psychology, 88,* 564-572.

Bowker, L. H. (1982). The academic dean. *Teaching Sociology, 9,* 257-271.

Brace, G. W. (1968). *The department.* New York: Norton.

Braskamp, L. A. (1980). The role of evaluation in faculty development. *Studies in Higher Education, 5,* 45–54.

Braskamp, L. A., Fowler, D. L., & Ory, J. C. (1984). Faculty development and achievement: A faculty's view. *Review of Higher Education, 7,* 205–222.

Braxton, J. (1983). Department colleagues and individual faculty publication productivity. *Review of Higher Education, 6,* 115–128.

Brookes, M.C.T., & German, K. L. (1983). *Meeting the challenges: Developing faculty careers.* Washington, DC: Association for the Study of Higher Education.

Buhl, L. C., & Greenfield, A. (1975). Contracting for professional development in academe. *Educational Record, 56,* 11–121.

Bullough, R. V., Knowles, J. C., & Crow, N. A. (1989). Teacher self-concept and student culture in the first year of teaching. *Teachers College Record, 91,* 209–233.

Busch, J. W. (1985). Mentoring in graduate schools of education: Mentors' perceptions. *American Educational Research Journal, 22,* 257–265.

Cameron, S. W., & Blackburn, R. T. (1981). Sponsorship and academic career success. *Journal of Higher Education, 52,* 369–377.

Caplow, T., & McGee, R. J. (1958). *The academic marketplace.* New York: Basic Books.

Cares, R. C., & Blackburn, R. T. (1978). Faculty self-actualization: Factors affecting career success. *Research in Higher Education, 9,* 123–136.

Carlberg, J. (1981). *Professional development through growth contracts handbook.* Wenham, MA: Gordon College.

Centra, J. A. (1978). Faculty development in higher education. *Teachers College Record, 80,* 188–201.

Chism, N. (1988). Collaborating with departmental TA coordinators: The next step? *To Improve the Academy, 7,* 181–188.

Ciampa, B. J. (1978, February). Faculty development: The "haves" and the "have nots." *Research in Education,* pp. 1–18.

Clark, S., & Lewis, D. (1985). *Faculty vitality and institutional productivity*. New York: Teachers College Press.

Cole, D. L. (1986). Attracting the best and brightest to teach psychology. *Teaching of Psychology, 13*, 107–110.

Collett, J. (1990). Reaching Afro-American students in the classroom. *To Improve the Academy, 9*, 177–188.

Cooper, J. (1990). What is cooperative learning? *Cooperative Learning and College Teaching, 1*(1), 2.

Cooper, K. J. (1991, March 3). Stanford president sets initiative on teaching. *Washington Post*, p. A12.

Covey, S. (1989). *The seven habits of highly effective people*. New York: Simon & Schuster.

Crane, D. M. (1969). Social class origin and academic success: The influence of two stratification systems on academic careers. *Sociology of Education, 42*, 1–17.

Creswell, J. W. (1985). *Faculty research performance* (ASHE-ERIC Higher Education Report No. 4). Washington, DC: Association for the Study of Higher Education.

Creswell, J. W., Wheeler, D. W., Seagren, A. T., Egly, N. J., & Beyer, K. D. (1990). *The academic chairperson's handbook*. Lincoln: University of Nebraska Press.

Crocker, J., & McGraw, K. M. (1984). What's good for the goose is not good for the gander. *American Behavioral Scientist, 27*, 357–369.

Cronin-Hillix, Y. T., Cronin-Hillix, W. A., Gensheimer, L. K., & Davidson, W. S. (1986). Student's views of mentors in graduate training. *Teaching of Psychology, 13*(3), 123–127.

Cross, K. P. (1977). Not *can*, but *will* college teaching be improved? In J. A. Centra (Ed.), *Renewing and evaluating teaching* (New Directions for Higher Education No. 17, pp. 1–15). San Francisco: Jossey-Bass.

Cross, K. P., & Angelo, T. A. (1988). *Classroom assessment techniques*. Ann Arbor, MI: National Center for Research to Improve Postsecondary Teaching and Learning.

Dailey, A. L., & Jeffries, C. A. (1983). Burnout strategy and intervention: Rationale and institutional strategies. *Journal of the College and University Personnel Association, 34*(1), 15–21.

Daley, S. (1991, January 9). Little girls lose their self-esteem on way to adolescence, study finds. *New York Times*, p. B6.

Daniels, A. K. (1979). Development of feminist networks in the professions. In A. M. Briscoe & S. M. Pfafflin (Eds.), *Expanding the role of women in the sciences* (Vol. 3, pp. 215-227). New York Academy of the Sciences.

Darley, J. M., & Zanna, M. P. (1987). The hiring process in academia. In M. P. Zanna & J. M. Darley (Eds.), *The compleat academic* (pp. 3-21). New York: Random House.

Deci, E. L., & Ryan, R. M. (1985). *Intrinsic motivation and self-determination in human behavior*. New York: Plenum Press.

Deneef, A. L., Goodwin, C. D., & McCrate, E. S. (1988). *The academic's handbook*. Durham, NC: Duke University Press.

Dewey, J. (1916). *Democracy and education*. New York: Macmillan.

Diamond, R. M., & Wilbur, F. P. (1990). Developing teaching skills during graduate education. *To Improve the Academy, 9*, 199-216.

Doherty, E. M., Nord, W. R., & McAdams, J. L. (1989). Gainsharing and organization development: A productive synergy. *Journal of Applied Behavioral Sciences, 25*, 209-229.

Eble, K. E. (1972). Preparing college teachers of English. *College English, 33*(4), 385-406.

Eble, K. E. (1988). *The craft of teaching: A guide to mastering the professor's art* (2nd ed.). San Francisco: Jossey-Bass.

Eble, K. E., & McKeachie, W. J. (1985). *Improving undergraduate education through faculty development: An analysis of effective programs and practices*. San Francisco: Jossey-Bass.

Eckstein, R., Boice, R., & Chua-Yap, E. (1991). An annotated bibliography of teaching assistant training. *Journal of Staff, Program, and Organization Development*.

Edwards, K., Frank, M., Huff, J., Lauda, D., Maggadino, J., Martinez, I., Moustafa, M., Rader, B., & Schlaich, J. (1986). Report on recruitment, orientation, and mentoring of new faculty, California State University, Long Beach, Task Force on Recruitment, Orientation, and Mentoring of Faculty.

Eison, J. A. (1989). Mandatory teaching effectiveness workshops for new faculty: What a difference three years make. *Journal for Staff, Program, and Organization Development, 7,* 59–66.

Elbow, P. (1973). *Writing without teachers.* New York: Oxford University Press.

Elbow, P. (1983). Embracing contraries in the teaching process. *College English, 45,* 327–339.

Ellenberger, H. (1970). *Discovery of the unconscious.* New York: Basic Books.

Epps, E. G. (1989, September–October). Academic culture and the minority professor. *Academe,* pp. 23–26.

Etzioni, A. (1976). *A comparative analysis of complex organizations.* New York: Free Press.

Evetts, J. (1989). Married women and career: Career history accounts of primary head teachers. *International Journal of Qualitative Studies in Education, 2*(2), 89–105.

Exum, W. M. (1983). Climbing the crystal stair: Values, affirmative action, and minority faculty. *Social Problems, 30,* 383–399.

Exum, W. M., Menges, R. J., Watkins, B., & Berglund, P. (1984). Making it at the top: Women and minority faculty in the academic labor market. *American Behavioral Scientist, 27,* 301–324.

Feinstein, S. (1988, January 22). Women and minority workers in business find a mentor can be a rare commodity. *Wall Street Journal,* p. 2.

Feldman, K. A. (1983). Seniority and experience of college teachers as related to evaluations they receive. *Research in Higher Education, 3,* 125.

Feldman, K. A. (1986). The perceived instructional effectiveness of college teachers as related to their personality and attitudinal effectiveness. *Research in Higher Education, 24,* 139–213.

Feldman, K. A. (1987). Research productivity and scholarly productivity of college teachers as related to their instructional effectiveness: A review and exploration. *Research in Higher Education, 26,* 227–298.

Feldman, K. A. (1988). Effective college teaching from the students' and faculty's view: Matched or mismatched priorities? *Research in Higher Education, 28,* 291–344.

Feldman, K. A. (1989a). The association between student ratings of specific instructional dimensions and student achievement: Refining and extending the synthesis of data from multisection validity studies. *Research in Higher Education, 30,* 583–645.

Feldman, K. A. (1989b). Instructional effectiveness of college teachers as judged by themselves, current and former students, colleagues, administrators, and external (neutral) observers. *Research in Higher Education, 30,* 137–194.

Fink, L. D. (1984). *The first year of college teaching* (New Directions for Teaching and Learning No. 17). San Francisco: Jossey-Bass.

Fink, L. D. (1988). Establishing a successful consulting program. In K. G. Lewis & J. T. Povlacs (Eds.), *Face to face: A sourcebook of individual consultation techniques for faculty/ instructional developers* (pp. 3–17). Stillwater, OK: New Forums Press.

Fink, L. D. (1991). New faculty members: The professoriate of tomorrow. *Journal of Staff, Program, and Organizational Development.*

Finkelstein, M. J. (1984). *The American academic profession: A synthesis of social inquiry since World War II.* Columbus: Ohio State University Press.

Finkelstein, M. J. (1990). Faculty development in higher education. In L. R. Mareus & B. D. Stickney (Eds.), *Politics and policy in the age of education* (pp. 77–91). Springfield, IL: Thomas.

Flannery, B., & Vanderpool, M. (1990). A model for infusing cultural diversity concepts across the curriculum. *To Improve the Academy, 9,* 159–175.

Flower, L. (1990). The role of task representation in reading-to-write. In L. Flower, V. Stein, J. Ackerman, M. J. Kantz, K. McCormack, & W. C. Peck (Eds.), *Reading-to-write* (pp. 33–75). New York: Oxford University Press.

Flower, L. S., & Hayes, J. R. (1984). Images, plans, and prose: The representation of meaning in writing. *Written Communication, 1,* 120–160.

Fox, M. F. (1985). Location, sex-typing, and salary among academics. *Work and Occupations, 12,* 186–205.

Francis, J. B. (1975). How do we get there from here: Program for faculty development. *Journal of Higher Education, 46,* 719–732.

Freudenthal, N. R., & DiGiorgio, A. J. (1989). New faculty mentoring: The institution as mentor. *Journal of Staff, Program, and Organizational Development, 7,* 67–71.

Fuller, J. A., & Evans, F. J. (1985). Recharging intellectual batteries: The challenge of faculty development. *Educational Record, 66*(2), 31–34.

Gabelnick, F., MacGregor, J., Matthews, R. S., & Smith, B. L. (1990). *Learning communities: Creating connections among students, faculty, and disciplines* (New Directions for Teaching and Learning No. 41). San Francisco: Jossey-Bass.

Gaff, J. G. (1975). *Toward faculty renewal: Advances in faculty, instructional, and organizational development.* San Francisco: Jossey-Bass.

Gaff, J. G., & Wilson, R. C. (1971). The teaching environment. *AAUP Bulletin, 57,* 475–493.

Gainen, J. (1991, March 26). *New faculty as teachers: Longitudinal studies and institutional responses.* Symposium chaired at the AAHE Conference, Washington, DC.

Gamson, Z. F. (1966). Utilitarian and normative orientations toward education. *Sociology of Education, 39,* 46–73.

Gappa, J. M. (1984). *Part-time faculty: Higher education at a crossroads.* Washington, DC: Association for the Study of Higher Education.

Gilkes, C. T. (1982). Successful rebellious professionals: The black woman's identity and community commitment. *Psychology of Women Quarterly, 6,* 289–311.

Goodman, C. H. (1980). Incentives and motivation for staff development. In P. L. Ward (Ed.), *The professional development of the librarian and information worker* (pp. 209–215). London: Aslib.

Gordon, E. W., & Meroe, A. (1991). Common destinies—continuing dilemmas. *Psychological Science, 2,* 23–29.

Grasha, A. F. (1977). *Assessing and developing faculty performance: Principles and models.* Cincinnati, OH: Communication and Education Associates.

Green, M. F. (1988). *Minorities on campus: A handbook for increasing faculty diversity.* Washington, DC: American Council on Education.

Hartley, J., & Branthwaite, A. (1989). The psychologist as wordsmith: A questionnaire study of productive British psychologists. *Higher Education, 18,* 423–452.

Hartley, J., & Davies, I. K. (1978). Note-taking: A critical review. *Learning and Educational Technology, 15,* 207–224.

Highet, G. (1950). *The art of teaching.* New York: Vintage Books.

Hilgard, E. R. (1977). *Divided consciousness.* New York: Wiley.

Hill, B. H. (1990). Fostering professional, personal, and family growth: Loyola University of Chicago. In J. H. Schuster, D. W. Wheeler, and Associates, *Enhancing faculty careers: Strategies for development and renewal* (pp. 212–229). San Francisco: Jossey-Bass.

Hill, S. E., Bahniuk, M. H., & Dobos, J. (1989). The effect of collegial support on faculty success: An analysis of support behavior, information adequacy, and communication apprehension. *Communication Education, 38,* 15–33.

Hilsen, L. (1990). Foreword. *To Improve the Academy, 9,* vii–viii.

Holmes, S. K. (1988). New faculty mentoring: Benefits to the mentor. *Journal of Staff, Program, and Organization Development, 6,* 17–20.

Hoover-Dempsey, K. V., Plas, J. M., & Wallston, B. S. (1986). Tears and weeping among professional women. *Psychology of Women Quarterly, 10,* 19–34.

Howard, A., & Bray, D. W. (1988). *Managerial lives in transition.* New York: Guilford Press.

Hoyt, D. P. (1977). *Interpreting the DECAD report.* Manhattan: Kansas State University, Center for Faculty Evaluation.

Hsia, J. (1988). Limits of affirmative action: Asian American access to higher education. *Educational Policy, 2,* 117–136.

Inwald, R. E. (1988). Five-year follow-up study of departmental terminations as predicted by 16 preemployment psychological indicators. *Journal of Applied Psychology, 73,* 31–39.

James, W. (1989). *Talks to teachers.* Troy, MO: Holt, Rinehart & Winston.

Jarvis, D. K (1988). Junior faculty and language department quality. *ADFL Bulletin, 19*(3), 32–37.

Jarvis, D. K. (1991). *Junior faculty development: A handbook.* New York: Modern Language Association.

Johnson, G. R. (1988). *Taking teaching seriously: A faculty handbook.* College Station: Texas A&M Center for Teaching Excellence.

Kanter, R. M. (1981, Summer). Career growth and organization power: Issues for educational management in the 1980s. *Teachers College Record,* pp. 553–556.

Katz, J. (Ed.). (1985). *Teaching as though students mattered* (New Directions for Teaching and Learning No. 21). San Francisco: Jossey-Bass.

Katz, J., & Henry, M. (1988). *Turning professors into teachers: A new approach to faculty development and student learning.* New York: Macmillan.

Kerner, O. (1968). *The report of the National Advisory Commission on Civil Disorders.* New York: Bantam Books.

Kerr, S. (1988). Some characteristics and consequences of organizational reward. In F. D. Schnoorman & B. Schneider (Eds.), *Facilitating work effectiveness* (pp. 43–76). Lexington, MA: Lexington Books.

King, A. (1990). Enhancing peer interaction and learning in the classroom through reciprocal questioning. *American Educational Research Journal, 27,* 664–687.

Knight, W. H., & Holen, M. C. (1985). Leadership and perceived effectiveness of department chairpersons. *Journal of Higher Education, 56,* 677–690.

Kozma, R. B., (1978). Faculty development and the adaptation and diffusion of classroom innovations. *Journal of Higher Education, 49,* 438–449.

Kram, K. E., & Isabella, L. A. (1985). Mentoring alternatives:

The role of peer relationships in career development. *Academy of Management Journal, 28,* 110-132.

Kunz, D. (1977). [Review of J. G. Gaff's *Toward faculty renewal*]. *AAUP Bulletin, 63,* 329.

Kurfiss, J. G. (1988). *Critical thinking: Theory, research, and possibilities.* Washington, DC: Association for the Study of Higher Education.

Kurfiss, J. G., & Boice, R. (1990). Current and desired faculty development practices among POD members. *To Improve the Academy, 9,* 73-82.

Labovitz, G. A. (1987). *Total quality improvement system.* Burlington, MA: Organizational Dynamics.

Langer, E. J., & Park, K. (1990). Incompetence: A conceptual reconsideration. In R. J. Sternberg & J. Kolligan (Eds.), *Competence considered* (pp. 149-166). New Haven, CT: Yale University Press.

Lavery, P. T., Boice, R., Thompson, R. W., & Turner, J. L. (1988). An annotated bibliography of mentoring for new faculty. *Journal of Staff, Program, and Organizational Development, 7,* 39-46.

Laws, J. L. (1975). The psychology of tokenism: An analysis. *Sex Roles, 1,* 51-67.

Leslie, D. W., and Gappa, J. (forthcoming). *Making effective use of faculty in higher education.* San Francisco: Jossey-Bass.

Lessow-Hurley, J., (1989). Recruitment and retention of minority faculty. *CUPA Journal, 40*(3), 22-26.

Lewis, C. C. (1990). Rethinking our educational assumptions. *Contemporary Psychology, 35,* 878-879.

Lewis, D. R., & Becker, W. E. (1979). *Academic rewards in higher education.* New York: Ballinger.

Lewis, K. G. (1988). Using an observation system to diagnose teaching problems. In K. G. Lewis & J. T. Povlacs (Eds.), *Face to face: A handbook of individual consultation techniques for faculty/instructional developers* (pp. 137-157). Stillwater, OK: New Forums Press.

Lewis, K. G., & Povlacs, J. T. (1988). *Face to face: A handbook of individual consultation techniques for faculty/instructional developers.* Stillwater, OK: New Forums Press.

Lewis, K. G., Svinicki, M. D., & Stice, J. E. (1985). Filling the gap: Introducing new faculty to the basics of teaching. *Journal of Staff, Program, and Organization Development, 3,* 16-21.

Lewis, L. S. (1975). *Scaling the ivory tower.* Baltimore, MD: Johns Hopkins University Press.

Lomperis, A.M.T. (1990). Are women changing the nature of the academic profession? *Journal of Higher Education, 61,* 643-677.

London, M. (1985). *Developing managers: A guide to motivating and preparing people for successful managerial careers.* San Francisco: Jossey-Bass.

London, M., & Bray, D. W. (1985). Measuring and developing young managers' career motivation. *Journal of Management Development, 5,* 3-25.

London, M., & Stumpf, S. A. (1986). Individual and organizational career development in changing times. In D. T. Hall & Associates, *Career development in organizations* (pp. 21-49). San Francisco: Jossey-Bass.

Lucas, A. F. (Ed.). (1989). *The department chairperson's role in enhancing college teaching* (New Directions for Teaching and Learning No. 37). San Francisco: Jossey-Bass.

Lucas, A. F. (1990a). Redirecting faculty through organizational development: Fairleigh Dickinson University. In J. H. Schuster, D. W. Wheeler, & Associates, *Enhancing faculty careers: Strategies for development and renewal* (pp. 230-253) San Francisco: Jossey-Bass.

Lucas, A. F. (1990b). Using psychological models to understand student motivation. In M. D. Svinicki (Ed.), *The changing face of college teaching* (New Directions for Teaching and Learning No. 42, pp. 103-114). San Francisco: Jossey-Bass.

Lucas, R. A., & Harrington, M. K. (1990). Workshops on writing blocks increase proposal activity. *To Improve the Academy, 9,* 139-146.

Mann, M. P. (1988). Individual consultation and the workshop: What's the connection? In K. G. Lewis & J. T. Povlacs (Eds.), *Face to face: A sourcebook of individual consultation techniques for faculty/instructional developers* (pp. 67–80). Stillwater, OK: New Forums Press.

Matier, M. W. (1990). Retaining faculty: A tale of two campuses. *Research in Higher Education, 31,* 39–60.

Mayhew, L. B., Ford, P. J., & Hubbard, D. L. (1990). *The quest for quality: The challenge for undergraduate education in the 1990s.* San Francisco: Jossey-Bass.

McCadden, J. F. (1989). *Adjunct faculty handbook.* Pemberton, NJ: Burlington College.

McKay, N. (1983). Black woman professor—white university. *Women's Studies International Forum, 6,* 143–147.

McKeachie, W. J. (1983). Faculty as a renewable resource. In R. G. Baldwin & R. T. Blackburn (Eds.), *College faculty: Versatile human resources in a period of constraint* (New Directions for Institutional Research No. 40, pp. 57–66). San Francisco: Jossey-Bass.

McKeachie, W. J. (1987). Tips on teaching. In M. P. Zanna & J. M. Darley (Eds.), *The compleat academic* (pp. 87–113). New York: Random House.

McMillen, L. (1985). Department chiefs are urged to change roles, give more time to raising funds, managing. *Chronicle of Higher Education, 29*(23), 27–28.

Menges, R. J. (1986, April). *Colleagues as catalysts for teaching.* Paper presented at the meeting of the American Educational Research Association, San Francisco.

Menges, R. J., & Brinko, K. T. (1986, April). *Effects of student evaluation feedback.* Paper presented at the American Educational Research Association, San Francisco.

Menges, R. J., & Brinko, K. T. (1990). A three-dimensional model for planning and assessing faculty development. *Journal of Staff, Program, and Organization Development, 8,* 133–142.

Menges, R. J., & Mathis, B. C. (1988). *Key resources on teaching, learning, curriculum, and faculty development: A guide to the higher education literature.* San Francisco: Jossey-Bass.

Mentkowski, M., & Chickering, A. W. (1987). Linking educators and researchers in setting a research agenda for undergraduate education. *Review of Higher Education, 11,* 137-187.

Mentor. (1987). *A handbook for teaching assistants.* Seattle: University of Washington, Center for Instructional Development and Research.

Merriam, S. B., Thomas, T. K., & Zeph, C. P. (1987). Mentoring in higher education: What we know now. *Review of Higher Education, 11,* 199-210.

Miles, B. W. (1983). Trials and tribulations of the academic chair. *College and University Personnel Association, 34*(4), 11-15.

Miller, L. H. (1989, September 13). Bold, imaginative steps are needed to link teaching with research. *Chronicle of Higher Education,* p. A52.

Milo, K. J. (1986, Spring). Faculty attitudes and involvement as regards educational marketing and student recruiting. *College and University,* pp. 180-193.

Mooney, C. J. (1990). Faculty generation gap brings campus tensions, debates over hiring rating of professors. *Chronicle of Higher Education, 36*(41), A18-A19.

Moore, K. M. (1983). *The top line: A report on presidents', provosts', and deans' careers.* University Park: Pennsylvania State University, Center for the Study of Higher Education.

Moore, K. M., & Johnson, M. P. (1989). The status of women and minorities in the professoriate: The role of affirmative action and equity. In G. G. Lozier and M. J. Dooris (Eds.), *Managing faculty resources* (New Directions for Institutional Research No. 63, pp. 45-63). San Francisco: Jossey-Bass.

Moore, W. (1988). Black faculty in white colleges: A dream deferred. *Educational Record, 69*(1), 117-121.

Morone, J. A. (1990). *The democratic wish.* New York: Basic Books.

Morris, V. C. (1981). *Deaning.* Champaign: University of Illinois Press.

Naditch, M. P. (1983). The stay well program: Health enhancement at work. In J.S.J. Manuso (Ed.), *Occupational clinical psychology* (pp. 245–254). New York: Praeger.

National Center for Education Statistics. (1989). *Digest of education statistics.* Washington, DC: U.S. Department of Education.

National Education Association. (1989). *A survival handbook for part-time & temporary faculty.* Washington, DC: National Education Association.

Nelson, W. C. (1981). *Renewal of the teacher-scholar.* Washington, DC: Association of American Colleges.

Neuman, G. A., Edwards, J. E., & Raju, N. S. (1989). Organizational development interventions: A meta-analysis of their effects on satisfaction and other attitudes. *Personnel Psychology, 42,* 461–489.

Neuman, Y., & Finaly-Neuman, E. (1990). The reward-support framework and faculty commitment to their university. *Research in Higher Education, 31,* 75–97.

Nixon, H. K. (1928). *Psychology for the writer.* New York: HarperCollins.

Noller, R. B. (1982). Mentoring: A renaissance of apprenticeship. *Journal of Creative Behavior, 16*(1), 1–4.

Noonan, J. F. (1980). An institute on teaching and learning for new faculty. In W. C. Nelsen & M. E. Siegel (Eds.), *Effective approaches to faculty development* (pp. 49–56). Washington, DC: Association of American Colleges.

Nurnberger, J. T., & Zimmerman, J. (1970). Applied analysis of behavior. *Behavior Therapy, 1,* 59–60.

Nyquist, J. D., Abbott, R. D., & Wulff, D. H. (1989). The challenge of TA training in the 1990s. In J. D. Nyquist, R. D. Abbott, & D. H. Wulff (Eds.), *Teaching assistant training in the 1990s* (New Directions for Teaching and Learning No. 39, pp. 15–22). San Francisco: Jossey-Bass.

Nyquist, J. D., Abbott, R. D., Wulff, D. H., & Sprague, J. (1991). *Preparing the professoriate of tomorrow to teach.* Dubuque, IA: Kendall/Hunt.

Olian, J. D., Carroll, J. D., Giannantonio, C. M., & Feren, D. B. (1988). What do proteges look for in a mentor? Results of three experimental studies. *Journal of Vocational Behavior, 33,* 15–37.

Painter, N. (1981, December 10). Hers. *New York Times*, p. 22.

Payne, N. J. (1989). Hidden messages in the pursuit of equity. *Academe, 75*, 19–22.

Pearson, D. A., & Seiler, R. E. (1983). Environmental satisfiers in academe. *Higher Education, 12*, 35–47.

Pellino, G. R., Blackburn, R. T., & Boberg, A. L. (1984). The dimensions of academic scholarship: Faculty and administrator views. *Research in Higher Education, 20*, 103–115.

Pelz, D. C., & Andrews, F. M. (1966). *Scientists in organizations*. New York: Wiley.

Peters, T. J., & Waterman, R. H. (1984). *In search of excellence*. New York: Warner Books.

Peterson, D., Kromrey, J., Borg, J., & Lewis, A. (1990). Defining and establishing relationships between essential and higher order teaching skills. *Journal of Educational Research, 84*, 5–12.

Pollack, J. S. (1986, January–February). The erosion of tenure in the California State University. *Academe*, pp. 19–24.

Power, F. C., Higgins, A., & Kohlberg, L. (1991). *Moral education through democratic communities*. New York: Columbia University Press.

Rabinbach, A. (1990). *The human motor*. New York: Basic Books.

Rausch, D. K., Ortiz, B. P., Douhitt, R. A., & Reed, L. L. (1989). The academic revolving door: Why do women get caught? *CUPA Journal, 40*, 1–16.

Relch, M. H. (1986, February). The mentor connection. *Personnel*, pp. 50–56.

Reskin, B. F. (1977). Academic sponsorship and scientists' careers. *Sociology of Education, 52*, 129–146.

Reynolds, M. C. (1989). *Knowledge base for the beginning teacher*. Oxford, England: Pergamon Press.

Ribot, T. (1906). *Essay on the creative imagination*. Chicago: Open Court.

Rice, B. (1985). Performance review: The job nobody likes. *Psychology Today, 19*(9), 29–35.

Rosser, S. V. (1989). Warming up the classroom climate for women. *Feminist Teacher, 4*, 8–12.

Rothblum, E. D. (1988). Leaving the ivory tower: Factors contributing to women's voluntary resignation from academia. *Frontiers, 10*(2), 14–17.

Rothblum, E. D. (1990). Fear of failure: The psychodynamic, need achievement, fear of success, and procrastination models. In H. Leitenberg (Ed.), *Handbook of social and evaluation anxiety* (pp. 497–537). New York: Plenum Press.

Rousseau, D. M. (1991). Solving the problems of work. *Contemporary Psychology, 36*(2), 131–132.

Royce, J. (1898). The psychology of invention. *Psychological Review, 5*, 113–114.

Rynes, S. L., & Boudreau, J. W. (1986). College recruiting in large organizations: Practice, evaluation, and research implications. *Personnel Psychology, 39*, 729–757.

Sacken, D. M. (1990). Taking teaching seriously. *Journal of Higher Education, 61*, 548–564.

Salancik, G. R. (1987). Power and politics in academic departments. In M. P. Zanna & J. M. Darley (Eds.), *The compleat academic* (pp. 61–84). New York: Random House.

Sands, R. G., Parson, L. A., & Duane, J. (1991). Faculty mentoring in a public university. *Journal of Higher Education, 62*, 174–193.

Scarr, S. (1982). An editor looks for the perfect manuscript. In D. Loeffler (Ed.), *Understanding the manuscript review process.* Washington, DC: American Psychological Association.

Schmidt, G. H. (1983). Problem-based learning: Rationale and description. *Medical Education, 17*, 11–16.

Schuster, J. H. (1989). The personal dimension: Faculty development. *Thought and Action, 5*(1), 61–72.

Schuster, J. H. (1990a, November 2). *Faculty development in the new millennium: What to do about it now.* Keynote presentation to the POD Conference, Lake Tahoe, CA.

Schuster, J. H. (1990b). Strengthening career preparation for prospective professors. In J. H. Schuster, D. W. Wheeler, & Associates, *Enhancing faculty careers: Strategies for development and renewal* (pp. 65–83). San Francisco: Jossey-Bass.

Schuster, J. H., Wheeler, D. W., & Associates. (1990). *Enhanc-*

ing faculty careers: Strategies for development and renewal. San Francisco: Jossey-Bass.

Schwartz, G. E. (1983). Stress management in occupational settings. In J.S.J. Manuso (Ed.), *Occupational clinical psychology* (pp. 229–244). New York: Praeger.

Scott, C. D., & Hawk, J. (1986). *Heal thyself: The health of health care professionals.* New York: Brunner/Mazel.

Seldin, P. (1984). *Changing practices in faculty evaluation: A critical assessment and recommendations for improvement.* San Francisco: Jossey-Bass.

Seldin, P. (Ed.). (1987). *Coping with faculty stress* (New Directions for Teaching and Learning No. 29). San Francisco: Jossey-Bass.

Seldin, P. (1988). *Evaluating and developing administrative performance: A practical guide for academic leaders.* San Francisco: Jossey-Bass.

Simeone, A. (1986). *Academic women: Working towards equality.* South Hadley, MA: Bergin & Garvey.

Simon, H. (1991). *Models of my life.* New York: Basic Books.

Simonton, D. K. (1988). *Scientific genius.* New York: Cambridge University Press.

Simpson, R. D., & Jackson, W. K. (1990). A multidimensional approach to faculty vitality: The University of Georgia. In J. H. Schuster & D. W. Wheeler (Eds.), *Enhancing faculty careers: Strategies for development and renewal* (pp. 167–187). San Francisco: Jossey-Bass.

Smart, G. R. (1978). *Career roles of research university faculty.* Paper presented at the meeting of the American Educational Research Association, Toronto.

Smart, J. C., & McLaughlin, G. W. (1978). Reward structures of academic disciplines. *Research in Higher Education, 8,* 39–55.

Smelser, N. J., & Content, S. G. (1980). *The changing academic market.* Berkeley: University of California Press.

Smith, P. (1990). *Killing the spirit.* New York: Viking Press.

Smith, S. L., & Borgstedt, K. W. (1985). Factors influencing adjustment of white faculty in predominantly black colleges. *Journal of Negro Education, 54,* 148–163.

Sorcinelli, M. D. (1985). Faculty careers: Satisfactions and discontents. *To Improve the Academy, 4,* 44–62.

Sorcinelli, M. D. (1988). Satisfactions and concerns of new university teachers. *To Improve the Academy, 7,* 121–133.

Sorcinelli, M. D. (1990, April 11). *Dealing with troublesome behavior in the classroom.* Workshop presented at University of Massachusetts, Amherst.

Sorcinelli, M. D., & Near, J. P. (1989). Relations between work and life away from work among university faculty. *Journal of Higher Education, 60,* 59–81.

Staton-Spicer, A. Q., & Darling, A. (1989). Socialization of teaching assistantships. In J. D. Nyquist, R. B. Abbott, & D. H. Wulff (Eds.), *Teaching assistant training in the 1990s,* (New Directions for Teaching and Learning No. 39, pp. 15–22). San Francisco: Jossey-Bass.

Sternberg, D. (1981). *How to complete and survive a doctoral dissertation.* New York: St. Martin's Press.

Sternberg, R. J. (1988). *The triarchic mind: A new theory of human intelligence.* New York: Penguin.

Sternberg, R. J. (1990). Prototypes of competence and incompetence. In R. J. Sternberg & J. Kolligan (Eds.), *Competence considered* (pp. 117–145). New Haven, CT: Yale University Press.

Sternberg, R. J., Okagaki, L., & Jackson, A. S. (1990, September). Practical intelligence for success in school. *Educational Leadership,* pp. 35–39.

Stice, J. E., Svinicki, M. D., & Lewis, K. G. (1990). *Teachers and students.* Austin: University of Texas, Center for Teaching Effectiveness.

Sue, D. W. (1981). *Counseling the culturally different.* New York: Wiley.

Suinn, R. M., & Witt, J. C. (1982). Survey on ethnic minority recruitment and retention. *American Psychologist, 37,* 1239–1244.

Svinicki, M. D. (Ed.). (1990). *The changing face of college teaching* (New Directions for Teaching and Learning No. 42). San Francisco: Jossey-Bass.

Svinicki, M., Kurfiss, J., & Stone, J. (1986). Foreword. *To Improve the Academy, 5,* iii–iv.

Taylor, S. E., & Martin, J. (1987). The present-minded professor: Controlling one's career. In M. P. Zanna & J. M. Darley (Eds.), *The compleat academic* (pp. 23–60). New York: Random House.

Thoreson, R. W., Kardash, C. M., Leuthold, D. A., & Morrow, K. A. (1990). Gender differences in the academic career. *Research in Higher Education, 31,* 193–209.

Thoreson, R. W., Roberts, K. S., & Pascoe, E. A. (1979). The University of Missouri-Columbia Employee Assistance Program. *CUPA Journal, 30,* 51–60.

Tobias, S. (1990). *They're not dumb, just different.* Tucson, AZ: Research Corporation.

Tremmel, R. (1989). Investigating productivity and other factors in the writer's practice. *Freshman English News, 17*(2), 19–25.

Tsui, A. S. (1984). Personnel department effectiveness: A tripartite approach. *Industrial Relations, 23,* 184–197.

Turner, F. C. (1977). Academic recruitment: Some thoughts on role models and self-image. *Improving College and University Teaching, 25,* 201–203.

Turner, J. L., & Boice, R. (1987). Starting at the beginning: Concerns and needs of new faculty. *To Improve the Academy, 6,* 41–55.

van der Bogert, V. B. (1991). Starting out: Experiences of new faculty at a teaching university. *To Improve the Academy, 10,* 63–81.

Wagner, R. K., & Sternberg, R. J. (1985). Practical intelligence in real-world pursuits: The role of tacit knowledge. *Journal of Personality and Social Psychology, 49,* 436–458.

Wallace, I. (1968). *The writing of one novel.* New York: Simon & Schuster.

Watkins, B. T. (1990a, March 7). Education-reform movement is here to stay, deans are told. *Chronicle of Higher Education,* p. A16.

Watkins, B. T. (1990b, May 16). New technique used to evaluate college teaching. *Chronicle of Higher Education,* pp. A15–A17.

Weaver, F. S. (1982). Teaching, writing and developing. *Journal of Higher Education, 53,* 586–592.

Weick, K. E. (1976). Educational organizations as loosely coupled systems. *Administrative Science Quarterly, 21,* 1–19.

Weimer, M. (1990). *Improving college teaching: Strategies for improving instructional effectiveness.* San Francisco: Jossey-Bass.

Wheeler, D. W. (1990). Providing career consulting services to midcareer faculty. In J. H. Schuster and D. W. Wheeler (Eds.), *Enhancing faculty careers* (pp. 84–105). San Francisco: Jossey-Bass.

Wheeler, D. W., & Schuster, J. H. (1990). Building comprehensive programs to enhance faculty development. In J. H. Schuster, D. W. Wheeler, & Associates, *Enhancing faculty careers: Strategies for development and renewal* (pp. 275–297). San Francisco: Jossey-Bass.

Wilhite, M. S. (1990). Chairs and conflict prevention. *Academic Leader, 2*(2), 111–121.

Winkler, K. J. (1988, November 9). Minority students, professors tell of isolation, anger in graduate school. *Chronicle of Higher Education,* pp. A15, A19.

Wittrick, M. C., & Farley, F. (1989). *The future of educational psychology.* Hillside, NJ: Erlbaum.

Wright, D. L. (1985). Improving classrooms for women: The faculty developer's role. *To Improve the Academy, 4,* 93–105.

Wulff, D. H., Nyquist, J. D., & Abbott, R. D. (1987). Students' perceptions of large classes. In M. G. Weimer (Ed.), *Teaching large classes well* (New Directions for Teaching and Learning No. 32, pp. 17–30). San Francisco: Jossey-Bass.

Wylie, N. R. (1985). *Third renewal proposal to FIPSE.* Unpublished report, Great Lakes Colleges Association.

Wylie, N. R. (1986). *Helping new faculty adjust to new careers at liberal arts colleges.* (ERIC Document Reproduction Service No. ED 298 843)

Wylie, N. R. (1990). A consortial approach: The Great Lakes Colleges Association. In J. H. Schuster, D. W. Wheeler, & Associates, *Enhancing faculty careers: Strategies for development and renewal.* San Francisco: Jossey-Bass.

Young, R. E. (1987). Faculty development and the concept of a profession. *Academe, 73,* 12–14.

Zanna, M. P., & Darley, J. M. (1987). *The compleat academic.* New York: Random House.

Zimpher, N. L. (1988). This issue: Mentoring teachers. *Theory into Practice, 27,* 174.

Name Index

Subject Index